# College Exploration on the Internet

## Second Edition
*College & Career Press*
*Chicago, Illinois*

## Project Staff

Managing Editor: Andrew Morkes
Editors: Felicitas Cortez, Nora Walsh, Laura Walsh
Additional Editorial Assistance: Amy McKenna
Interior Design: The Glasoe Group
Cover Design: Meyers Design, Inc.

**Photo Credits:** - Cover(Comstock, PhotosToGo, Photos.com), xxxv (Photos.com), 1 (Photos.com), 120 (Photos.com)

Copyright © 2009 College & Career Press, LLC
ISBN 10: 0-9745251-4-6
ISBN 13: 978-0-9745251-4-3

**Library of Congress Cataloging-in-Publication Data**
Morkes, Andrew.
  College exploration on the internet : a student and counselor's guide to more than 1,000 websites and resources / by Andrew Morkes and Amy McKenna.
    p. cm.
  Includes bibliographical references and index.
  ISBN 978-0-9745251-4-3
  1.  College choice--United States--Computer network resources. 2. Universities and colleges--United States--Computer network resources--Directories. 3.  Universities and colleges--United States--Admission. 4. Web sites--Directories.  I. McKenna, Amy, 1969- II. Title.
  LB2350.5.M67 2009
  378.73028'5--dc22

                                         2008028982

**Published and distributed by:**
College & Career Press, LLC
PO Box 300484
Chicago, IL 60630
773/282-4671
www.collegeandcareerpress.com

Printed in the United States of America
08-09

# Quick Guide to Resources

Use this section like an extended table of contents to help you locate information on campus tours, college admissions, financial aid, community colleges, college majors (such as astronomy, computer science, and zoology), and more than 145 other topics related to college education. Section names ("College Resource Websites" and "Association Web Resources"), website names, and corresponding page numbers are listed for each topic so that you can easily track down the information that you need.

## Agriculture (cont.)

## Alcohol Abuse

**College Resource Websites:**

## Alternative Health Care

**Association Web Resources:**

## Alternatives to College

**College Resource Websites:**

## Animal Science

**Association Web Resources:**

## Animation

**Association Web Resources:**

## Anthropology

**Association Web Resources:**

## Application Essays

**College Resource Websites:**

## Archaeology

**Association Web Resources:**

# Architecture

## Association Web Resources:

# Art

## Association Web Resources:

# Astronomy

## Association Web Resources:

# Athletics (see Student-Athletes)

# Automotives

## Association Web Resources:

# Aviation

## Association Web Resources:

# Biology

## Association Web Resources:

## Counselor Resources

**College Resource Websites:**
While all the sites in this book provide general information that will be useful to counselors and educators, the following websites have specific counselor- and educator-oriented sections or publications that will be especially helpful.

## Funeral Services

### Association Web Resources:

## Gap Year

### College Resource Websites:

## Genealogy

### Association Web Resources:

## General

### College Resource Websites:
General websites include information on most aspects of college
preparation, including searching
for and choosing a college, test
preparation, financial aid, and
other topics.

### Association Web Resources:

## Health Care and Health Education (cont.)

## Health Care and Health Education (cont.)

## Journalism (cont.)

**Association Web Resources:**

## Laboratory Science

**Association Web Resources:**

## Law/Legal Services

**Association Web Resources:**

## Law School

**College Resource Websites:**

**Association Web Resources:**

## Library and Information Science

**Association Web Resources:**

Note: Information on religious colleges and universities can be found under "Religion/Theology.".

# Introduction

High school students planning to go to college cite the Internet as the second most important resource available to them, after their guidance counselors, according to a survey by the Art & Science Group.

The Internet has had a profound effect on the way we do business, gather information, and communicate with one other. Consider the Web's groundbreaking impact on college exploration. Less than 15 years ago, high school students had to research and plan for college via snail mail, telephone calls to college officials, or through costly and time-consuming campus visits.

Today, students can use the Internet to find information about almost any college-related topic imaginable. They can use the Web to help choose a major; research admissions requirements; apply for scholarships; and tour colleges via online videos, photographs, and audio recordings. There are websites that feature student reviews of professors and schools that are brutally honest in their assessment. Students can even use the Web to apply to college! In short, there are literally thousands of college-related websites on the Web.

Unfortunately, quantity doesn't always mean quality. Many "college websites" are merely advertisements for fee-based services or offer information that is outdated or too vague to be of use to students and educators.

To provide you with the most useful college resources on the Web, we have visited more than 2,000 websites to create *College Exploration on the Internet: A Student and Counselor's Guide to More Than 685 Websites*.

Using this book will help you save time, money, and avoid dated or incorrect information. The 685+ Web resources presented in *College Exploration on the Internet* are the most useful websites available today. They provide information on:

| | |
|---|---|
| ✔ College admissions | ✔ Internships |
| ✔ Choosing a major | ✔ Study abroad opportunities |
| ✔ Campus visits | ✔ Religious colleges |
| ✔ U.S. and Canadian college search tools | ✔ Graduate school |
| ✔ Scholarships, grants, loans, and other financial aid | ✔ Campus crime, alcohol abuse, and depression |
| ✔ Minority resources | ✔ Professor reviews |
| ✔ Community colleges | ✔ Accreditation |
| ✔ Students with disabilities | ✔ Fraternities and sororities |
| ✔ Women's issues | ✔ Other postsecondary options including apprenticeships and military training |
| ✔ Distance and online education | |

Some of these websites (such as ACT, Peterson's, and The Princeton Review) are household names, but others (such as College is Possible, Making It Count, and Super College) are hidden gems that will provide you with excellent advice and resources.

Use *College Exploration on the Internet* to find useful websites and college-related information, but don't forget that Web research is no substitute for visiting a college campus, talking with a counselor or teacher about your college plans, or discussing your goals with parents and friends.

We hope that *College Exploration on the Internet* becomes a valued and trusted resource as you navigate the challenges of college!

## How This Book is Organized

*College Exploration on the Internet* has two main sections: College Resource Websites and Association Web Resources. The Quick Guide to Resources serves as a type of extended Table of Contents that will help you locate websites and resources on more than 145 college-related topics. This book also features a list of national and state associations for counselors, a list of state financial aid and college planning associations and websites, a glossary, a list of financial aid abbreviations, and career title and website indexes. The following paragraphs provide more information on the contents of the book.

### College Resource Websites

This section features reviews of the best college-related websites on the Internet for students, parents, school and independent counselors, and other education professionals. See page 1 for a detailed overview of this section.

### Association Web Resource

This section lists nearly 1,000 online resources and publications relating to college planning, majors, and careers. They are offered by more than 360 professional association and government agencies. See page 120 for a detailed overview of this section.

### Counselor Associations on the Internet

This section features a list of the names and websites of national and state counselor associations as an informational resource for counselors.

### State Financial Aid and College Planning Associations and Websites

This section features a list of the names and websites of state financial aid and college planning organizations and websites.

### Glossary

The Glossary defines more than 170 terms that students and educators will encounter frequently as they research college options on the Web.

### Career Title and Website Indexes

We all know that students attend college to expand their knowledge and prepare for a career. To assist high school and community college students who may already have a career interest, we have provided a Career Title Index that students can use to locate further information on the career of their choice.

A Website Index lists all of the websites referenced in this book.

## Issues to Remember as You Use This Book:

**Website Content Changes Constantly.** The Web is constantly changing: section titles get changed, websites are redesigned, new information is added . . . you get the idea. If you have trouble locating any of the websites listed in this book, try shortening the Web address to its basic address. For example, if you are having trouble finding the Associated Colleges of the Midwest's high school resources website (www.acm.edu/admiss), shortening the address to its most basic format (e.g., www.acm.edu) will usually allow you to access the site and locate the information at the site's home page or by using its search feature.

**Keep Up With Technology.** While the resources at most websites can be read in basic text or html format, you may need some additional tools to access certain resources. One of the more popular ways to distribute information electronically is the Portable Document Format (PDF). PDF files are compatible with Windows, Macintosh, and Unix-based systems. They retain all the formats of the original version and can be read on screen and printed with nearly any computer and printer. You may already have a copy of this popular software on your computer, but if you don't, you can visit the Adobe Systems Inc. website (www.adobe.com/products/acrobat/readstep2.html) to download a free copy of the software and begin viewing documents.

Other software programs that you might need as you surf the Web for college information include the Macromedia Flash Player (www.adobe.com/shockwave/download/download.cgi), which allows users to view moving or static images on the Web; and the QuickTime Media Player (www.apple.com/quicktime/download) and the RealOnePlayer (www.real.com), which allow users to access video and audio resources on the Web. All three of these programs can be downloaded for free. Installing and using these free resources will make your visits to college-related websites easier and more enjoyable.

# College Resource Websites

This section features reviews of 205 of the best college-related websites on the Internet for students, parents, school and independent counselors, and other educational professionals. These websites were created by for-profit and non-profit companies, trade and professional associations, and governmental agencies.

Each website review has three sections:

The **What** section provides a brief description of the following:

✔ The website's major sections

✔ Information on the website's sponsor

✔ Audience best served by the website

The **Best Points** section details the website's most useful sections. Examples of resources spotlighted in this section include helpful online articles, essays, and other publications; college search engines; college and financial aid planning worksheets and checklists; sample admissions tests; glossaries of college-related terms; scholarship search engines; student interviews; and online chat rooms, message boards, blogs, podcasts, and forums that focus on college-related issues.

The **What You Should Know** section serves as a bottom-line summary of the website's merits. It also discusses the level of access that is available to

## The 10 Best College Resource Websites

The 10 websites below are our picks for the best of the best general college resources. These attractive websites (listed in alphabetical order) offer comprehensive information on preparing for college, admissions, college search, majors, and financial aid. Note: There are many other excellent sites that focus on a particular topic such as financial aid or study abroad. For more information on these specialty websites, check the Quick Guide to Resources on page v.

**Adventures in Education**
www.adventuresineducation.org

**College is Possible**
www.collegeispossible.org

**CollegeConfidential.com**
www.collegeconfidential.com

**CollegeData**
www.collegedata.com

**Hobson's College View**
www.collegeview.com

**Making It Count**
www.makingitcount.com

**Peterson's Planner**
www.petersons.com

**The Princeton Review**
www.princetonreview.com

**Super College**
www.supercollege.com

**Ten Steps to College With the Greenes**
www.pbs.org/tenstepstocollege

the casual user. The following categories are used to describe websites in this book:

✔ **Full access available.** This means that the materials and resources at this website can be used by anyone free of charge with no registration required.

✔ **Limited access available.** This means that while users have access to some areas of the website, registration is required for other areas of the site. To register, you will need to provide personal information such as your name, mailing address, telephone number, and email address. There is usually no cost associated with this registration, but some users may feel uncomfortable providing personal information at these websites.

✔ **Registration required for all areas of this site.** Free registration is required to access all of the resources at this website.

✔ **Fee-based service.** Although certain features may be free to visitors, the majority of the content at this type of website requires a usage fee. The handful of fee-based websites in *College Exploration on the Internet* are included because they offer a considerable amount of free college-related resources. Our listing of these websites suggests no endorsement of their fee-based goods or services (as well as any other types of advertisements displayed at websites). In short, it is up to you to decide whether it is worth spending your money on these fee-based services.

# 4College Women: Health Our Way

### www.4collegewomen.org

**What:** The site was created by students at Brandeis University and supervised by Dr. Susan Blumenthal, professor and U.S. assistant surgeon general, and Shulamit Reinharz, director of the Women's Studies Research Center at the University. Future and current female college students looking for information about adopting healthy lifestyles on and off campus will find this website useful.

**Best Points:** The site covers a wide variety of women's health concerns, including general health and prevention, reproductive health, emotional and mental health, diseases and conditions, safety and violence issues, alternative and complementary medicine, minority women's health, disabilities, and health insurance issues. The site also provides information on health-related careers, links to a wealth of trusted health information, and health information in Spanish. In addition, there is even a subsite that covers men's health issues.

**What You Should Know:** Full access available. This is a very useful resource for all women—whether they plan to attend college or not.

# About.com: Business School

### http://businessmajors.about.com

**What:** About.com offers "high-quality, original content" on more than 50,000 subjects. It also provides nearly one million links to other resources on the Web that illuminate a topic. The main site is divided into sections, known as channels (e.g., Education, Jobs & Careers, News & Issues, etc.), that are managed by a Guide who arranges and gathers information, links, and other materials pertinent to the topics—in this case, business majors.

**Best Points:** If you're interested in majoring in business, a visit to this site should be one of your first stops on the Information

### Did You Know?

*BusinessWeek* recently released its list of the top undergraduate business programs. Here are the top five: University of Pennsylvania, University of Virginia, University of Notre Dame, Cornell University, and Emory University. Visit www.businessweek.com for information on selection criteria.

Superhighway. The site has a wealth of information about majoring in business. Sample article titles include: Business Majors 101, Applying to Business School, Undergrad Business Majors, SAT Info/Prep, Deciding on an MBA, GMAT Info/Prep, and Business School Rankings. Visitors to this site, whether business professionals or students, can also contribute to this growing web of information by suggesting ideas, stories, and websites on the topic.

**What You Should Know:** Full access available. This is a very useful site for aspiring business majors.

# About.com: College Admissions

http://collegeapps.about.com

**What:** About.com offers "high-quality, original content" on more than 50,000 subjects. It also provides nearly one million links to other resources on the Web that illuminate a topic. The main site is divided into sections, known as channels (e.g., Education, Jobs & Careers, News & Issues, etc.), that are managed by a Guide who arranges and gathers information, links, and other materials pertinent to the topics—in this case, college admissions in the United States.

**Best Points:** A wealth of information exists on every admissions topic conceivable, including college rankings, affirmative action, campus visits, virtual tours, SAT/ACT prep, college essays, scholarships and other financial aid, and distance education. Site visitors can also contribute to this growing web of information by contributing ideas, stories, and websites on admissions-related topics. A Chat feature allows users to exchange ideas and advice with other visitors to the site.

**What You Should Know:** Full access available. This site is an excellent clearinghouse for information on admissions.

# About.com: Graduate School

http://gradschool.about.com

**What:** About.com provides "high-quality, original content" on more than 50,000 subjects. It also provides nearly one million links to other resources on the Web that illuminate a topic. The main site is divided into sections, known as channels (e.g., Education, Jobs & Careers, News & Issues, etc.), that are managed by a Guide who arranges and gathers information, links, and other materials pertinent to the topics—in this case, graduate school.

**Best Points:** This site offers many useful features on graduate school-related issues, including specialized information for more than 20 subject areas including computer science, mathematics, and sociology; a database of graduate schools; and interesting articles such as Graduate School Admissions 101, Guide to the GRE, Preparation and Your Admissions Essay, and Graduate Application Time Table. Site visitors can also contribute to this growing collection of information by contributing ideas, stories, and websites on graduate school.

**What You Should Know:** Full access available. This site provides excellent resources for students considering graduate school.

## Academics: You Can Do It!

www.nasfaa.org/SubHomes/DoItAffordIt/doitcover.html

**What:** This website is brought to you by the National Association of Student Financial Aid Administrators. On it, you'll find information on setting life and career goals, preparing for college, and choosing the right school.

**Best Points:** In addition to general college and career resources, the site offers useful worksheets for comparing schools and to-do check-lists for students in grades eight through 12. A Glossary of Terms defines words you will come across during your college search.

**What You Should Know:** Full access available. What this site lacks in visual appeal and ease of use, it makes up for in content. Give this site a visit for the checklists and comparison worksheets.

## Accepted.com

http://accepted.com

**What:** Accepted.com is a for-profit admissions consulting and application essay editing service. It offers free information and other features for aspiring undergraduate and graduate students. Sections include MBA, Medical School, Law School, Grad School, College Admissions, and Resume Advice.

**Best Points:** The advice in each section is uniformly strong.

Sections offer advice on getting accepted (Essay Dos and Don'ts, Tips for Better Writing, and Approaching Recommenders), sample college admissions essays, and tips for writers of letters of recommendation. The Business School Admissions section even has an MBA Interview Feedback Database, where students who are about to attend an admission interview can get inside information from past interviewees. More than 120 schools are listed, including Arizona State, Duke, Yale, and the London Business School. This site also offers a Chat Room where you can talk to admissions counselors and other education experts about your college concerns.

**What You Should Know:** Full access available (free portion of the website). This is an excellent site for information on admissions.

# ACT

**www.act.org/education**

**What:** ACT, Inc., the provider of one of the most popular college admissions tests in the United States, provides assessment tests and research tools for education and workforce development. Visit this site for information on the ACT college entrance exam and career and college guidance.

> **FYI**
> More than 1.4 million high school graduates—or 43 percent of all graduating seniors—took the ACT test in 2008, according to the ACT.

**Best Points:** At the home page, click on Students for tips on the ACT exam and sample questions in English, math, reading, and science. Online sample tests are interactive and easy to use. Another section worth visiting is College Planning, which features a College Planning Checklist (that includes tips on what steps to take during your high school and early college years) and more information about the benefits of college and admissions practices. Other useful features: Financial Aid, Student Blog, and ACT Podcast.

**What You Should Know:** Full access available. This is a great site for information on the ACT exam as well as general college preparation resources. Parents may also want to check out www.act.org/path/parent for resources to help their child choose a college, prepare for the workforce, or explore career options.

# Adventures in Education

### www.adventuresineducation.org

**What:** Sponsored by the Texas Guaranteed Student Loan Corporation, this site helps students and families achieve their higher education goals.

**Best Points:** This website has a wealth of information for anyone looking to learn more about college. It is easy to find your way around this site, as it is organized into sections including Middle School Student, High School Student, College Student, Parent, Counselor, Teacher, and Librarian. By clicking on State Education Resources, you can access a map of U.S. states, that lists specialized college planning information that is available from your state. The High School Student section provides detailed advice on subjects that may seem overwhelming to both students and parents at first, such as finding the right school. This site also provides extensive information on financial aid and money management concerns (such as how to borrow responsibly before, during, and after college). The financial aid calendar, scholarship search, and budget worksheets are useful tools to help you keep money matters organized. Another feature of this site is AIEmail, which is a free weekly email newsletter that helps students, parents, and counselors plan for college.

**What You Should Know:** Full access available. This site is an excellent source of financial information for both students and parents, and it is also available in Spanish.

# Allied Health Careers

### www.ama-assn.org/ama/pub/category/14598.html

**What:** Allied Health is a broad field of study encompassing diverse health care professions—from art therapy to dietetics to genetic counseling—that does not include physicians, nurses, dentists, or podiatrists. The American Medical Association's website has free, downloadable informational flyers on these popular career choices.

**Best Points:** Each flyer includes an overview of the occupation, including an occupational/job description, employment characteristics, employment outlook, and educational programs necessary to enter the field. Links to register for the organization's free monthly allied health professions e-newsletter and to order paid publications are also available. Such paid publications include the *Health Professions Career and Education Directory,* from which the free informational flyers are excerpted. The book, in full, provides invaluable information on 65 different allied health careers, including professional descriptions along with in-depth listings of all of the educational programs and institutions that provide degrees in these fields.

**What You Should Know:** Limited access available; you must register to receive the e-newsletters. This website is a useful resource for students who are in the beginning stages of exploring career options in the allied health professions, and it is worth a visit.

## BabyMint

**www.babymint.com**

**What:** BabyMint is a college savings program that is linked to the credit card(s) you use every day. When you purchase goods or services from BabyMint partners, you receive money back for your child's future college education.

**Best Points:** Rewards are granted from various partners, from retail giant Eddie Bauer to Royal Caribbean. Money back from purchases can be sent to you via check, directed into another BabyMint member's account, or deposited directly into your college savings account, such as state 529 plans or Coverdell Educational Savings Accounts. You can also read general information and advice on saving for college and enrolling in college savings plans.

**What You Should Know:** Registration required for all areas of this site. Registration is free and relatively easy, and, according to the site, your privacy is fully protected.

## *The Black Collegian* Online

**www.black-collegian.com**

**What:** This is the online version of *The Black Collegian* magazine, which has been providing African-American students with college-related information since 1970. The site provides graduate school and career information to students of color.

**Best Points:** Though the site does not cover undergraduate college concerns (such as choosing the right school and applying for and getting financial aid) in detail, it features many articles about the importance of graduate school, as well as links to many grad programs.

**What You Should Know:** Full access available. This site will be most useful to African-American and other students of color who are already in college and are considering graduate school.

# Braintrack

**www.braintrack.com**

**What:** If you're hoping to study abroad but are not sure where, this site is a good place to learn about schools located all over the world.

**Best Points:** This site contains more than 8,300 links to higher education institutions in 194 countries. You can search by region (by continent or country) and by school name. Not all school pages can be viewed in English, but many can, and most include contact pages where you can request more information. This list includes colleges, universities, theological seminaries, polytechnics, institutes of technology and research, and other educational institutions.

**Did You Know?**
According to the IIE, the most popular study abroad destinations for American students include the United Kingdom, Italy, Spain, France, Australia, Mexico, and China. However, more students are now opting to study in Latin America, Africa, the Middle East, and Asia.

**What You Should Know:** Full access available. This site is a good comprehensive resource for those looking to study abroad or in the United States.

# Brokescholar

**http://brokescholar.com**

**What:** Brokescholar is a free searchable database of more than 650,000 scholarships; it is operated by a subsidiary of JPMorgan Chase Bank. You can browse through $2.5 billion worth of undergraduate and graduate scholarships awarded based on academic merit, ethnicity, extracurricular activities, religion, and interests.

**Best Points:** Your scholarship search will create a list of applicable awards and all details such as the type, dollar amount, deadlines, and links to the scholarship's website. A calendar can be created listing all approaching deadlines. Another handy feature: a computer-generated application request letter that can be customized for each particular award—click, print, and mail! The site also has information geared towards parents—including articles on college finances, types of loans, and how to discuss such costs with the entire family.

**What You Should Know:** Limited access available; free registration is required to use the database. The registration process is a bit lengthy, but yielded some lesser-known scholarships due to the detailed profile you'll create.

## Campus Security Data Analysis Cutting Tool

http://ope.ed.gov/security

**What:** The Office of Postsecondary Education, part of the U.S. Department of Education, provides this website so students and parents can search the crime statistics of colleges located nationwide. You can browse schools by name, region, state, city, instructional program, type of institution, and size. Crime information for each school is organized by type of crime and year. You can get data for one school or aggregated data for a group of schools.

**Best Points:** You can access each school's statistics on on- and off-campus criminal offenses. Each listing also includes the name and contact information for the school's director of security.

**What You Should Know:** Full access available. This is an extremely useful website for parents and students concerned with campus safety. Note that statistics reflect criminal events that have been reported. Data do not always reflect convictions or prosecutions.

## CampusStarter.com:
## Universities and Colleges in Canada

www.campusstarter.com

**What:** Sponsored by The EI Group (a for-profit career and educational resource company), this website offers information on education in Canada. It has the following sections: Compare

Programs, Virtual Tours, Request Info, Regional Portals, and Campus Portals. There is also a scholarship search feature, a college search feature, a glossary of college-related terms, and information on careers.

**Best Points:** The Compare Programs section allows you to compare up to three business, engineering, fine arts, science, or teacher education programs to determine which is the best fit for you. The college search engines allow you to search by name, field of study, degree type, and province/city.

**What You Should Know:** Full access available. Visit this site to perform basic research on colleges and universities in Canada.

# CampusTours

**www.campustours.com**

**What:** CampusTours LLC, a for-profit company, has created this website to allow students to tour 850 college campuses from the comfort of their homes. Visitors to the site can take three types of tours: the standard virtual tour, the virtual reality tour, and a multimedia tour. Tours include text descriptions, photographs, maps, videos, and Webcams.

**Best Points:** After searching schools by name or state, you can explore tour features from a separate pop-up window, allowing for easy navigation. Tours are well documented, and accompanying photographs illustrate academic and residential buildings, social life, students, and athletic facilities. Many school listings also have video clips as well as links to the school's website. Information is also provided on tuition, majors offered, admission requirements, and sports offered. At the home page, click on College Viewbooks to request school catalogs or applications.

**What You Should Know:** Full access available. You will need two Web browser plug-ins, QuickTime and RealPlayer (both free downloads), to view tours and video segments. Although the founders of CampusTours stress that no student should actually pick a college without first visiting it in person, they feel that the site is extremely useful for students in the early stages of information gathering, those who are about to take actual tours, and those who might seek additional information after returning from actual tours.

*Two physicians discuss a case. (Photo courtesy of Comstock)*

## Career Guide to Industries

**www.bls.gov/oco**

**What:** The *Career Guide to Industries* is published by the U.S. Department of Labor to educate people about industry employment options and educational requirements. It is revised every two years.

**Best Points:** Information on career options, educational requirements, employment, earnings, and outlooks in 43 U.S. industries is covered in this useful publication. Some of the industries covered include construction, air transportation, Internet, software publishers, advertising and public relations services, health care, and federal government.

**What You Should Know:** Full access available. This is an excellent resource for those interested in learning about industries, career options, and educational requirements to enter various field.

## The Career Key

**www.ncsu.edu/careerkey**

**What:** This site, created by a professor emeritus of education at North Carolina State University, will be useful if you're feeling a bit overwhelmed about your future, as it allows you to take a personality test to help you decide which career path will be the best fit.

**Best Points:** Once you take this site's professional career test—which measures your skills, abilities, values, interests, and personality—you can view lists of jobs that fit your personality type. Clicking on job titles in these lists will link you to the U.S. Department of Labor's *Occupational Outlook Handbook,* which provides information on job duties, college majors, and educational requirements. The site also includes guidance information for counselors and educators.

**What You Should Know:** Fee-based service (to take the test). This is a quick and easy tool for those looking to learn more about themselves, and it has consistently received positive ratings from middle school, high school, and college students.

# Career-College.com

**www.career-college.com**

**What:** Career-College.com, sponsored by EDge Interactive Publishing, is a source for students interested in information on Canadian career colleges (or vocational schools). Use this site to research schools and programs (including virtual campus tours) and learn about financial aid options.

**Best Points:** The Search by School section lists schools alphabetically, with each listing providing one of more of the following: a link to the school's website, program information, online application, virtual tour, and email addresses. The Search by Career section allows users to find colleges based on their career interests.

**What You Should Know:** Full access available. This is a basic clearinghouse of information on Canadian career schools.

# CareerOneStop: Financial Aid Center

**www.careeronestop.org/FINANCIAL/FinancialAidHome.asp**

**What:** CareerOneStop is sponsored by the U.S. Department of Labor. It is designed to help students and job seekers find information regarding education, employment, and career development. The site's Financial Aid Center pinpoints all sources of assistance for college ranging from government programs, scholarships, and training providers.

**Best Points:** There's a lot of information here—links to web resources for financial aid, articles on college and career planning, and a search tool for opportunities with the Workforce Investment Act. Check out the Financial Aid Advisor, an interactive tool designed to find out all options you can use to pay for your college education or work training.

**What You Should Know:** Limited access available. The Financial Aid Center requires completion of a questionnaire regarding your financial status. If you are deemed a dependent, then you'll have to provide financial information about your parents as well. These questions may seem intrusive, but necessary to qualify for key government programs such as a Pell Grants.

# CAREERS & COLLEGES

www.careersandcolleges.com

**What:** This site provides college planning resources for students. It is operated by Alloy Education, a provider of targeted media and promotional programs.

**Best Points:** Sections include Search for Scholarships, Explore Colleges, Find Student Loans, Consider Career Schools, and Discover Careers & Majors. There is also an Ask the Dean feature, articles on college-related issues, a Students Perspective Blog, and information on a scholarship offered by the site's operator.

**What You Should Know:** Limited access available. You must register for all of the main sections, but you can read the articles and access the blogs and Ask the Dean section without registering.

# CareerVoyages.gov

www.careervoyages.gov

**What:** This site, a collection of education and career information, is the joint effort of the U.S. Departments of Labor and Education. Although much of the information it provides is career-related, a good deal of it concerns the training and education needed to attain one's career of choice. The site is also available in Spanish.

**Best Points:** The Students section has easy to understand information, laying out a variety of choices for students to explore. This includes information on fast-growing industries and career options by education level; careers in the military, apprenticeships and volunteer opportunities; the financial benefits of going to college; and links to many resources to help students obtain financial aid and explore careers. The Parents section has resources that show parents how they can assist their children in making college and career decisions, as well as how to finance their education. The Career Advisors section offers links to education and training opportunities, assessment tests, job placement tools, and general references that will help them assist their students in making education and career decisions. Students can also read online versions of *InDemand* magazine, which details careers and educational requirements in fast-growing industries.

**What You Should Know:** Full access available. This is a very useful site for students, parents, and counselors/educators.

## Cash for College

**www.nasfaa.org/AnnualPubs/CashforCollege.pdf**

**What:** Brought to you by the National Association of Student Financial Aid Administrators, this online publication provides a wealth of information about college costs and how to manage them.

> **Did You Know?**
> Seventy-five percent of undergraduates at U.S. colleges and universities received some form of financial aid in 2004-05, according to the U.S. Department of Education.

**Best Points:** With its question-and-answer format, *Cash for College* is simple and easy to read. Questions range in complexity from what colleges cost to how to compare different financial aid packages. The Financial Aid Checklist offers a handy worksheet to keep your college application and aid deadlines in order.

**What You Should Know:** Full access available. Some of the information presented is pretty basic and lacks detail, but this is a good place to learn about paying your way through college. Note: This document is in PDF format. You will need to download a copy of the free Adobe Acrobat Reader to view the publication. (See the Glossary for more info.)

## Center for Student Opportunity: College Center

**www.csocollegecenter.org**

**What:** The College Center is a website sponsored by the non-profit organization, the Center for Student Opportunity. Its purpose is to help promote college access and educational opportunities for first generation college students or those belonging to underserved groups.

**Best Points:** This is a great site for first generation college students, but especially so for their parents. Basic information such as a search for the best schools and the application process is available but with detail to calm even the most nervous parent. You'll want to check out the fast facts profile for each college which includes student and faculty ratio, multi-cultural offerings, and lists all distinguished first generation or minority alums. Another helpful section is Programs in Practice, a database which lists organizations or programs promoting college-bound awareness to young students belonging to minority groups, or underserved populations, many of whom may someday be first generation college students.

**What You Should Know:** Limited access available; free registration is required to target schools best suited to your interests and educational needs.

## Choosing a Career or Vocational School

**www.ftc.gov/bcp/edu/pubs/consumer/products/pro13.shtm**

**What:** This article, provided by the U.S. Federal Trade Commission, offers advice to students considering a private vocational or correspondence school.

**Best Points:** The article covers the importance of researching the qualifications of schools, how to compare schools based on their cost and quality, and how to file a complaint against a school if you feel you've been a victim of consumer fraud. Websites and other contact information are provided for more information on protecting yourself from fraudulent, deceptive, or unfair business practices.

**What You Should Know:** Full access available. Although brief in length, the information presented at this website is highly useful.

## ChristianCollegeMentor.com

**www.christiancollegementor.com**

**What:** ChristianCollegeMentor.com is an online resource created by the National Association of Christian College Admissions Personnel and the Council for Christian Colleges & Universities. It provides students and their families with information on selecting a Christian college, applying for admission, and financing higher education. The site has the following sections: What Is ChristianCollegeMentor?, Plan for College, Select a School, Financial Aid, Online Applications, Career Center, Ask an Expert, and My Mentor.

**Best Points:** Each section of this website is useful, but the most helpful sections are Select a School, Online Application, Career

Center, and My Mentor. Users of the Undergraduate Matching Assistant in the Select a School section can search for Christian colleges by undergraduate enrollment, geographical region, sports teams, graduate programs offered, religious affiliation, and major. This section also offers a comparative college feature where you can compare Christian colleges by location, percent of students receiving financial aid, average class size, and setting. The Online Application section allows you to apply to more than 85 Christian colleges and universities. The Career Center helps students evaluate their interests and aptitudes and match them to appropriate college majors as well as Christian universities that offer the suggested majors. The My Mentor section allows you to store and organize the information you have gathered by accessing different parts of the site.

**What You Should Know:** Limited access available; free registration required for certain areas (Plan for College, Online Applications, and My Mentor) of this site. This is a very useful site for students interested in learning more about college-related issues and attending a Christian higher education institution.

# College & Career Programs for Deaf Students

http://gri.gallaudet.edu/ccg

**What:** This is an online version of a print publication produced by the National Technical Institute for the Deaf and Gallaudet University, a leading academic institution for deaf, hard of hearing, and hearing students in Washington, DC. It lists postsecondary programs for deaf students and information on admissions and support services.

**Best Points:** The site provides detailed information on more than 100 college programs for deaf students. Information is provided on the type of institution, tuition and other costs, enrollment, admission requirements, and other categories. Educational and support services for deaf students—such as classroom communication practices, the availability of tutors and notetakers, and sign language classes—are also listed. Full contact information is provided for each college. The site also offers an excellent list of questions deaf students should ask when choosing a college.

**What You Should Know:** Full access available. This is an excellent resource for deaf and hard of hearing students interested in learning more about postsecondary options.

## College and University Rankings

http://door.library.uiuc.edu/edx/rankings.htm

**What:** Americans love lists, so it was inevitable that someone would compile rankings of best colleges. This site, created by professionals at the Education and Social Science Library at the University of Illinois at Urbana-Champaign, gathers links to many of the most popular and offbeat college lists.

**Best Points:** The site breaks lists down into the following categories: General/Undergraduate, Graduate Research Programs, Business, Law, International, and Humor and Satire. After viewing more credible lists from The Princeton Review or *Kiplinger's*, check out the Humor section to read more whimsical entries such as the Academic Squirrels of California and Beyond site (which ranks colleges by the size, girth, and health of their squirrel population).

**What You Should Know:** Full access available. College rankings are not without controversy. Many students and educators question the validity and usefulness of any college ranking system. To address these concerns, the site offers a Caution & Controversy page that lists more than 30 articles about the pros and cons of rankings and how to use them wisely.

## The College Blog Network

www.thecollegeblognetwork.com

**What:** This site serves as an index for all blogs written by college students concerning topics ranging from campus life to political groups to the latest Hollywood offerings.

**Best Points:** No need to surf the web to find blogs meaningful to your own situation and interests. This site organizes blogs and makes them accessible to students throughout the world. You are also encouraged to rate your fellow students' blogs—bumps are good, dumps are not. This result in a daily top five blogs list as well as those most dumped.

**What You Should Know:** Limited access available; free registration is required. Note that in order to register, you must have an educational email address (an address that ends in ".edu"). This ensures that all participating bloggers are actual students. The site claims schools are joining daily, which would result in more bloggers entering the network, however, currently for example, only one school in the entire state of Arizona is represented.

# College Board.com

www.collegeboard.com

**What:** The College Board is a nonprofit association of more than 5,4,00 schools, colleges, universities, and other educational organizations. Its SAT, PSAT, and AP tests are widely used throughout the United States to gauge academic achievement.

**Best Points:** This site offers very detailed information about the SAT and will be especially helpful to high school students as it contains PSAT information and articles such as "Getting College Credit Before College." Plan for College features planning guides for high school students and useful articles such as "Twenty Questions to Ask Your School Counselor." The Pay for College section will help parents and students get an idea of what to expect financially. Try out College MatchMaker (click on Find a College), which finds colleges with similar characteristics to ones you already know that you like. You can apply to more than 500 colleges and universities through this site, and you will find many helpful articles. Also on this site, you can get free email newsletters and alerts that give you updates about the SAT, PSAT, and AP exams, as well as test preparation tips from the test makers.

**SAT Scores**
The College Board reports that the average combined scores (mathematics and critical reading) for the high school graduating class of 2007 who took the SAT declined to the lowest point in nearly 10 years. The average score on the reading section was 502 (out of a possible 800 points) and the average math score was 515 (out of a possible 800 points).

**What You Should Know:** Limited access available; registration required for certain areas of this site. This site should help ease your fears about taking college admissions tests.

## College Bound Network

**www.collegebound.net/content**

**What:** This website contains feature articles on topics such as finding a college, Greek life, financial aid, college myths, testing skills, and scholarships.

**Best Points:** The articles are varied and interesting to read, with information specifically catered to students' concerns. There are 40 article categories, including College Degree Breakdown, College Trends, College Admissions, College Scholarships, and SAT/ACT Test Prep & College Exams.

**What You Should Know:** Full access available. This site contains a wide variety of informative articles on college-related topics.

## College Drinking: Changing the Culture

**www.collegedrinkingprevention.gov**

**What:** This site was created by the National Institute on Alcohol Abuse and Alcoholism in response to the growing problem of alcohol abuse among college students. Visit the site to read articles and statistics about the dangers of alcohol abuse and its prevalence on college campuses.

**Did You Know?**
According to Facts on Tap, nearly 160,000 first-year college students drop out of school each year due to reasons related to drugs and alcohol abuse.

**Best Points:** Click on How to Cut Down on Your Drinking to read short articles about how to know if you or someone you know is an alcoholic and get tips on how to cut down on your alcohol consumption (of course, you must be 21 or older to legally drink alcoholic beverages) or completely eliminate drinking. If you click on Students from the home page, you can read interactive and useful information about common myths about alcohol and its effects on the body.

**What You Should Know:** Full access available. This is an informative (and at times alarming) site about the often-overlooked dangers of alcohol and the widespread alcohol abuse that occurs at colleges across the country. Check out this site to educate yourself before you even think about attending your first keg party.

# College is Possible

**www.collegeispossible.org**

**What:** This website, sponsored by the American Council on Education, is full of resources for parents, students, and education professionals. It is divided into three main sections: Preparing for College, Choosing the Right College, and Paying for College.

**Best Points:** Preparing for College offers A Guide for Parents: Ten Steps to Prepare Your Child for College, a list of recommended courses for middle and high school students (including minimum years and types of classes), and websites and books for further exploration. Choosing the Right College has an admissions and financial aid timeline, links to college search websites, and information for international students. Under Paying for College, read about financial aid and scholarship options, but be sure to read the warnings about scholarship scams and how to avoid them.

**What You Should Know:** Full access available. This is an excellent resource with information for all those involved in the college and university search.

# College Navigator

**http://nces.ed.gov/collegenavigator**

**What:** This website, which was developed by the National Center for Education Statistics, allows you to search for colleges based on name of school, state, zip code, program/major, level of award, and other criteria.

**Best Points:** The search tool is user friendly, allowing you to use as many search criteria as you want. For example, you could create a list of all schools in one state or search for all four-year non-profit institutions with fewer than 5,000 students. Each school listing provides a link to its website and includes information on enrollment, application fees, tuition costs, degrees offered, federal aid options, and more.

**What You Should Know:** Full access available. This site is a good general search and research tool. Also note that because a school is listed on this site doesn't mean the institution or its programs has been approved by the U.S. Department of Education.

# College Parents of America

## www.collegeparents.org

**What:** A national membership association that assists parents as they prepare for and put their children through college.

**Best Points:** Parents who become members of this association receive information on financial aid, savings strategies, the application and admissions process, and other college-related issues.

**What You Should Know:** Fee-based service. Many of the resources at this site require membership in the association. Free materials include a small list of articles on college-related issues, college search engines, a blog for parents, *Decade of Decisions* (a newsletter about college planning for parents) and a list of Web links to financial aid, admissions, and campus safety websites.

# College Planning

## http://collegeplan.org

**What:** This site was developed by the College Planning Network, a nonprofit college and career planning organization based in the U.S. Pacific Northwest.

**Best Points:** The site provides good advice for both high school students with just a few years to college and younger students with college in their more distant sights. It covers the general admission and selection process, offers tips for paying for tuition and applying for scholarships and loans, and includes links to additional information. Also included is a scholarship search engine that allows students to browse scholarships that match their characteristics and preferences. Archives of the College Planning Network's online newsletter, *Beyond High School,* are also available.

**What You Should Know:** Full access available. The online scholarship and general college information is useful and applicable to all students, not just those living in the Pacific Northwest.

# College Results Online

## www.collegeresults.org

**What:** Are you still working on your final round of college applications? Do you want to see how your college of choice compares to other schools? Do you wonder what your chances are of graduating "on time"? If so, check out this website. College Results offers a wealth of information on universities and colleges nationwide, their faculty, and students. Created by The Education Trust, a nonprofit advocate for quality education, this website presents data gathered by the U.S. Department of Education's Graduation Rate Survey.

**Best Points:** The interactive search tool is the most useful part of this website. Simply pick your school, or search for a group of schools. You can also search according to student characteristic such as an ethnicity or institutional characteristic such as a sports program. Information is presented in table or graph format, and also compares your school with up to 50 other similar colleges. So what can you learn? Everything! Besides the school's vital stats—size, locale, finances, ethnic diversity—you can also research the percentage and types of degree conferred, the graduation rate of students, part-time vs. full time students, number of Pell Grant recipients, and more. You can even compare your ACT or SAT scores with those of currently enrolled students.

**What You Should Know:** Full access available. While the focus of this website is on a school's graduation rate, the information regarding the school itself and its student body is equally important and helpful. It's certainly worth a look—especially if you need help making that final college choice.

# College Savings Plans Network

**www.collegesavings.org**

**What:** This website, from the National Association of State Treasurers, offers information on college savings plans, searchable by state.

**Best Points:** In addition to searching plans, you can also read answers to frequently asked questions about the differences between savings plans and prepaid tuition programs, who is eligible for plans, how to file for tax exemptions, and more. The website also hosts a lengthy guide to understanding 529 savings plans, available for viewing as both HTML and PDF documents.

**What You Should Know:** Full access available. There is not a lot of information on the site (and most of what is presented has been picked up from other sites), but the savings plan search and comparison option is easy to use and yields detailed results.

*(Photo courtesy of Dynamic Graphics)*

# CollegeConfidential.com

**www.collegeconfidential.com**

**What:** College Confidential is a for-profit company that seeks to demystify the college admissions process and provide information on other college issues. Its editorial team consists of admissions counselors, a parent with a child who has participated in the admissions process, and authors of books on college admission. The website has four useful main sections: College Search, College Admissions, College Discussion, and Financial Aid & Planning. Each section offers articles written by the staff or other professionals and links to books and websites.

**Best Points:** There is a wealth of information presented here about college admissions and other college-related topics. The Ask the Dean section features answers to questions such as Is applying to college electronically safe?, How do I go about finding a good women's college?, How do I compare larger universities and smaller colleges?, and Is a college visit necessary? The College Discussion Forums are full of lively interaction among students interested in learning more about various aspects of college.

**What You Should Know:** Full access available. This website has excellent information for students interested in learning more about college. Note: The site also advertises fee-based professional services offered by the site's staff.

# CollegeData

**www.collegedata.com**

**What:** Brought to you by 1st Financial Bank, CollegeData has a wealth of information for students, parents, counselors, and others who advise students about college. The site has three main sections: College 411-Making Your College Match, Prepare and Apply-The Goods on Getting In, and Pay Your Way-Financing Your College Education. The site also has a scholarship finder, a college search feature, a newsletter, and a link to the Common

Application that students can use to apply to more than 300 colleges and universities.

**Best Points:** Each section of this site offers comprehensive information and articles that will help students make important decisions about their education. *College Buzz,* an online magazine, offers interesting stories from students about the application process and articles on time management, dealing with stress, and managing financial issues. A Data Locker feature allows visitors to save interesting articles, college information, and scholarships for further review. Users can even use this feature to write themselves notes on followup issues and use electronic labels to sort and categorize their lists. Users of the College Chances feature can enter information about their academic qualifications and extracurricular involvement and receive an estimate of their chances of admittance into a specific college or university.

**What You Should Know:** Limited access available. Visitors must register to use the College Chances, Common Application, and Data Locker. This is an excellent site for students and others interested in learning more about college.

# CollegeJournal

### www.collegejournal.com

**What:** Brought to you by *The Wall Street Journal,* this site features articles and reviews direct from the newspaper.

### Best Points:

The home page includes feature stories that are updated daily, covering interesting subjects such as how to choose the right college major, increasing competition for college admission, and colleges' efforts to fight violence on campus.

**What You Should Know:** Full access available. This site provides a wealth of timely and interesting information on college issues.

# CollegeNET: It Pays to Think

### www.collegenet.com

**What:** Are you good with words and looking for a novel way to earn money for college? If so, you've come to the right place at CollegeNet. All it takes is for you to register at CollegeNet, find a discussion forum that interests you, and write about the topic in questions (or post a video that is also judged by other members). If your writing or video wows the other members, you receive points that accrue toward scholarships. Members who receive the most points earn scholarships. CollegeNET also offers a College Search engine, a Scholarship Search engine, and a section where you can apply online to multiple colleges.

**Best Points:** The discussion forum/video scholarship is a great idea if you are a creative person. The College Search tool allows students to browse colleges by type of institution (two-year, four-year, vocational, medical, etc.), location, enrollment, major, tuition, sports offered, and average GPA. The Scholarship Search offers detailed search criteria to help you find scholarships.

**What You Should Know:** Limited access available. If you plan on applying to schools online and compete for CollegeNet scholarships, you will need to register.

# CollegeNews.org

**www.collegenews.org**

**What:** Brought to you by The Annapolis Group, a nonprofit alliance of the nation's leading independent liberal arts colleges, this site delivers the latest news, developments, and trends occurring at liberal arts colleges across the nation.

> **Did You Know?**
> Nineteen percent of U.S. presidents attended a residential liberal arts college, according to The Annapolis Group.

**Best Points:** This resource is a good way to learn about the goals and issues of liberal arts schools in general. The home page is well organized, featuring recent news and editorial pieces. You can also access links to other websites with information on general issues of higher education. A list of member schools (and links) is also provided.

**What You Should Know:** Full access available. This resource may be more useful to journalists seeking information on liberal arts colleges than to a high school student researching his or her options. However, if you are looking for an overview of the benefits of a liberal arts education, this site will be most useful.

# CollegeRoommates.net

### www.collegeroommates.net

**What:** CollegeRoommates.net provides a lighthearted look at finding and successfully interacting with a college roommate.

**Best Points:** The site features advice—as well as humorous and sometimes horrific stories—about living with college roommates in dorms and in on- and off-campus apartments. The site also discusses the pros and cons of living alone. There is also a very short section on how to locate a good roommate and a link to a for-profit company that helps match up college roommates.

**What You Should Know:** Full access available.

# CollegeSource Online

### www.collegesource.org

**What:** Sponsored by the Career Guidance Foundation, CollegeSource Online features more than 42,560 college catalogs in complete, original page format. You can download and view each college's catalog as a Portable Document File (.PDF). General information, such as institution type, degree levels, tuition costs, and enrollment is also listed for each college and university.

**Best Points:** If you want to research vital statistics on schools, simply type in school names and click on the Profile logo to compare tuition costs, enrollment, and admissions requirements. However, the highlight of this site is its thousands of online academic catalogs. View the latest catalogs, or study archived versions.

**What You Should Know:** Limited access available. Registration required for most areas of this site. To view school catalogs, you need to register for a free trial account, which allows you to view up to three school documents. But if you would like full access to this site, you will need to subscribe.

# CollegeSurfing.com

### http://collegesurfing.com

**What:** Brought to you by the CollegeBound Network, this site provides a useful college search engine that allows you to browse 4,000 schools by name, location, and major, as well as articles on college- and career-related topics.

**Best Points:** Besides the general search feature, the site also includes information on more than 300 career schools.

**What You Should Know:** Full access available. This is a quick and easy way to browse several different colleges and universities and compare and contrast available programs, costs, requirements, and student body compositions. However, to ensure the accuracy and currency of these statistics, you should visit the actual websites of the schools in which you are most interested.

## CollegeToolkit.com

### www.collegetoolkit.com

**What:** CollegeToolkit provides information on scholarships via a search engine (and touts its website as unique because it provides "direct access to online scholarship applications"). CollegeToolkit also offers a $1,000 scholarship to high school seniors and college students.

**Best Points:** The scholarship search engine is a great way to learn more about financial aid. Users can search by their personal profile, geography, heritage/religion, extracurriculars, family affiliations, and other categories. By registering, students can save their scholarship searches in a "Briefcase" and be notified when new scholarships become available that match their personal profile and interests. In addition to a comprehensive scholarship search feature, this site also features a searchable college database (by state, major, etc.), career assessment tools that help users determine their best career fit, calculators (cost of college, college savings, expected family contribution, financial aid award, etc.), a Scholarship & College Advice Blog, a Career Interest Profiler, and useful articles about financial aid and college admissions.

**What You Should Know:** Limited access available. You must register to use the scholarship search feature or to save your results after searching for college. This is a good resource to learn more about college funding, colleges, and related topics.

## CollegeZone

### http://collegezone.com

**What:** Sponsored by the Illinois Student Assistance Commission (an official agency of the state of Illinois), this website offers detailed information on college for students, parents, and counselors.

**Best Points:** The website has specialized information for students in grades 6-8 and 9-12 and those who are already pursuing undergraduate and graduate studies. The section for high school students has five subsections: Planning (which features a college-bound checklist, a college cost calculator, and information on the importance of extracurricular activities as you prepare to apply to colleges), Finding/Applying (which describes the types of colleges and degrees), Financing (information on scholarships, grants, loans, and other types of financial aid), FAQs, and Helpful Links. Students and parents can also sign up for E-Messaging, an email service that provides information on financial aid deadlines and other college-related topics.

**What You Should Know:** Full access available. This website has useful information for almost anyone interested in planning for, applying to, and attending college. CollegeZone will be especially useful to those interested in attending academic institutions in Illinois. Detailed information (including educational offerings, contact information, and costs) about Illinois colleges is available at the site. This website is also available in Spanish.

# Collegiate Choice Walking Tours

**www.collegiatechoice.com**

**What:** This for-profit site, created by independent college advisors in Bergen County, New Jersey, offers price lists and ordering information for video tours of hundreds of college campuses located around the world. There are also free resources, such as tips on taking college campus tours, basic college prep advice, lists of school rankings from popular magazines, and humorous articles on the college application process.

**Best Points:** After visiting and filming hundreds of college campuses, the authors of this site have good advice for you to make the most of your campus trips. The advice on whether to apply for early admission and how to best craft your college essay is also informative. After visiting the "serious" sections of the site, definitely read through the funny acceptance and rejection letters sent in by actual students and their parents for laughs.

**What You Should Know:** Fee-based service; free resources available. Though the videotaped tours might be useful, they should only be used to complement an actual visit to a school that you are interested in. If you visit this site, use it for the free resources, then browse the list of schools and product reviews from the *Chicago Tribune, Los Angeles Times, Boston Globe,* and other publications to help you determine if the tapes would make a good investment.

## The Common Application

**www.commonapp.org**

**What:** Administered by the National Association of Secondary School Principals, the Common Application program allows students to complete one application to send to all participating different colleges and universities of interest.

**Best Points:** Simplifying the application process for students who apply to multiple colleges, the Common Application has eliminated repetitive work, varying and confusing deadlines, and mailing issues. Nearly 350 colleges accept this form, and all participating schools pledge to weigh it equally against the school's own application. Using Common Application Online, you can register and set up your own account, save your application, and send it electronically to schools of your choice. You can also choose to send the Common Application through the mail by printing out the finished application and sending the hard copy to schools directly.

**What You Should Know:** Full access available. Not all schools participate in the program, so be sure to check the list of schools before starting to fill out your forms. In addition, some colleges and universities require that you complete supplemental forms in addition to the Common Application. The website provides a list of schools requiring these additional forms, many of which can also be completed online. You may want to check with the school directly to verify requirements.

## Common Black College Application

**www.eduinconline.com/eduweb/apply.htm**

**What:** EDU, Inc. offers the Common Black College Application for students who are interested in attending a Historically Black College or University.

**Best Points:** Students can apply to up to 34 Historically Black

Colleges and Universities at this website.

**What You Should Know:** Fee-based service; there is a fee of $34.95 to use the service and apply to the colleges online.

# Cultural Experiences Abroad

**www.gowithcea.com**

**What:** This for-profit organization organizes study abroad programs in Australia, Costa Rica, England, France, Ireland, Italy, Mexico, Spain, and other countries. At its website, you can learn about programs, view photos, and read students' accounts of their travels and tips for studying abroad. Other available features include RSS feeds, blogs, podcasts, and a live chat feature.

**Best Points:** This website is well organized and informative. Detailed information is provided on financing, transferring college credits, study abroad safety issues, and other topics.

**FYI**
According to Open *Doors 2007,* the following colleges sent the most students abroad in 2005-06: New York University, Michigan State University, the University of Texas-Austin, Penn State University, the University of Illinois-Urbana-Champaign, the University of Minnesota-Twin Cities, the University of California-Los Angeles, the University of Florida, the University of Georgia, and Ohio State University.

**What You Should Know:** Full access available. Unlike many other study abroad organizations, Cultural Experiences Abroad offers programs to college students of all ages—not just juniors. This organization also emphasizes that studying abroad can be simple and doesn't have to break the bank. If you always thought studying abroad was out of reach because of financial reasons, a visit to this website might change your mind.

# Database of Institutions and Programs Accredited by Recognized United States Accrediting Organizations

**www.chea.org/search**

**What:** This site, sponsored by the Council for Higher Education Accreditation (CHEA), offers a searchable database of approximately 7,000 degree-granting and non-degree-granting institutions that have been recognized either by the CHEA or by the U.S. Department of Education or both.

**Best Points:** The database provides comprehensive information on accredited programs. This site also provides details on more than 17,000 individual college programs in 62 fields of education, such as business, health care, interior design, law, library science, nursing, social work, and veterinary medicine. Both the Accredited Institutions and Accredited Programs databases are searchable by institution name, US state/territory, foreign country, and accreditor—making information gathering a snap.

**What You Should Know:** Full access available. This is a very useful resource and the place to go for information on accredited colleges and universities and educational programs.

## Design Schools Directory

**www.design-school-directory.com**

**What:** This website, created by Career Advantage, provides a directory of schools offering programs in graphic design, fashion design, interior design, Web design, game design, and online design.

**Best Points:** Under each design category, you can browse schools by state. School listings include a short description of the school's degree programs and a link to request more information. Also check out the Resources link (located on the bottom of the home page) for links to pages detailing design careers, industry trends, and how to select a design school.

**What You Should Know:** Full access available. The school listings are useful, but the most valuable area of this site is the easy-to-miss Resources page. This is a handy site for students just starting to explore their options in the design field.

## DiscoverNursing.com

**www.discovernursing.com**

**What:** Created by Johnson & Johnson Services, this website is a comprehensive tool for aspiring nurses.

**Best Points:** The site features the following sections that will be useful to aspiring nurses: What, which details more than 40 nursing specialties and the benefits of becoming a nurse; How, which details educational paths for aspiring nurses and offers a Nursing Program Search (searchable by state, school type, enrollment, degree type, and online education availability), a Nursing Program Search (searchable by state, school type, enrollment, degree type, and online education availability), a Preparing for Nursing School section (that provides information on choosing a program and summer nursing camps for high school students), a Nursing Scholarship Search (searchable by state, GPA, ethnicity, and academic level), and a Nursing Programs Without Waiting Lists (a key resource because many

*Employment for registered nurses is expected to grow much faster than the average for all careers through 2016. (Photo courtesy of Dynamic Graphics)*

nursing schools are turning away aspiring nursing students due to faculty shortages and other factor).

**What You Should Know:** Full access available. This site is a invaluable tool for high school students and others who are interested in careers in nursing.

# DistanceStudies.com

### www.distancestudies.com

**What:** This site provides information on distance education programs in the United States and Canada. You can search more than 860 programs and read articles on featured programs, admissions information, and the benefits of distance education.

**Best Points:** You can search for schools by field of study or degree offered. Listings include school contact information, a virtual tour, and program descriptions. Program profiles cover the certificate type, program duration, whether there is an on-campus requirement (or if you can take all classes online), prerequisites, and tuition costs. After researching schools, be sure to visit the Distance Learning Articles section, which addresses the application process, choosing a career, the basics of distance learning, securing financial aid and/or scholarships, job searching, and study habits.

**What You Should Know:** Full access available. This resource is worth a visit for the articles alone, but the distance education search engine is useful as well. Recommended for students who are undecided about living on campus.

## Diversity Pipeline Alliance

www.diversitypipeline.com

**What:** The Diversity Pipeline Alliance (an affiliate of the Graduate Management Admission Council) is a nonprofit organization that seeks to encourage African American, Hispanic American, and Native American students to pursue business education from middle school to the MBA and beyond. Its website offers useful information for high school and college students interested in learning more about business education and careers.

**Best Points:** The Destination College section has many useful areas, including Getting Into College, which offers suggested classes and preparation activities for high school freshmen, sophomores, juniors, and seniors, and Paying for College, which provides an overview of financial aid and available resources and sources of additional information. The site also features useful information and statistics for teachers, guidance counselors, and parents about the dearth of minorities studying business and efforts by the Alliance to encourage young people to study business. Additional sections provide resources for undergraduates majoring in business and an overview of the MBA.

**What You Should Know:** Full access available. Although this site focuses on encouraging minorities to pursue education and careers in business, many of its resources will be of use to students from all ethnic backgrounds.

## Dr. Mom's Guide to College

www.lions.odu.edu/~kkilburn/dr_mom_home.htm

**What:** This unique website, created by Kerry S. Kilburn, Ph.D. (a professor at Old Dominion University in Norfolk, Virginia), has personal advice for students heading to college. Read tips on interacting with roommates, students, and teachers, balancing work with play, and staying organized.

**Best Points:** The site is organized into main bullet points, each of which links you to a new page of content. Kilburn's advice on handling yourself in the classroom is insightful and funny: "No cell phones or beepers unless your life, or a family member's life, depends on it. Pizza delivery and party plans, strange as this may seem, don't count." Though you may have heard much of her advice before (perhaps from your own mom), Kilburn's points may be more easily digested from this site.

**What You Should Know:** Full access available. Kilburn's writing is conversational and at times humorous and should keep your attention as you browse through her main points. Definitely give this site a quick read through regardless if you're a high school student, just beginning college, or a college senior wanting to milk the most of your last year in school.

# Dynamy

### http://dynamy.org

**What:** Dynamy, Inc. is a non-profit educational organization located in Worcester, Massachusetts, and focused since 1969 on helping young people find their place and purpose in life. This is achieved through internship programs, a youth academy, and a wilderness expedition. There are also some seminars offering college credit through nearby Clark University.

**Best Points:** If you've considered the possibility of spending a gap year, check out this site. Dynamy links many internship possibilities in many areas ranging from culinary/hospitality to government. The site does a good job of explaining all details—how to apply, type of jobs, housing, and other financial concerns—which will put many parents at ease!

**What You Should Know:** Full access available to view the site. However, a written application, including references, transcripts, and personal interviews are required for consideration into the Dynamy program.

# eCampusTours.com

### http://ecampustours.com

**What:** This site has been developed by EdFinancial Services, a private, nonprofit corporation interested in helping students learn more about college and financial aid options. As its name suggests, the main focus of this website is 360 degree x 360 degree tours of more than 1,200 college campuses in all 50 states and the District of Columbia. In addition to the campus tours, the site also offers sections on College Planning, Campus Life, Careers, and Paying for College.

**Best Points:** For students unable to physically visit their college choices, this website is an excellent resource. Tours include college buildings, dorms, biology labs, libraries, student activity centers, and athletic fields. The College Planning section offers a variety of articles on applying to, choosing, and excelling in college. The Paying for College section provides basic information on loan programs, application information, and repayment options, a scholarship planner, info on how to avoid scholarship scams, a search engine for state-based financial aid, and a scholarship search of more than 10,000 programs that distribute more than 150,000 awards worth more than $36 million. The School Counselors section (click on For Educators) features a variety of useful educational handouts for students.

**What You Should Know:** Full access available. The site is well organized and designed and provides much helpful information to aspiring college students. The campus tours feature is useful, but, of course, it should not replace actual physical campus tours and additional research (visits to a school's website, requests for college catalogs and other brochures, conversations with teachers and former students, etc.) on academic institutions.

**FYI**
*Kiplinger's* magazine prepares an annual list of best colleges that provide a "combination of outstanding academic quality plus an affordable price tag." Here are the top five schools from a recent list: the University of North Carolina-Chapel Hill, the University of Florida, the University of Virginia, the College of William and Mary, and New College of Florida.

# Education Planner

**www.educationplanner.org**

**What:** Developed by American Education Services, a student loan guarantor, this website allows you to search for schools, apply to colleges online, research loan options, prepare and plan for your career, and more. The site is also available in Spanish.

**Best Points:** Useful sections include Thinking About College, Choosing a College, and Paying for College. There is also a scholarship search feature.

**What You Should Know:** Full access available. There is a wealth of helpful articles, tools, and other resources available at this site.

# Education UK

www.educationuk.org

**What:** This site was developed by the British Council, the U.K.'s organization for educational opportunities and cultural relations with more than 100 countries worldwide. You can search schools by location, program length or season, or academic offerings. The site also has an undergraduate and graduate scholarship database, helpful information on required documents, and advice on traveling to England.

**Best Points:** After you've browsed schools, check out *Club U.K.,* an online magazine aimed at international students interested in studying in England. You can read news articles on English tourism, education, technological developments, and more. Under Living in the U.K., read about culture issues, or check out the U.K. Study section to read profiles of students who have previously studied in England.

**What You Should Know:** Full access available. If you want to save your past searches or information of interest, or apply to schools online, you will need to create a free account. However, this is not necessary for browsing most areas of this site.

# Educational Testing Service

www.ets.org

**What:** To get the facts on admissions tests, try this site. It is run by Educational Testing Service, a private educational testing company that develops and administers admissions tests in the United States and 180 other countries.

**Best Points:** You can search this site's database to find information on more than 40 standardized tests, including AP exams, the SAT, the GRE, and the GMAT.

**What You Should Know:** Full access available. This site doesn't contain general college information, but it does provide information for students and educators about standardized tests.

## EduPASS: The SmartStudent Guide to Studying in the USA

**www.edupass.org**

**What:** This site, developed by a college and financial planning expert, is aimed at international students interested in attending college in the United States.

**Best Points:** Information is organized into sections on college admissions, financial aid, language skill requirements, visas and passport information, societal differences, and other things international students need to consider before deciding to study at a U.S. school. The Cultural Differences section is an interesting read and covers everything from overcoming American stereotypes (as loud, boisterous, lazy) to converting international dress and shoe sizes to those used in the United States.

**What You Should Know:** Full access available. Nothing on this site is groundbreaking, but it is a good one-stop resource for international students thinking of studying away from their home countries.

*An agricultural engineer (center) and technician (kneeling) prepare a microturbine for operation with a wind-hybrid system for supplying electric power to remote villages, while another agricultural engineer measures emissions from a diesel generator. (Photo courtesy of Stephen Ausmus, USDA)*

## Engineering K12 Center

**www.engineeringk12.org**

**What:** The American Society for Engineering Education sponsors this site, which is loaded with information for high school students who are interested in pursuing engineering careers. There are section for students and K-12 educators.

**Best Points:** This site features many useful sections for high school students interested in engineering, including The Engineering Alphabet (which describe more than 20 engineering disciplines, including ocean engineering and fire protection engineering); Finding and Affording the Right School (tips on selecting and applying to engineering colleges and universities); College Search Database (which allows users to search by location, city size, enrollment size, distance from home, and key-word); and Outreach Program Database (a directory of K-12 pre-college engineering outreach programs).

**What You Should Know:** Full access available. This site is a top spot for exploring engineering programs and schools.

# Essay Edge.com

**http://essayedge.com**

**What:** Essay Edge is a for-profit company that offers assistance with application essays. The site offers information for people applying to private high school, college, or gradu-ate school.

**Best Points:** You can check out 100 free sample essays at this site and take a Free Admissions Essay Help Course. Additionally, the Admissions Center sec-tion offers a College Search Engine, an SAT Mini Test, and infor-mation on college interviews, scholarships, asking for a recom-mendation, and other topics.

> **Did You Know?**
> According to the National Association for College Admission Counseling, the most important factors used by admissions officers to evaluate college applicants are (in descending order): grades in college prep classes, strength of curriculum, scores from standardized admissions tests, overall GPA, strength of the application essay or writing sample, class rank, and counselor recommendations.

**What You Should Know:** Fee-based service, but there is a good amount of free information available to visitors, especially people interested in learning more about writing college essays and other college-related topics.

# FAFSA4caster

**www.fafsa4caster.ed.gov**

**What:** FAFSA4caster is an online tool from the U.S. Department of Education that helps high school students and their families explore their financial aid options earlier than the student's senior year of high school. The site is also available in Spanish.

**Best Points:** Users of the FAFSA4caster can receive an early esti-mate of their eligibility for federal student aid. Once students are ready to apply for aid, they can transition from FAFSA4caster to FAFSA on the Web. Much of the information that a user has entered into the FAFSA4caster is then added to the FAFSA on the Web application—saving the user time. In addition to helping students estimate the amount of financial aid they will receive, the site also provides an overview of financial aid, types of financial aid, and the steps in the financial aid process.

**What You Should Know:** Limited access available; you will need to provide your Social Security Number and first and last name exactly as they appear on your Social Security Card to use this website. High school students who want to get the early edge when it comes to learning about and applying for financial aid will find this site to be a great resource.

# FASTaid

**www.fastaid.com**

**What:** FASTaid offers a huge database of private sector scholarships, grants, and awards.

**Best Points:** Your search begins by identifying academic disciplines of interest, such as sociology and its subspecialty of paleontology, as well as any particular schools you wish to attend. A list of applicable scholarships and awards are compiled using information given. Scholarship information is well organized, including description, dollar amount, registration deadline, and important contact information. The website also offers basic information for parents—tips on saving for college, a directory of most U.S. colleges and universities, as well recommended publications to help college-bound families.

**What You Should Know:** Limited access available; free, though lengthy, registration is required. When using the scholarship search feature, make sure you identify all possible topics of interest—even if you only have a remote interest in archeology, mark it! Otherwise your list of potential scholarships may be limited.

# FastWeb

**www.fastweb.com**

**What:** This site offers scholarship, college, and job search engines. Based on your responses to questions about your interests, financial need, and location, FastWeb generates a list of colleges, jobs, or scholarship opportunities for further exploration. FastWeb is an affiliate of Monster.com, a popular, for-profit online career network.

**Best Points:** The Find Scholarships search tool is useful to narrow your search and pinpoint funding sources from specialty groups (such as religious organizations and other nonprofits) that match your interests and group memberships. The Choose a College search engine similarly generates a list of schools that match your location preferences, career goals, and academic needs.

**What You Should Know:** Registration required for all areas of this site. You will need to enter personal information such as your name, email address, and mailing address to use the scholarship and college search tools. This process is not only time consuming, but it also is a bit invasive. If your online privacy is important to you, look elsewhere for college and scholarship search assistance.

# Federal Citizen Information Center

**www.pueblo.gsa.gov**

**What:** This organization, part of the U.S. General Services Administration, provides news releases on everything from health and finances to government services and automobiles to careers and education.

**Best Points:** Under the Education menu, you can read timely and interesting articles about education developments and concerns for students of all ages. College topics include financial planning and exploring alternative education options such as getting college credit through the GED program. All resources are available for purchase (for a small fee) or can be read online at no charge. One online publication worth reading is *Think College: Me? Now?* Though aimed at younger students, the information is presented in a simple manner that may be appreciated by older students as well. For example, to show the benefits of going to college, the authors use this helpful scenario: a college graduate who works as a physical therapist assistant can earn enough in one day to buy groceries for a week. On the other hand, a high school graduate who works as an aerobics instructor would have to work three days to buy the same amount of groceries.

**What You Should Know:** Full access available. Visit this site for basic resources on college and other education topics.

# Federal Cyber Service: Scholarship for Service

**www.sfs.opm.gov**

**What:** Federal Cyber Service: Scholarship for Service is an official website of the U.S. government, operated by the Office of Personnel Management. This site is geared towards students interested in someday working as civilians to help protect and strengthen the nation's information infrastructure. Merit-based scholarships cover all expenses for up to two years of college, with a one-year minimum service obligation for a federal agency. Agencies can also search this database for qualified students eligible for internship positions and future employment.

**Best Points:** The FAQs section is thorough and gives information helpful to students and their parents. Some areas covered include the application process, scholarship, and internship details.

**What You Should Know:** Limited access available. Only those students approved by a participating school, and enrolled in the SFS program will receive a user code to gain full access to the system.

# Federal Student Aid

**www.studentaid.ed.gov**

**What:** When it comes to financial aid facts, this site, which is run by the U.S. Department of Education, is near the top of the list.

**Best Points:** This comprehensive financial aid site is divided into six main categories: Preparing for Your Education, Choosing a School, Applying for Admission, Funding Your Education, While Attending School, and Repaying Your Loans. There are many free publications available on this site, such as *Myths About Financial Aid and Do You Need Money for College?* In addition, *The Student Guide,* which includes information on scholarship scams, is available at no cost. Other useful sections include a Financial Aid and Scholarship Wizard, a scholarship search engine, and a Scholarship Matching Wizard.

**What You Should Know:** Full access available. Since this is a federal website, students, parents, and educators will have to look elsewhere to find information on private loans and scholarships.

# Finaid: The SmartStudent Guide to Financial Aid

**www.finaid.org**

**What:** If you're looking for the facts on all sorts of financial aid, this award-winning site, created by financial aid and college planning author Mark Kantrowitz, will be a perfect fit.

**Best Points:** This website is loaded with facts on how to financially plan for college. It is divided into Student, Parent, and Educator sections for easy access to specific information, such as how to create a savings plan. The Savings section features tips on everything from prepaid tuition to an extensive College Savings Checklist. This site's many Calculators are especially useful, including the College Cost Projector and the Student Budget Calculator. Student, parent, and private loans are described in detail, as is loan consolidation. The Military Aid section provides information on the Armed Forces recruiting programs, as well as aid programs for veterans and their children. The Ask the Aid Advisor section answers FAQs and allows users to email questions to experts. Also on this site, you can sign up to receive other free financial aid publications.

> ### The Hidden Costs of College
>
> College costs don't end with tuition and room and board. In fact, *Forbes* reports that the average college student spends an additional $5,000 per year on clothing, transportation, textbooks, dorm furnishings, school supplies, and other extras.

**What You Should Know:** Full access available. This is a comprehensive site for anyone seeking college financial aid information.

# Financial Aid Officer

**www.financialaidofficer.com**

**What:** This privately managed resource site is part of the Student Loan Network, a collection of Internet sites created to inform students and parents about loan and financial aid options.

**Best Points:** The majority of the site is informational, with extensive coverage of the types of financial aid available, how to determine eligibility, steps and deadlines for applying for financial aid, and how to organize a budget for education costs. The authors of this site succeed in breaking down the often confusing information about aid and loan options. This is a great resource to not only learn about financial aid, but also to apply for programs, either through links to federal aid websites or by registering for assistance from the Student Loan Network. You can also sign up your email address to receive a monthly online newsletter about new and exciting scholarships, news, and links to other useful sites.

**What You Should Know:** Full access available. The informational part of this website is free, easy to navigate, and extremely comprehensive. However, if you are interested in applying for financial assistance through the Student Loan Network, you will need to give your name, contact information, and eligibility requirements to start the application process.

*Many first-time college students attend a community college. According to the U.S. Department of Labor, the following careers that require an associate degree or postsecondary vocational award offer the best employment prospects: registered nurse, nursing aide, preschool teacher, automotive service technician, and computer support specialist. (Photo courtesy of Dynamic Graphics)*

## First in the Family: Advice About College

**www.firstinthefamily.org**

**What:** First in the Family offers advice and encouragement to young people who are the first in their families to attend college. It is sponsored by What Kids Can Do, a national nonprofit child advocacy group and the Lumina Foundation for Education.

**Best Points:** This site offers tips on planning for college and finding success once you are there, grade-level appropriate planning checklists, useful videos that profile students who were the first in their families to attend college (including immigrants and those from inner-city schools who faced special challenges), and links to related websites and books.

**What You Should Know:** Full access available. This is a useful website for students who seek guidance and inspiration as they face one of the biggest challenges of their lives—becoming the first in their families to attend college.

# FraternityInfo.com

### www.fraternityinfo.com

**What:** This site, sponsored by the North-American Interfraternity Conference, provides general information on Greek life, contains links to websites for all national fraternities, and addresses some of the stereotypes of Greek life.

**Did You Know?**
Forty-eight percent of U.S. presidents, 42 percent of U.S. senators, and 30 percent of U.S. Congressmen were members of fraternities, according to the North-American Interfraternity Conference.

**Best Points:** The FAQs page is useful for students and parents alike. This page covers issues such as hazing rituals and other negative perceptions that many associate with fraternity life. Also discussed are the benefits of belonging to a fraternity, and the financial costs. From the home page, you can also sign up for a chance to win a $500 scholarship (participation in a Greek organization is not required).

**What You Should Know:** Full access available. This is an informative site on the myths and truths of Greek life. However, browsers should be aware that because the site is sponsored by a coalition of fraternities, it may be more than a little biased toward Greek life.

# Free Application for Federal Student Aid on the Web

### www.fafsa.ed.gov

**What:** This is an online version of the U.S. Department of Education's Free Application for Federal Student Aid (FAFSA), which students must complete to be eligible for government financial aid programs. The website is available in English- and Spanish-language versions.

**Best Points:** The site's three main sections are for students who are considering their federal aid options, for those who are ready to file, and for those who have already filled out the FAFSA. Under Before Beginning a FAFSA, you can read about eligibility requirements, deadlines for applications, and other options for financial assistance. When you are ready to fill out the application, this site takes you through several steps that ask about you, your academic plans, and your financial situation. Finally, after you have filed, you can use the third section of this site to check on the status of your application or make any necessary corrections.

**What You Should Know:** Full access available. While the paper version of the FAFSA is still available, there are many benefits to filing online. According to the site, filing the FAFSA on the Web is faster, requires applicants to answer fewer questions, and offers students the chance to double-check their application before final submission and avoid having to file again because of missing or incorrect information.

# FreSch!

### www.freschinfo.com

**What:** FreSch! has a database of approximately 450,000 financial awards from thousands of organizations and foundations. At this site, you can browse scholarships, read advice on finding and applying for awards, and research other financial aid options.

**Best Points:** Under the main scholarship section, search for awards based on your responses to questions about your student status, ethnic background, location, and interests. Before filling out any award applications, make sure to read the site's warnings about scholarship scams and how to spot them. Though this site doesn't have original information about colleges and tuition costs, you can link to other online resources that have search engines and other needed resources to explore schools.

**What You Should Know:** Full access available. This site is loosely organized and somewhat hard to view at times due to distracting banner advertisements. However, you can find plenty of information on scholarships, loans, and grants as well as answers to your frequently asked questions about managing financial costs.

# Fulbright Program

### http://fulbright.state.gov

**What:** The Fulbright Program, run by the U.S. Department of State, is designed to "increase mutual understanding between the people of the United States and the people of other countries." More than 250,000 graduate students (all with excellent academic and leadership skills) have been chosen to study and teach abroad.

**Best Points:** The home page offers plenty of information on the history and details of the program and contact information for more details. From the main menu, you can learn more about the application process for graduate students, scholars/professionals, and teachers/administrators.

**What You Should Know:** Full access available. This is an informative and entertaining site that, if nothing else, will give you the urge to travel!

# The Gates Millennium Scholars

**www.gmsp.org**

**What:** This program, funded by the Bill and Melinda Gates Foundation, encourages minority students to attend college and graduate school. Top students are awarded scholarships to attend the college of their choice (for all disciplines) or pursue a graduate degree in computer science, education, engineering, library science, mathematics, public health or science.

**Best Points:** The Gates Millennium Scholars program had funded more than 12,000 Scholars since its inception. At its website, you can view photos and read short profiles of nearly 20 of these top students. The site allows you to submit your name and address to receive information by mail. You can also read answers to frequently asked questions about eligibility and view links to other scholarship opportunities.

**What You Should Know:** Limited access available; applicants must register in order to apply for this program. Scholarships are available only to students who are African American, American Indian/Alaska Native, Asian Pacific Islander American, or Hispanic American. Students are judged based on their academic achievement, community service, and leadership potential.

# Getting Ready for College Early

**www.ed.gov/pubs/GettingReadyCollegeEarly**

**What:** This U.S. Department of Education website is a guide on preparing for college while in middle school or junior high. The site is organized into four sections that are easy to understand and navigate: Making the Decision, Getting Ready, Planning Ahead, and Paying for College.

**Did You Know?**
There are approximately 7,000 accredited two- and four-year academic institutions in the United States, according to the Council for Higher Education.

**Best Points:** Check out Making the Decision to read a list of jobs that are obtainable with varying levels of education. In Getting Ready, read a list of suggested courses that will best prepare you for a challenging high school curriculum that will, in turn, prepare you for college-level classes. In Planning Ahead, you can read about how you can begin to explore your financial aid opportunities ahead of time. In the last section, Paying for College, read about the different forms of aid that are available and browse lists of scholarship and federal aid sources.

**What You Should Know:** Full access available. Though this site, last updated in 2000, is considered "archived information," much of the data presented are still relevant and deserve a read.

## GoCollege

**www.gocollege.com**

**What:** You can browse schools, search colleges with simple or advanced criteria, research scholarship and government loan options, find out about distance learning programs, and prepare yourself for admissions tests. The site has the following sections: Prepare & Admissions, Education Options, Financial Aid Guide, and College Survival. There is also a Digital Student Blog.

**Best Points:** The information provided in each section is universally strong. You can use this site as a primer for almost any college-related topic imaginable—from scholarships essay writing tips and the ACT and SAT, choosing a major and excelling on campus.

**What You Should Know:** Full access available. This is an excellent site with plenty of information to offer. Its founders claim to have been mentioned on the television news program *20/20,* and after browsing the site, we can believe it. If it's good enough for *20/20,* it should be good enough for you!

## Going2College.org

**http://going2college.org**

**What:** Going2College, from the nonprofit organization Mapping Your Future, offers a variety of college planning resources.

**Best Points:** Plan for College offers advice to elementary, middle, and high school students to help them plan for college; month-by-month planning information is provided for 11th and 12th graders. The section also lists school-based mentor and tutor programs, financial aid/college information events, and college entrance exams. The Find a College section offers tips on locating the best college fit, including campus visits and applying to colleges and for financial aid. Pay for College provides information on the various types of financial aid and advice on estimating costs, comparing awards letters, and finding additional sources of financial aid. State List is the best resource at the site. Users can select their state of residence and find out what governmental programs (including financial aid) are available to help them plan for college.

**Did You Know?**
Nearly 67 percent of high school students enroll in college within one year of graduation, according to *RedEye*.

**What You Should Know:** Full access available. This is an excellent clearinghouse of college and career information.

# GovBenefits.gov

**www.govbenefits.gov**

**What:** This site, the result of a partnership of federal, state, and local government organizations, gives students access to government-sponsored assistance programs.

**Best Points:** Students can search more than 1,000 programs designed to aid in career development and education and training. Links are provided for many scholarships and awards to help students in the grade school level up to graduate school. You can target your search of benefits by category, or those given by state or federal agencies. This site is especially beneficial for those with a disability, as it provides links for a variety of government programs geared for physical or emotional hardships.

**What You Should Know:** Limited access available; users must complete a questionnaire to use this site. The list of questions is extensive, including those covering personal and family history, educational and employment history, and any government loans or assistance.

# GradSchools.com

### www.gradschools.com

**What:** If you're considering grad school, make this website one of your first stops. It is run by EducationDynamics, an interactive marketing and information services company.

**Did You Know?**
There are approximately 1,800 graduate school programs in the United States, according to The Council of Graduate Schools. Education and business are the most popular programs, with health science programs enjoying the fastest growth.

**Best Points:** Useful sections include Why Grad School (which details the differences between undergraduate and graduate study and offers tips on choosing a program), Find a Program (a database of graduate programs searchable by field of study, location, and keyword), Finance Your Study (which provides information on financial aid resources), and Get Informed (which provides a wealth of articles on applying to and surviving graduate school).

**What You Should Know:** Limited access available; you must register at the site to save searches and manage your list of prospective graduate schools. This site is a valuable resource for anyone considering graduate school.

# Graduate Guide

### www.graduateguide.com

**What:** This site, sponsored by School Guide Publications (a for-profit company that provides high schools with information on colleges and universities), offers a graduate school search engine; college fair and conference schedules; GRE, GMAT, LSAT, and MCAT testing tips; and information on school accreditation and financial aid.

**Best Points:** Use the search engine to browse graduate programs by name, location, or field of study. School listings include contact information and degree programs. There is also a separate search engine for distance learning programs. The Agg Graduate Fairs calendar list events by date and include contacts for additional information. The testing section lists test locations and dates for the most popular graduate-level entrance exams. Check out the Financial Aid section for information on government and private sources for aid and how to fit graduate school into your budget.

**What You Should Know:** Full access available. This site has a little bit of everything, but it does not go into much detail. Use it for the basic search engine, but make sure to explore individual schools' sites and other online resources for details on programs and comparison tools. The financial aid information on this site is also worth a look.

# Graduate Record Examination

**www.gre.org**

**What:** Administered by the Educational Testing Service, this site provides news, advice, and registration help for the Graduate Record Examination (GRE), which is a test required for entrance into graduate degree programs.

**Best Points:** The home page is simple and easy to navigate. Depending on your interest, you can browse information on the General GRE, subject tests, or writing assignments. The General Test contains verbal, quantitative, and analytical writing sections that, according to the website, "test skills that have been acquired over a long period of time and that are not related to any specific field of study." Subject tests are available in eight areas: biochemistry, cell and molecular biology; biology; chemistry; computer science; literature in English; mathematics; physics; and psychology. You can also learn more about both the computer and paper versions of the exams, read answers to FAQs, and access free and low-cost test prep materials.

> **FYI**
>
> The most popular fields of graduate study in 2006 were Education, Business, Health Sciences, Social Sciences, and Physical Sciences, according to the Council of Graduate Schools.

**What You Should Know:** Full access available. Because this is the GRE official website, it's an excellent place to learn about the exam. Take full advantage of the practice tests and other preparatory resources listed under each section of the GRE.

# GrantsNet

**www.grantsnet.com**

**What:** If science is your strong point, this site can help you find funds. It is sponsored by the Howard Hughes Medical Institute, the American Association for the Advancement of Science, and the Japan Society for the Promotion of Science.

**Best Points:** You can search this site's grant database to find funds for undergraduate and graduate science education and biomedical training. The Funding News section will help you stay up to date on the latest information on science research, internships, and grants.

**What You Should Know:** Full access available.

# Greek Pages.com

**http://greekpages.com**

**What:** Greek Pages.com, which bills itself as "the original, the definitive fraternity and sorority website," has links to national and local chapters of fraternities and sororities on campuses nationwide. Students can search by Greek group or by campus. Also included are other online resources for Greeks and shopping links for the latest in Greek wear and other goods.

**Best Points:** This site is simple and easy to use. You can search fraternities and sororities by letter (Greek or Arabic) or by campus. Each college listing presents the Greek groups present (all-men, all-women, and coed) and includes links to each group's personal site, if one exists.

**What You Should Know:** Full access available. With more than 10,000 group listings, this site is pretty extensive; however, because not all campus groups have their own website, many organizations may be left off college listings. This would be a good starting place to research Greek life, but be sure to double-check data with information found on the websites of individual colleges.

# Health Resources and Services Administration (HRSA) Division of Health Careers Diversity and Development: Student Assistance

**www.bhpr.hrsa.gov/dsa**

**What:** This part of the HRSA's website offers information on scholarships, grants, and specialized loans to students interested in studying in various areas of medicine. It is sponsored by the Bureau of Health Professions of the U.S. Department of Health and Human Services.

**Best Points:** The site is compact and quick to browse through. You can search financial assistance opportunities by the following branches of medical study: allied health, behavioral and mental health, chiropractic, dentistry, medicine, nursing, optometry, pharmacy, physician assistant, podiatry, public health, or veterinary medicine. You can also browse a complete listing of student assistance programs, organized by type and intended audience.

> **> Did You Know?**
> Nurses are considered the most honest and ethical workers in the United States, according to an annual poll conducted by Gallup. Eighty-four percent of Americans rate nurses' ethics as "very high" or "high." Medical professionals—including pharmacists, veterinarians, medical doctors, and dentists—make up four of the next five highly regarded professions, with engineers rounding out the top six professions.

**What You Should Know:** Full access available. This site offers useful information and links to other financial aid resources for students interested in careers in health care.

# HEATH Resource Center

**www.heath.gwu.edu**

**What:** This site, sponsored by George Washington University, is a clearinghouse of information on postsecondary education for people with disabilities. The site features *Information From HEATH,* a useful electronic newsletter that offers full-length articles, book reviews, and more.

**Best Points:** Users can read answers to FAQs as well as email (askheath@heath.gwu.edu) staff members with their own questions. Read the online newsletter for Did You Know segments featuring new events and developments in the field of disabilities and listings of new print, video, and Internet resources. *Creating Options: A Resource on Financial Aid for Students with Disabilities* is an online resource paper that describes federal financial aid programs for students with disabilities.

**What You Should Know:** Full access available. This site has comprehensive resources, well-written articles, and useful links to other resources for students with disabilities.

## FYI

In 2004, the total number of minority students attending college reached 4.7 million, a 146 percent increase since the number was last tallied in 1984. According to the National Center for Education Statistics, Hispanics had the highest rate of enrollment growth—237 percent, followed by Asians with 177 percent; American Indians, 106 percent; and Blacks with a 93 percent increase.

# Hispanic College Fund (HCF)

**www.hispanicfund.org**

**What:** The HCF offers scholarships to college-bound Hispanic students interested in studying business, finance, engineering, and the sciences. Its website has information for high school and college students and their parents.

**Best Points:** The scholarship page is easy to browse and includes links to many other funding organizations. Under the Resources section, you can learn about the pros and cons of attending a community college, state university, or private university; get information on financial aid resources (including links to outside providers); and learn more about internships.

**What You Should Know:** Full access available. This is a good site for Hispanic American students seeking financial aid.

# Hispanic Scholarship Fund (HSF)

**www.hsf.net**

**What:** According to its website, the "HSF was founded in 1975 with a vision to strengthen the country by advancing college education among Hispanic Americans, the fastest-growing segment of the U.S. population." At this site, students can browse scholarships, get tips on financial aid, and read about the benefits of attending college.

**Best Points:** This site offers more than scholarships. Visit the Students section to access Destination University (a 40-page, fully bilingual guide to applying to and paying for college), The Money Manual (which offers advice on financial aid), the Roadmap to College Admissions (which provides specialized college planning advice for high school students by grade level), and Getting Ready for College (which provides comprehensive information on planning for and attending college).

**What You Should Know:** Full access available. This is a great resource for Hispanic students who want to learn about their financial options and other advice about applying to school, choosing a major, and getting involved in campus and community groups.

## HBCU Mentor

**www.hbcumentor.org**

**What:** This website was developed by XAP Corporation for students aiming to attend Historically Black Colleges and Universities (HBCUs). This site has information on schools, tools for planning and preparing for college and financial aid options, and it includes links for career advice and online applications.

**Best Points:** After creating an online account, check out HBCU Mentor Modules. This page will allow you to create personalized planners to help you sign up for the right classes while in high school and meet all your college application deadlines. You can also compare schools to help you narrow your choices. Choose Comparative View to compare statistics of your chosen schools. Financial aid and scholarship information is also included on this site. Under Financial Aid, you can research aid options and search for scholarships.

**What You Should Know:** Limited access available; registration required for certain areas of this site. To fully benefit from this site, you need to create a free account. This account can be used to store information about your college research, class planning, and more.

## Hobson's College View

**www.collegeview.com**

**What:** College and career experts from Hobson's developed this site that includes professional advice and a comprehensive college search engine of more than 3,800 schools in the United States and Canada. Other sections include Financial Aid, Application Process, Campus Life, Careers & Majors, as well as videos, podcasts, and student blogs.

**Best Points:** The search engine allows students to customize their school selections with 12 options, such as location, athletics, disabilities, and religious affiliation. Each listing provides an overview of the school. In addition to the search feature, students can read about college life, study abroad options, and specific courses of study, such as pre-med or technical programs. The site also offers useful sections for high school counselors and parents.

**What You Should Know:** Full access available. This site has so much information, it may be overwhelming for some students. You could spend hours at this site, either using the search feature or browsing the online college advice. All in all, an excellent site for both general and specific college research.

> **> Did You Know?**
> 529 plans are state-operated investment plans that help students and their families save for college costs. 529 plans are named after Section 529 of the Internal Revenue Code. Every state has at least one 529 savings plan.

# HowStuffWorks— How 529 Plans Work

http://money.howstuffworks.com/ personal-finance/529.htm

**What:** HowStuffWorks provides reliable, straightforward explanations of how things work. Visitors to this site can learn more about air bags, Nostradamus, credit cards, and, yes, college 529 plans, which allow students and their parents to get a tax-free jump on saving for college.

**Best Points:** Detailed information on 529 plans is presented in an attractive format. Sections include Introduction to How 529 Plans Work, The Cost of College, The 529 Plan, State-to-State Variations, The Benefits, The Drawbacks, Investment Control, and Choosing the Right Plan.

**What You Should Know:** Full access available. This is a well-presented introduction to 529 savings plans.

# HowStuffWorks—How College Admission Works

http://people.howstuffworks.com/college-admission.htm

**What:** HowStuffWorks provides reliable, straightforward explanations of how things work. Visitors to this site can find out the inside scoop on the "Jaws of Life," fax machines, rip currents, and the college admissions process.

**Best Points:** The sub-site presents detailed information on college admissions in an attractive format. Sections include Selecting a College, College Applications, SAT Scores and Minority Students, and College Admissions. There is even a profile of Duke University's admissions process that features an interview with its director of undergraduate admissions.

> **> Did You Know?**
> Four-year public colleges accepted 70 percent of applicants in 2005, according to the National Association for College Admission Counseling, while four-year private schools accepted 68 percent of applicants.

**What You Should Know:** Full access available. This is a basic introduction to the college admissions process.

# HowStuffWorks—How College Financial Aid Works

http://money.howstuffworks.com/personal-finance/
college-financial-aid.htm

**What:** HowStuffWorks provides reliable, straightforward explanations of how things work. Visitors to this site can find out the inside scoop on Internet radio, irrigation, sunburns, and college financial aid.

**Best Points:** Detailed information on scholarships, work-study, grants, loans, and other types of college financial aid is presented in an easy-to-use format. Sections include What is Financial Aid?, How Do I Apply for Need-Based Aid?, Formulas and Applying, Scholarships, Reserve Officer Training Corps, and What About Loans?

**What You Should Know:** Full access available. This is a nicely organized website on college financial aid.

# HowStuffWorks—How Online Degrees Work

http://people.howstuffworks.com/online-degree.htm

**What:** HowStuffWorks provides reliable, straightforward explanations of how things work. Visitors to this site can learn more about quicksand, nuclear power, Mars, and online degrees.

**Best Points:** If you are one of the 26 percent of Americans who believe that online bachelor's degrees are as credible as traditionally earned bachelor's degrees, according to Vault.com, this site will be a good resource. It presents detailed information on online degrees in a well-organized format. Sections include The Employer's View; Online Learning Programs; Evaluating the Program; and The Good, the Bad, and the Accredited.

**What You Should Know:** Full access available. This is a useful primer for those interested in learning more about online and distance education.

# HowStuffWorks—How SATs Work

http://people.howstuffworks.com/sat.htm

**What:** HowStuffWorks provides reliable, straightforward explanations of how things work. Users of this site can find out the inside scoop on electric cars, Botox, mortgages, and the SAT, the most popular college entrance exam in the United States.

**Best Points:** Detailed information on the SAT (offered by The College Board) is presented at this site in a well-organized, easy-to-use format. Sections include Introduction to How the SAT Works, What's the SAT II?, What Kind of Questions Can I Expect on the SAT?, Can I Study for the SAT?, What Else Do I Need to Know About Test Day?, and When Will I Know My Scores?

**What You Should Know:** Full access available. Other than The College Board's website (www.collegeboard.org), few sites provide as much detail and advice on taking this very important test as How SATs Work.

# INROADS

www.inroads.org

**What:** According to its website, the mission of INROADS is "to develop and place talented minority youth in business and industry and prepare them for corporate and community leadership." This nonprofit organization's website provides information on INROADS school and career planning services for high school and college students.

**Best Points:** High school seniors can research INROADS programs and services such as supplemental academic instruction, ACT/SAT preparation, leadership development, career guidance, and business skill workshops. College students can learn more about INROADS programs, such as business simulations, seminars, and other workplace training. After graduating, students can participate in two- to four-year internships with participating corporate sponsors.

**What You Should Know:** Full access available; however, preference for INROADS assistance goes to students of color. You must be at least a high school senior to apply for INROADS. College students need to have a GPA of 2.8 or better. High school seniors must have a GPA of 3.0 or better and either have an ACT composite score of 20 or more, have an SAT combined score of 1,000 or better, or rank within the top 10 percent of their class.

# IIEPassport

**www.iiepassport.org**

**What:** The Institute of International Education (IIE) is a nonprofit organization that bills itself as "the world's most experienced global higher education and professional exchange agency." This site serves as a search engine for various study abroad opportunities.

**Best Points:** Check out the home page to read about the featured country of the month. Each listing provides fast facts about the country

### Good Advice
The Institute of International Education advises students to learn as much as they can about their country of study to avoid culture shock when they arrive. It suggests that students speak to alumni about their experiences at the school, obtain information about the country from embassies or consulates, and attend organized, pre-departure events offered by their school or the organization sponsoring the program.

and online resources for more information. If the featured country doesn't appeal to you, simply click on the search engine, which will ask you to pick a country, field of study, or your choice of language. You can also use an advanced option to refine your search. Using the advanced search tool, you can specify a world region (instead of a specific country), the time of year you plan to travel, and the duration of the program.

**What You Should Know:** Full access available. This is a good place to start researching your many options for studying abroad. Even if you're not set on the study abroad experience, check out this site to read the Student Guide for Studying Abroad, which covers the benefits of studying in a different culture, how to pick the right program for you, and things to consider before you leave home.

# International Education Financial Aid

**www.iefa.org**

**What:** This site, which is a member of the International Student Network (a for-profit provider of educational and consulting services), offers financial aid information for students hoping to study abroad.

**Best Points:** You can search for scholarships on this site by field of study, location of study, or host institution. You can also sign up to receive a free newsletter or participate in a message board that focuses on topics such as financial aid, scholarships, and studying in the United States and other countries.

**What You Should Know:** Full access available.

# International Education Site

**www.intstudy.com**

**What:** The site, created by a for-profit British digital media company, offers information about studying abroad. Sections include a College Search feature, Course Center (which features articles on academic subjects), and Living & Learning Abroad. There are also links to useful articles and an application service in which students can contact multiple colleges and universities for more information.

**Best Points:** There is a wealth of information on study abroad topics at this site. At the College Search section, you can read articles about choosing a college, studying in a specific country, and searching for and contacting international academic institutions to gather more information. The Living & Learning

Abroad section allows you to learn more about the climate, entrance requirements, visa/immigration requirements, accommodations, tuition/fees/living expenses, and educational system of a specific region or country.

**What You Should Know:** Full access available. You must register to contact colleges. Due to the plethora of information available, this site is occasionally difficult to navigate. Despite the information overload, this is a useful site for patient people interested in studying abroad.

# International Scholarships Online

**www.internationalscholarships.com**

**What:** Visit this site for financial aid and scholarship resources aimed at students wishing to study abroad. Listings cover all fields of study and include grants, scholarships, loan programs, and other awards. The site is sponsored by the Edvisors Network, a for-profit provider of educational and consulting services.

**Best Points:** The scholarship search engine is user friendly and yields results for many criteria options. You can search awards by your academic field or by the country in which you hope to study. Results depend on the criteria you use; be open to many countries or search for a broad industry to yield the most scholarship opportunities. Each listing includes contact information of the host institution, award type, dollar amount, and other details.

**What You Should Know:** Full access available. This site looks like it offers more than a scholarship search tool, but most of the other content available is advertisements and links to other sites. If you are a student hoping to study abroad, use this resource primarily for the search tool.

# International Student Loan Program

**www.internationalstudentloan.com**

**What:** Sponsored by the Envisage International Corporation (a for-profit provider of educational and consulting services), International Student Loan Program offers financial information and options (Stafford Loans, FFEL, or ISLP loans) for both American and Canadian students planning to study abroad and international students planning to study in the United States.

**Best Points:** The easy-to-navigate home page directs U.S., Canadian, and international students to areas of the site applicable to their situation. Each of these sections describes the loans available to the student group, a FAQ section, and sources for additional information. For U.S. students, available loan options depend on whether they plan to study at a foreign institution or study abroad through a school in the United States. U.S. students can search loan information for both undergraduate- and graduate-level programs.

**What You Should Know:** Full access available.

# International Student

www.internationalstudent.com

**What:** This site, sponsored by the Envisage International Corporation (a for-profit provider of educational and consulting services), offers information on schools across Europe, the Americas, Asia, and Australia and advice for students interested in studying abroad.

**Best Points:** The home page has a wealth of useful content, such as information on schools across the globe, travel health insurance, international scholarships, discounted airfare, travel and working permit requirements, and even how to call home. More general school and career advice is also available, such as test-taking tips and suggestions for writing college essays or resumes. You can submit your email address to receive additional information and periodic newsletters.

**What You Should Know:** Full access available. Whether you're a student from Missouri hoping to study in Ireland or a French student hoping to study in Texas, this site is for you. However, because of the broad nature of this site, you may also want to visit websites that have information specific to your host country.

# InternJobs.com

www.internjobs.com

**What:** Brought to you by the large online network, AboutJobs.com, this website offers a basic search engine for paid and unpaid internships around the world. Positions are aimed at current college students and recent graduates. The site also offers fee-based resume writing assistance.

**Best Points:** The search engine is free and easy to use and includes opportunities in the United States and in countries around the world. Each internship listing includes the name and contact information for application as well as a detailed description of the position and company. The site also includes useful articles, such as From Internship to Career: Leap Ahead in the Job Market and Top Ten Tips for Finding Your Dream Internship.

**What You Should Know:** Full access available.

# InternWeb.com

### www.internweb.com

**What:** This site allows students to browse internships based on their location and work preferences. It also includes articles on choosing the right internship, applying for jobs, and resume and cover letter advice.

**Best Points:** In addition to allowing you to search for traditional internship opportunities, this website also features articles about landing an internship.

**What You Should Know:** Full access available.

# Jackie Robinson Foundation

### www.jackierobinson.org

**What:** The Jackie Robinson Foundation is a national, nonprofit organization that "assists increasing numbers of minority youths through the granting of four-year scholarships for higher education." Its website describes these scholarship awards in detail.

**Best Points:** Under Apply, you can read about the eligibility requirements and deadlines for application. In addition to financial help, the Foundation also offers scholarship winners career guidance and leadership development services. For those interested in learning about Jackie Robinson, check out the section, About Jackie, to read about his life and lasting contributions.

> **> Did You Know?**
> Jackie Robinson (1919-72) was the first black baseball player in Major League Baseball. He had a stellar career with the Brooklyn Dodgers and was elected to the Baseball Hall of Fame in 1962. After he retired from baseball, Robinson worked tirelessly to improve the civil rights of blacks and other minorities in the United States.

**What You Should Know:** Full access available. Awards are limited to minority high school seniors with leadership potential and eligible SAT and ACT scores.

# Kaplan Online

**www.kaplan.com**

**What:** If the thought of standardized admissions tests makes you squeamish, then possibly a prep class will help to ease your fears. Kaplan offers tons of test prep options and other college resources on its website.

**Best Points:** At the Kaplan home page, choose the Test Preparation/College Admissions section to access ways (e.g., books, software, and online classes) to prepare for college admissions tests. Sample questions and detailed explanations can be found for all college-related tests. Check out the College Success link, which includes articles on choosing the right school, applying properly and on time, paying for school, packing for school, and other useful topics. Parents and students alike may be interested in Kaplan's Premier Tutoring, which is fee-based, one-on-one tutoring for standardized tests.

**What You Should Know:** Limited access available; Kaplan's test preparation materials and Premier Tutoring require a fee. Despite this, there are a lot of free college planning resources at this website.

# KnowHow2GO

**www.knowhow2go.org**

**What:** "College doesn't just happen; you have to work to make it a reality," says KnowHow2GO, which was created by the American Council on Education and the Lumina Foundation for Education. The site is available in English and Spanish.

**Best Points:** The site seeks to help young people plan ahead so that they will be able to be academically prepared, as well as pay for college, via four main sections. Be a Pain encourages students to never give up when it comes to seeking mentors and information that will help them prepare for college. Push Yourself covers recommended high school classes that will help students become appealing candidates for college. Find the Right Fit offers advice on choosing a college and major. Put Your Hands on Some Cash provides an overview of financial aid and offers tips on landing cash for college. The website also has useful sections for students by academic level, such as middle school, freshman, sophomore, etc. Useful websites, articles (such as The Top Myths About College, The Top Myths About Financial Aid, and The ABCs of Standardized Tests), an e-newsletter that offers college planning tips, planning guides, and other resources are provided.

**What You Should Know:** Limited access available; you can browse most of this site without registration, but you will need to register to access the e-newsletter. This is an excellent resource for students.

# LearnOverseas.com

### www.learnoverseas.com

**What:** This site, developed by The EI Group (a for-profit career and educational resource company), has a massive database of foreign schools searchable by location, length of study, academic focus, and costs. You can also read facts about various countries and access other helpful links.

**Best Points:** Program listings are searchable and include name and host organization, contact information, a link to the program's website, and the option of requesting more information by mail. You can read about each program's details, academic concentration, registration deadlines, semester dates, admission requirements, costs, and housing options. Also be sure to check out the Articles section, which covers general questions about traveling and studying abroad, managing costs, and making sure credits transfer to your home institution. The Resources section has links to country profiles, embassy contact information, currency conversion tips, and more.

**What You Should Know:** Full access available. You can create an account to save your research, but registering is not necessary to access any sections of the site. This is a useful resource to help you choose a program and prepare yourself, emotionally and academically, before studying abroad.

# Making It Count

### www.makingitcount.com

**What:** Are you a high schooler looking to start your college search? This site, sponsored by Monster.com, contains loads of ideas on how to prepare for everything from campus visits to

**FYI**

The growing competitiveness of the college admissions process has prompted an increase in the number of Early Decision and Early Action applications. According to the National Association for College Admission Counseling, 60 percent of colleges that offer Early Decision admission reported an increasing number of applications from 2005 to 2006. And 70 percent of colleges that offered Early Action applications reported an increase in applications from the previous year.

research paper topics. It has four main sections: High School, Road to College, College Success, and Jobs & Careers, as well as a scholarship database and a college search feature sponsored by FastWeb.

**Best Points:** The college and scholarship search features are effective tools to gather information. The College Planning Timeline lets you know exactly what steps you should be taking in the fall and spring of each of your four years of high school. Several good tips are listed in Time Management Tips, such as "Schedule early classes" and "Study after class before dinner." You can also get expert advice on writing a college essay, read student articles such as The Truth About Small Schools, and tips for campus tours, such as bringing a journal and asking strangers questions about the school.

**What You Should Know:** Limited access available; registration required for certain areas of this site. This site is an excellent planning tool for students because the advice given from students and experts is not generic—it is similar to advice that an older sibling might give.

## Mapping Your Future

**www.mapping-your-future.org**

**What:** Sponsored by a group of agencies that participate in the Federal Family Education Loan Program, this nonprofit site offers specialized college and career information for middle school, undergraduate, graduate, and adult students; parents; middle school and high school counselors; and financial aid professionals. The site is available on both English- and Spanish-language versions.

**Best Points:** You can browse this site either by selecting a tab at the top of the opening page that matches your student status (high school student, undergraduate, etc.) or by choosing one of the main menu options. This menu has four informative sections: Prepare for College, Pay for College, Manage Your Money (which lists steps to financial success and includes calculators to help you manage anything from your checkbook to your school loans), and Explore Careers. You can also complete online student loan counseling at this site, which is a prerequisite for loan disbursement.

**What You Should Know:** Full access available (although you must register to participate in online student loan counseling). This site has plenty of information for students of all ages and their parents. Whether you are researching colleges, trying to pay off student loans, or searching for a job, this site will have useful resources for you.

## MBA.com

www.mba.com

**What:** Developed by the Graduate Management Admission Council, this site offers everything you need to know before obtaining your master's in business administration (MBA). You can research schools, learn about the GMAT exam, or read information on budgeting for tuition costs.

**Best Points:** The home page is visually appealing with links to different sections depending on your needs, such as Assess Careers and the MBA, Find Your Program, Take the GMAT, Apply Effectively, and Make Your Decision. Highly useful is the Take the GMAT section, which includes contact information for regional testing facilities, a general overview of the exam, sample questions, and scoring information.

**What You Should Know:** Full access available. This site does a good job in presenting all the things you should consider before starting your MBA search or study. One caveat: the school search engine is limited in scope. As a result, you may want to use this site more for the broad and useful information it offers rather than to help you choose an MBA program.

## Middle States Commission on Higher Education

www.msache.org

**What:** This organization is one of six regional institutional accrediting commissions in the United States. It accredits colleges and universities in Delaware, the District of Columbia,

Maryland, New Jersey, New York, Pennsylvania, Puerto Rico, the U.S. Virgin Islands, and several locations internationally.

**Best Points:** The Institution Directory allows users to search by institution name, state, type of school, and degree awarded. Contact information (including Web address), enrollment, type of institution, accreditation status, and distance education options are provided for each listing. You can also learn more about the accreditation process and get answers to frequently asked questions.

**What You Should Know:** Full access available. Aside from the directory of accredited schools, this site is geared more toward board members of the Commission than the general public.

> **Hot Majors**
FastWeb.com reports that the following majors are becoming popular on college campuses: New Media, Biotechnology, Organic Agriculture, Homeland Security, E-Business/E-Marketing, Computer Game Design, Forensic Accounting, Human-Computer Interaction, Society and the Environment, and Nanotechnology.

# MonsterTrak: Major to Career Converter

**http://jobshadow.monster.com/converter**

**What:** This website allows you to see what types of careers are most often associated with a particular major.

**Best Points:** You can search on nearly 50 majors—such as Biology & Toxicology, Finance, Mathematics, and Special Education—to find possible career choices. For example, a search on Mathematics generated a list of 38 possible careers, including air traffic control specialist, mathematics editor, and systems analyst.

**What You Should Know:** Full access available to all. This site provides a very general overview of careers that you can pursue with a specific degree. To learn more about the careers listed at this site, visit www.bls.gov/oco.

# My College Guide

**www.mycollegeguide.org**

**What:** This site provides a flashy, colorful, and humorous approach to searching for and applying to colleges. A print version of My College Guide is mailed to 130,000 high-achieving high school students each September.

**Best Points:** Well-written and funny articles cover various concerns facing college-bound students. Interesting topics include improving your chances of getting into schools, how to evaluate a college outside of its name and given reputation, and even relating your own college search to your parents' college experiences. Also included is a basic college search engine that allows students to research schools using criteria such as location, class size, and school type. There is also a discussion forum for students.

**What You Should Know:** Full access available. You might think the college search is tedious and potentially dull, but give this site a try and you might even catch yourself laughing. The only thing slightly off-putting about this site is the lack of source information. That said, take this site's advice with a grain of salt, but enjoy it all the same.

# My Future

**www.myfuture.com**

**What:** This site, presented by the U.S. Department of Defense, is designed for the high school graduate looking for advice on what to do next—ranging from entering the military to attending college.

**Best Points:** Beyond High School offers advice on finding a job, joining the military, performing volunteer work, entering an apprenticeship, or pursuing voc-tech training. The Career Toolbox provides advice on

*A military pilot climbs the ladder to his F-18 Fighting Falcon. (Photo courtesy of Tech Sgt. Ben Bloker, U.S. Air Force)*

finding success in the workforce (acing cover letters, resumes, interviews, etc.). The Money Matters section offers helpful scholarship tips (such as following up over the phone after you send in each application and keeping copies of your completed applications) and financial advice for students about to live on their own for the first time (by laying out typical budget categories such as rent, Internet service, and groceries). The site also provides basic money budgeting tips for students, advising them to buy a notebook and write down every purchase made over a one-week period. This site is loaded with information on military college programs, including tuition assistance and travel opportunities, and it even includes videos from military schools.

**What You Should Know:** Full access available. While a significant portion of this site focuses on military and other non-college options for high school graduates, the site does include some excellent information for the college-bound, such as scholarships and budgeting tips.

## Did You Know?

High school students who are wondering what college major they should choose might be interested in CNNMoney.com/ *Money*'s list of best jobs in America. The winners (in descending order): Software Engineer, College Professor, Financial Advisor, Human Resources Manager, Physician Assistant, Market Research Analyst, Computer/IT Analyst, Real Estate Appraiser, Pharmacist, and Psychologist. The editors of the list selected these careers because they provided workers with higher pay, more upside, and more control over their career paths than other careers.

## My Majors

www.mymajors.com

**What:** The site creates a free list of up to five recommended majors by gathering and analyzing data input by users. Users are asked to provide their grade level, GPA, grades in high school classes, interest in various high school classes, Advanced Placement credit, personal interests, preferences and values, and other background information. There is also a section for counselors and advisors.

**Best Points:** Approximately 105 majors are covered at the site. Information provided with each major includes an overview of the field, specialties, typical courses, employment settings, and featured institutions.

**What You Should Know:** Limited access available; you must provide personal information, including your email address, to use MyMajors. Additionally, there is a $5 charge for a printable advisement report that merely summarizes the user's responses, but lists up to 12 majors recommended by My Majors. While the site is a good basic resource to help students assess their interests in various majors, students would be wise to take the featured institutions with a grain of salt, as this handful of schools—while reputable and accredited—surely do not represent the only options in these fields. Students who need help choosing a major will find My Majors to be a useful, introductory tool. Use the free, basic research tool to help you match your interests with college majors, but seek out free resources for more detailed information on majors.

# myFootpath

**www.myfootpath.com**

**What:** This site, created by a group of former guidance professionals, offers information about preparing for school and managing college life, as well as information on careers. There is also a section (registration-required) that provides students with detailed information on admissions policies for top colleges and universities.

**Best Points:** Useful sections include Colleges (which offers informative articles on preparing for and applying to schools, taking standardized tests, adjusting to life on campus, and more), College Funding, Jobs (job search information), and Careers (detailed information on careers).

There were 4,216 universities and colleges in the United States in 2006, according to the *Chronicle of Higher Education*—an increase of nearly 2,000 institutions since 1966. About 17,648,000 million students were enrolled in 2006—11.2 million more than in 1966.

**What You Should Know:** Limited access available. You must register (free) to obtain reports on admission policies from the nation's top colleges. However, you can use the free areas of this site for answers to questions you may have about the college planning and preparation process.

# MySchool101.com

**www.myschool101.com**

**What:** This site, by EDge Interactive (a Canadian media company), provides information on schools, scholarships, and careers. Though this site is geared toward Canadian students, much of the information is relevant to all students.

**Best Points:** Visit the three main sections, My101Education, My101Scholarships, and My101Career, to use a a college search feature and read articles on schools, popular programs, financial help, and choosing a career. For a fun reward after all your serious browsing, check out MyClubs, a section of message boards that are grouped by category (or club). If you are Canadian, check out the book exchange (found under My Exchange) and see if other students have books to sell that you may need for your own classes.

**What You Should Know:** Limited access available; users must register for certain sections of the site (My101 Scholarships and My Exchange). Though the articles are informative, the message boards are the most interesting areas of the website. Chat with other students about subjects as varied as picking schools to picking a place to eat on campus.

## MyStudentBody.com

### www.mystudentbody.com

**What:** Developed by health communications company Inflexxion and funded by the National Institutes of Health, this site spells out the dangers of alcohol consumption as it relates to college students. Future sites in the MyStudentBody.com suite will focus on preventing STDs/HIV, promoting good nutrition, avoiding or quitting smoking, and alleviating stress.

**Best Points:** Both health experts and actual college students contribute to the site's material, making it not only informative, but also easy to understand and relate to. You can customize your own drinking profile (if you are drinking legally at age 21 or above) and compare it to national and regional averages, talk to other students about their experiences with peer pressure or other topics, and get information on how to say no, knowing your limits, and preventing alcohol abuse.

**What You Should Know:** Limited access available. You need a "school code" to use this site, which means your school first needs to be registered with MyStudentBody.com. If you feel it's a worthwhile investment after exploring the site, you may want to talk to a school administrator or counselor about registering for full access.

## NACME Backs Me

### www.nacmebacksme.org/nacmebacksme

**What:** This site, developed by the National Action Council for Minorities in Engineering (NACME), is aimed at minority high school students interested in careers in engineering. Visit it for information on engineering careers, colleges and graduate programs, and more. Sections are available for students (middle school through college), parents, educators, and mentors.

**Best Points:** At this site, you can learn about what engineers do and practice specialties, get tips on recommended high school classes and academic paths, and find out how to pay for engineering education. The NACME Programs section details outreach programs for middle school through college students. High school students, for example, can take advantage of pre-engineering scholarships and a mentorship program offered by the Council.

**What You Should Know:** Full access available. This is a great website not just for minorities, but all students, to explore engineering.

# National Catholic College Admission Association: Find the Perfect Catholic College For You

**www.catholiccollegesonline.org**

**What:** The Association's website offers a wealth of students who are interested in learning more about Catholic colleges, which are located in 40 states, the District of Columbia, and Puerto Rico. There are sections for students, parents, and counselors. The site is also available in Spanish.

**Best Points:** The Prospective Students section features a planning timeline, facts about Catholic colleges and universities, advice on finding financial aid, and the top 10 reasons for attending a Catholic college or university. The site also has a searchable database of the NCCAA's 186 member colleges. Users can search by academic program, total student enrollment, campus settings, region, degrees offered, selectivity, tuition, extracurricular activities, and other criteria. Each school profile contains an overview of the institution, contact information, and a list of academic programs, sports teams, and activities (such as cultural organizations, fraternities/sororities, honor societies, and service organizations) available at the school.

**What You Should Know:** Full access available. This site will be especially useful for those interested in attending a Roman Catholic college, but some of the information (such as the planning timeline and advice on financial aid) will be useful for students attending any type of college.

## National Center for Education Statistics (NCES) Students' Classroom

http://nces.ed.gov/nceskids

**What:** This site, from the NCES (a department of the U.S. Department of Education), is a fun, creative resource for exploring high schools and colleges, brushing up on your math and science skills, or browsing national educational statistics.

> **> Did You Know?**
> Nearly 33 percent of freshmen surveyed by UCLA's Higher Education Research Institute reported that they were attending their second-choice college. Students cited the high cost of tuition at their first-choice college as one of the main factors behind this decision.

**Best Points:** The college search page allows you to browse schools by state, region, type of institution, and size. Each school listing provides contact information as well as facts on tuition, size, faculty/student ratios, and diversity of student body. When you've finished college searching, check out the section titled Explore Your Knowledge (look for the frog at the bottom of the home page). Here you can test your basic math and science skills with 10-question online quizzes.

**What You Should Know:** Full access available. This is a fun and informative site for students of all ages.

## National Consortium for Graduate Degrees for Minorities in Engineering and Science (GEM)

www.gemfellowship.org

**What:** GEM seeks to increase the number of American Indians, African Americans, Latinos, Puerto Ricans, and other Hispanic Americans pursuing graduate degrees in engineering, natural sciences, and physical sciences.

**Best Points:** Under the GEM Fellowship page, you can learn more about GEM's scholarships as well as paid summer internships. This page also lists university Consortium members. You can apply for fellowships online and track your application in a personalized online account.

**What You Should Know:** Full access available. If you want to apply to become a GEM Fellow, you must create (register) an account at the website.

# National Endowment for Financial Education (NEFE) High School Financial Planning Program (HSFPP)

http://hsfpp.nefe.org/home

**What:** Financial literacy is a skill often overlooked by students as they plan for college and beyond. This site helps students develop these skills, as well as provides resources for instructors. The materials are also available in Spanish.

**Best Points:** The NEFE has created a five-part lesson plan that covers topics such as financial planning, developing a budget, and the costs and benefits of higher education. Games, puzzles, and other interactive teaching devices are used to reinforce the financial lessons discussed at the website. Additionally, print editions of the HSFPP are available free of charge to public and private school teachers, counselors, and students.

**What You Should Know:** Full access available. The HSFPP is a useful tool to help students establish financial literacy and discipline as they navigate college and enter careers.

# National Institutes of Health Undergraduate Scholarship Program

http://ugsp.info.nih.gov

**What:** This government program offers financial assistance to students from disadvantaged backgrounds who "are committed to biomedical, behavioral, and social science research careers at the National Institutes of Health." Some information at this site is available in Spanish.

**Best Points:** The website describes the scholarship program and eligibility requirements and includes application forms so you can apply online. You can also read about the National Institutes of Health and browse profiles (including photos) of recent scholarship winners. You can also access a list of related websites that may be of interest, such as a link to the Minority Health Professions Foundation website, http://minorityhealth.org.

**What You Should Know:** Full access available. To be eligible for the program, you must come from a disadvantaged background, which is described as coming from a low-income family. (Visit the site for details on this requirement.)

## Nellie Mae

**www.nelliemae.com**

**What:** Nellie Mae offers undergraduate and graduate school loans for students and parents. Students can choose from both federal and private loan options.

**Median Annual Earnings by Educational Attainment, 2005**

Professional degree: $100,000
Doctoral degree: $79,400
Master's degree: $61,300
Bachelor's degree: $50,900
Associate degree: $40,600
Some college, no degree: $37,100
High school graduate: $31,500

Source: College Board (data for workers ages 25 and older)

**Best Points:** Besides applying for loans, you can access a wealth of information on balancing your budget, applying for financial aid, and knowing all your options. Useful advice is presented for different audiences, such as Tips for Late Savers (example: maintain good grades to increase your chances of merit-based aid) and Helpful Hints on Using Credit Cards. (example: don't let a free t-shirt be the only reason you apply for a card). Students and parents can use the Calculators section to compare educational and financial aid costs at multiple schools, reduce the cost of borrowing, and evaluate repayment options. There are also many useful resources in the Library section (under Nellie Mae Brochures), including Steps to Success: A Comprehensive Guide to Preparing and Paying for College, Financing Your Child's Future: A Parent's Guide to Planning and Paying for College, and Entrance Counseling Guide for First-time Borrowers. There is a useful Glossary of financial aid terms.

**What You Should Know:** Full access available. Even though this is a loan provider hoping to sell its services, its website offers sound advice and budgeting tools for students simply interested in exploring their financial options.

## New England Association of Schools and Colleges

**www.neasc.org**

**What:** This organization is one of six regional institutional accrediting associations in the United States. It accredits colleges and universities in Connecticut, Maine, Massachusetts, New Hampshire, Rhode Island, Vermont, and American/international schools in more than 60 nations around the world. The Association also accredits career and technical schools via its Commission on Technical and Career Institutions (http://ctci.neasc.org).

**Best Points:** The membership directory lists accredited institutions by U.S. state or country. Information is provided on types of degrees awarded and accreditation status.

**What You Should Know:** Full access available. Other than the school directory, this site is geared more toward members of the Association than the general public.

## NewsLink

http://newslink.org/statcamp.html

**What:** This site features links to college newspapers across the United States.

**Best Points:** Students who are interested in studying journalism or English in college, or who just want to learn what's happening at a particular college, will enjoy this site. It features links to college newspapers across the United States. For example, a search of college newspapers in Illinois found the *Daily Illini* (University of Illinois-Urbana), the *Northern Star* (Northern Illinois University), and the *DePaulia* (DePaul University), among others.

**What You Should Know:** Full access available. Although this site nicely gathers links to college newspapers, it does not provide any original content. Keep in mind that most college papers are published only occasionally during the summer months, so be sure to visit this site during the school year for the latest news and information.

## *The Next Step Magazine*

www.nextstepmagazine.com

**What:** *The Next Step Magazine* has been published since 1995 and a print edition is distributed to high school students throughout the United States. The website's main sections feature articles culled from the print edition of the magazine. It also features lists of college open houses and fairs, a U.S. and Canadian college search database, a scholarship search feature, and a discussion board for students. Visitors can also enter a random drawing for a $1,000 scholarship.

### Did You Know?

Approximately one-third of U.S. undergraduates change colleges at least once during their college careers, according to the U.S. Department of Labor. At least 20 percent of this group transfer from one four-year college to another.

**Best Points:** The articles at the site offer great information on campus tours, choosing a major, college sports, early admission, paper and electronic applications, financial aid, and countless other topics. The Ask a College Planning Expert section lists the names and email addresses of college admission professionals that you can write to for general advice about college or specific information about their schools.

**What You Should Know:** Limited access available. Registration is required for the scholarship search, but all the other sections of this site are available to everyone. This attractive website is chock full of useful information for students interested in college and other post-high school options.

## North Central Association of Colleges and Schools—Higher Learning Commission

www.ncahigherlearningcommission.org

**What:** This organization is one of six regional institutional accrediting commissions in the United States. It accredits colleges and universities in Arkansas, Arizona, Colorado, Iowa, Illinois, Indiana, Kansas, Michigan, Minnesota, Missouri, North Dakota, Nebraska, Ohio, Oklahoma, New Mexico, South Dakota, Wisconsin, West Virginia, and Wyoming.

**Best Points:** A basic directory of accredited institutions is available online, allowing students to browse schools by name and state. You can also read about the accreditation process and the evaluators who make up the Commission.

**What You Should Know:** Full access available. Aside from the directory of accredited schools, this site is geared more toward board members of the Commission than the general public.

## Northwest Commission on Colleges and Universities

www.nwccu.org

**What:** This organization is one of six regional institutional accrediting commissions in the United States. It accredits colleges and universities in Alaska, Idaho, Montana, Nevada, Oregon, Utah, and Washington.

**Best Points:** The Directory of Institutions lists member colleges, information on degree-levels offered, and links to their websites. A FAQ page covers the meaning and process of accreditation, how to register a complaint about one of the member schools, and how complaints are handled.

**What You Should Know:** Full access available. Aside from the directory of accredited schools, this site is geared more toward board members of the Commission than the general public.

# Number2.com

### www.number2.com

**What:** This site was created by graduate students and college professors who have aced college prep tests or have taught others to do the same. Number2.com allows you to take free practice tests to prepare for the ACT, SAT, or GRE exams.

**Best Points:** First and foremost, the service is free. The site is also comprehensive and easy to navigate. Each exam section provides practice tests, tutorials, questions of the day, and vocabulary words to learn. You can work on the practice tests at your own pace while the tutorial program tracks and monitors your progress and varies the skill level of questions. Not only will you gain experience and confidence taking these tests, but you can also learn from your mistakes as you go along. When you answer a test question incorrectly, the tutorial program provides hints and suggestions to direct you towards the right answer. Tutorial programs also maintain a progress report so that every time you log into the site, you can quickly see the areas of the test in which you still need help.

**What You Should Know:** Limited access available; free registration required for certain areas of this site. However, you can tour the site and check out some sample questions before sharing any personal information. Another important thing to note is that sample questions are developed by the Number2.com staff, so no questions are from the actual tests.

## *Occupational Outlook Handbook*

**www.bls.gov/oco**

**What:** The *Occupational Outlook Handbook* (*OOH*) is published by the U.S. Department of Labor to educate people about career options and educational requirements. It is revised every two years. *A Teacher's Guide to the OOH* is also available.

**Best Points:** Hundreds of careers are covered in this book—from accountants and radiologic technologists, to nurses and teachers. Detailed information is provided on job duties; training, other qualifications, and advancement; work environments; earnings, and employment outlook. Readers of this book will find the Training, Other Qualifications, and Advancement section of each article to be especially useful. The section details minimum educational requirements to enter a field, typical classes, and the number of colleges and universities that offer training in the field. Tomorrow's Jobs is another excellent resource. It details employment and societal trends that students should be aware of when thinking about career options. The Employment Projections section provides detailed information on career trends and answers questions such as What are the fastest growing occupations?, What are the occupations with the most job growth?, What are the fastest growing industries?, and What are the industries with the most job growth? Opportunities in the armed forces are also covered in this publication.

*Business is one of the most popular college majors at colleges and universities in the United States. (Photo courtesy of Dynamic Graphics)*

**What You Should Know:** Full access available. This excellent resource should be one of students first stops when it comes to researching careers and educational requirements.

## ParentPLUSLoan

**www.parentplusloan.com**

**What:** This site, part of a larger group of sites called the Student

Loan Network, offers general information about financial aid and specific loan options, including the PLUS Loan that is aimed at parents of college-bound children. The Network also offers a $10,000 scholarship to high school seniors and college students.

**Best Points:** This site offers answers to frequently asked loan questions and things to consider when applying for financial assistance. Visit the Financial Aid Resources section before you explore other areas of the site. It offers information on 529 savings plans, calculating college costs and completing the FAFSA, a financial aid glossary, and links to scholarship search engines. Other useful features include information on loan application deadlines, budget breakdowns for typical education expenses, and a link to apply for the PLUS Loan online.

**What You Should Know:** Full access available. Don't be fooled by the name of this site; it's not just aimed at parents. Students planning to attend college with the aid of scholarships, grants, and/or loans will find this site helpful, as will parents. If you are interested in applying for the PLUS Loan online, you will need to enter personal details to determine your eligibility for assistance. You will also need to register to be eligible for the scholarship.

# Peterson's BestCollegePicks

**www.bestcollegepicks.com**

**What:** This online service from Peterson's helps students match their career goals and interests with colleges.

**Best Points:** To use BestCollegePicks, you will first need to create a free account (name, address, etc.). Then you will be asked a series of survey questions about your educational goals, career interests, personal skills and values, university type and location preferences, and expected tuition. These will be used to create a list of possible colleges, which can be saved for future reference. For each college selected, information is provided on enrollment, majors offered, student life, tuition, financial aid, and athletics. Students can also apply online to many of these schools via links at this site.

**What You Should Know:** Limited access available; registration is required to use this website. This is another excellent college planning resource from Peterson's.

## Peterson's Planner

www.petersons.com

**What:** Peterson's provides comprehensive information on the college search, undergraduate and graduate education, test preparation, admissions essays, financial aid, and more.

> ### Big Schools!
> Miami-Dade College is the largest brick-and-mortar degree-granting campus in the United States—with 54,169 students. Other large schools include Arizona State University-Tempe (51,612), the University of Minnesota-Twin Cities (51,175), and Ohio State University-Main Campus (50,504).

**Best Points:** The college search section features a database that is searchable by location, tuition, major, selectivity, and other criteria. The graduate school section offers a database of accredited graduate programs. For tips on college and graduate admissions tests and sample tests for practice, check out the Prepare for Tests section. Finally, if you need help financing your college education, check out Pay for School for advice on applying for financial aid, expense and savings calculators, a scholarship database, and links to useful organizations. The website also has information on distance learning and study abroad opportunities.

**What You Should Know:** Limited access available; users must register to use the scholarship search. This site has a little bit of everything for students at all points in their education. Considering that Peterson's charges money for its educational books, online products, and services, this free site is a great resource.

## Pick-a-Prof

www.pickaprof.com

**What:** This website offers student reviews of college professors at more than 400 colleges and universities in the United States. Registered users can access grading histories and student reviews of professors. They can also use the Degree Planner feature, which allows them to plan their education course by course and track their grades and course credits. Sections of this website are compatible with the popular Facebook social networking website.

**Best Points:** This website is one of those great ideas you wish you had thought of! Developed by recent college graduates, Pick-a-Prof truly has student interests in mind. As long as your college is covered in the site (which continues to grow), you can read reviews and ratings of professors before signing up for their classes. Reviews are written by students themselves, and all content is reviewed by the site's founders for clarity and appropriateness. Information included in many reviews is the teacher's typical homework load, lecture style, exam preferences, and attendance policy as well as study tips.

**What You Should Know:** Fee-based service; an annual subscription fee of $10/year is required to use this site. Keep in mind that reviews should be used for more than finding teachers who are "easy graders." Instead, students can use the site to choose professors who will fit their learning style and schedule.

# Preparing for College

http://preparingforcollege.usc.edu

**What:** Provided as a public service by the University of Southern California, this site is a useful tool for anyone applying to any college. Sections for parents and school counselors are also included.

**Best Points:** This website is easy to navigate, with information organized under headings such as current high school year, money management, and financial aid. Check out the Myths and Tips pages to clear up some common misconceptions about college expenses and admissions practices.

**What You Should Know:** Limited access available. Though this site has plenty of information to browse anonymously, you may want to register your name and email address to be able to use a personalized Preparing for College Planner, where you can record your class schedule, make to-do lists, and receive email alerts when deadlines for college applications and other forms approach. Registration is free and relatively simple.

### Free College Tuition!
The following colleges and universities do not charge tuition: Berea College (KY), College of the Ozarks (MO), Cooper Union for the Advancement of Science and Art (NY), Deep Springs College (CA), Franklin W. Olin College of Engineering (MA), U.S. Air Force Academy (CO), U.S. Coast Guard Academy (CT), U.S. Merchant Marine Academy (NY), U.S. Military Academy (NY), U.S. Naval Academy (MD), and Webb Institute (NY).

# Preparing Your Child for College

**www.ed.gov/pubs/Prepare**

**What:** Developed by the U.S. Department of Education, this site is a useful and easy-to-browse resource for parents of college-bound students.

**Best Points:** The home page, simply a table of contents of the print publication that was created in 2000, presents information on the following topics: general questions about college, preparing for college, choosing a school, financing education, planning for the long term, additional resources, and activities for parents and students to work on together.

**What You Should Know:** Full access available. Though labeled "archived information" and not the most attractively designed, the site is reliable and covers practically any question a parent may have about sending his or her child to college. Beware of outdated tuition costs; this edition of the guide uses information from 1998 and earlier. (For the most recent information on college costs, see the College Board's *Trends in College Pricing,* www.collegeboard.com.

# The Princeton Review

**www.princetonreview.com**

**What:** The Princeton Review is a highly respected for-profit educational company that has been in operation since 1981. Its website is loaded with information on college admissions, paying for college, careers and majors, and attending graduate school.

**Best Points:** This site is one of the most thorough and informative college websites out there. One of its best features is Counselor-O-Matic (found in the College subsection). This search engine first asks you questions about your academic record, extracurricular activities, and interests, as well as your school preferences, such as size, atmosphere, location, and majors offered. Counselor-O-Matic then assesses your responses and comes up with a list of schools that may be right for you. The resulting schools are divided into Good Match, Reach, and Safety Schools, so you get specific possibilities, plus a general idea of which types of schools you might realistically attend. This site also includes articles on many practical topics such as Freshman Fear and Necessities for Every College Student. There are free

ACT and SAT practice tests that you can take, lists of college rankings in multiple categories, a College Recruiter feature that allows students to contact schools that would be good fits for their academic interests, and information on more than 200 college majors. From advice on applications to news on how the SAT is changing, this site covers all the bases about college.

**What You Should Know:** Limited access available; free registration required for certain areas of this site. This is by far one of the best college websites in existence.

## The Princeton Review: Guide to Business School

### www.princetonreview.com/mba

**What:** This site, like the main Princeton Review site (www.princetonreview.com), has many helpful resources for students. You can research business schools, learn about admissions practices, practice for the GMAT, and explore your financial aid options.

**Best Points:** The School Search section matches students' educational interests with graduate programs in the United States and abroad. The website also offers advice about filling out applications and paying for school, as well as complete practice tests. You can also learn about The Princeton Review's fee-based on-site or online classes and seminars and their availability in your area. Finally, read about your school financing options and how to avoid getting into major debt.

**What You Should Know:** Limited access available; registration required for certain areas of this site. This site will be helpful to any student considering business school because of the wide range of information covered. Whether you're looking for help with the GMAT or help with picking a school, this site will be of assistance.

## The Princeton Review: Guide to Graduate School

### www.princetonreview.com/grad

**What:** Visit this site for information on choosing, preparing for, and applying to graduate school. Read about the importance of researching schools, applying online to programs, taking the GRE exam, and managing tuition costs.

**Best Points:** The school search engine allows you to browse schools by location, degrees offered, concentration, cost, test scores, class size, and student body diversity. In the GRE section, you can take a full-length practice test or sign up for online tutorials to prepare.

**What You Should Know:** Limited access available; registration required for certain areas of this site. Even if you are unsure about going to graduate school or have yet to decide what sort of degree you want to obtain, this site will be useful to give you a better sense of your educational goals and the benefits of an advanced degree.

## The Princeton Review: Guide to Law School

www.princetonreview.com/law

**What:** This site offers advice and other online resources for students planning to attend law school. You can access practice LSAT questions, read advice about preparing school applications, and research financial aid sources.

### FYI

In Fall 2007, there were 55,500 first-year students in law school, according to the Law School Admission Council. Slightly more than 70 percent of this group were White, 8.2 percent Asian American, 7.9 percent Hispanic American, 7.1 percent African American, and 0.8 percent Native American. Forty-six percent were female.

**Best Points:** This website offers a useful law school search engine, a section on first-year curriculum, information on financial aid, and advice on preparing for the LSAT.

**What You Should Know:** Limited access available; registration required for certain areas of this site. For any student considering law school, this site is worth a visit. Articles are thorough and informative and will educate you about law school options.

## The Princeton Review: Guide to Medical School

www.princetonreview.com/medical

**What:** This Princeton Review site has information on schools, the various medical degrees offered, entrance exams, class prerequisites, and financial aid options.

**Best Points:** This website features a medical school search engine, a medical school timeline, information on preparing for the MCAT entrance exam, and tips on surviving medical school.

**What You Should Know:** Limited access available; registration required for certain areas of this site. This is a good source for general and specific information on preparing for medical school and finding financial assistance to help out with the substantial costs of medical school.

> **> Did You Know?**
> There are 129 accredited M.D.-granting U.S. medical schools. In 2007, 70,225 students were enrolled in medical school, according to the American Association of Medical Colleges. Sixty-three percent of this group were White, 21 percent Asian American, 8 percent Hispanic American, 7 percent African American, and 0.9 percent Native American. Nearly 49 percent of students were female.

# RateMyProfessors.com

www.ratemyprofessors.com

**What:** Since its introduction in 1999, this website has collected more than six million student-written professor ratings from more than 6,000 schools in the United States and Canada. Students can anonymously rate their professors based on the following criteria: helpfulness, clarity, easiness, and overall quality. Features on this website are compatible with the popular Facebook social networking website.

**Best Points:** The number of schools and professors included on this site is impressive. To top it off, this website might also make you laugh. After conducting serious research, read over some of the more memorable reviews that have been submitted through the years (e.g., "He will destroy you like an academic ninja").

**What You Should Know:** Full access available. This site covers many more schools than similar websites, such as Pick-a-Prof (which is fee-based), which is also reviewed in this book. However, the scope of reviews is more limited than on other sites. Students use number scales to rate professors and generally include less commentary than what is found on other sites.

# Ron Brown Scholar Program

www.ronbrown.org

**What:** Funded by the CAP Charitable Foundation, the Ron Brown Scholar Program awards scholarships to bright, motivated

African-American high school seniors who are in financial need. (The late Ron Brown was the Secretary of Commerce in the Clinton Administration.) Students are awarded $40,000 for college and receive career counseling and guidance. The program also offers summer study abroad opportunities and internship positions.

**Best Points:** After browsing through the scholarship and program details, be sure to look at the profiles of past winners. Each winner has his or her own page, which includes the winner's photo, information on the winner's high school and chosen college, and a short biography. The stories are interesting and inspiring.

**What You Should Know:** Full access available. If you are an African-American high school senior with an excellent academic record, visit this website to see if you are eligible for financial assistance for college.

According to a 2007 poll by Zogby International, 30 percent of respondents said that they were taking or had taken an online course; another 50 percent said they would consider taking one. (Photo courtesy of Comstock)

## Sallie Mae: College Answer

http://salliemae.collegeanswer.com

**What:** Sponsored by SallieMae, one of the nation's leading providers of education funding, this website covers the college planning process from start to finish. There are sections for students and counselors. College Answer is also available in Spanish.

**Best Points:** The site has six main sections: Preparing, Selecting, Applying, Paying, Deciding, and Financing. The Preparing section offers information on personality/interest assessment tests, test prep, and advice from new college students. The Selecting section features college search databases and information on types of colleges and how to narrow your list of schools to a manageable number. The Applying section features information on everything students need to know about the admissions process, including writing essays, letters of recommendation, and transcripts. The Paying section offers details on loans, grants, and scholarships. The Deciding section offers tips on choosing a college and an Online Award Analyzer (free registration required), and the Financing section provides great suggestions on how students can pay for college. The site also has financial aid calculators, checklists, and answers to frequently asked questions. Finally, there is an excellent sub-site for high school counselors that features free Go-to-College Handouts and other useful resources.

**What You Should Know:** Limited access available; you must register to use the Online Award Analyzer. College Answer is highly recommended.

## SavingforCollege.com

www.savingforcollege.com

**What:** Savingforcollege.com, which is operated by the for-profit company Bankrate, Inc., offers information on financial aid and loan options, specifically 529 plans. You can browse frequently asked questions about 529 plans, such as how to decide which one is right for you and how to enroll.

**Best Points:** Check out the main area of the site, Your Guide to Saving for College, for basic information on what these plans entail and what options are available in your particular state. This section also allows you to browse plan listings by state, which include reviews of the plans and program details. Other useful resources include financial aid calculators, a message board, and a blog from Joe Hurley, a certified public accountant and "529 Guru."

**What You Should Know:** Full access available. Information is clearly presented and easy to navigate. This is not the site if you are looking for detailed information on all your financial aid options (including scholarship opportunities). However, if you or your parents want comprehensive coverage of 529 plans, check this site out.

## Scholarship Scams

www.ftc.gov/bcp/conline/edcams/scholarship

**What:** This site has been developed by the Federal Trade Commission to educate students about scholarship scams. The site offers some original content and includes links to other sites about scholarship scams. A Spanish-language version of the site is also available.

**Best Points:** For a real wake-up call, check out the List of Defendants in Project ScholarScam. You can read about recent prosecutions of individuals and fictitious companies that have scammed millions out of students who thought they would receive financial aid. At this page, you can also file a complaint online if you think you have been a victim of a scam.

**What You Should Know:** Full access available. While there is not a lot of information available on this site, its message should still be heard: be wary of any scholarship offer that seems too good to be true! Visit this website to learn more about protecting yourself against false promises.

# ScholarshipCoach

www.scholarshipcoach.com

**What:** Scholarship Coach provides students and parents with directions for financing college and their educational dreams. Information regarding saving for college, applying for scholarships, and even writing essays are sent in the form of email newsletters. The site's creator, Ben Kaplan, is a well known author, speaker, and businessman. Kaplan's advice has credibility since he was able to raise his entire Harvard tuition in just one year's time.

**Best Points:** The site's creator appears as an animated scholar-ship coach, the site's gimmick, to give commentary on numerous topics ranging from tuition reduction to athletic scholarships, depending on your current website location. His tips appear in the form of informative articles, tools, and database links.

**What You Should Know:** Limited access available with free registration. This website also serves as a vehicle for promoting Ben Kaplan and his seminars, books, and other products geared towards college-bound students and their families. The cartoon of Ben Kaplan is entertaining, though after a while you may be forced to turn off the volume…

# ScholarshipExperts.com

www.scholarshipexperts.com

**What:** This website features a scholarship database of 2.4 million scholarships worth more than $14 billion.

**Best Points:** The scholarship database, but you will need to register to access the resources in the database. Detailed information is provided for each scholarship along with an option to apply online. A basic school search is also available.

**What You Should Know:** Full access available. If you are willing to complete the lengthy registration process, you will be rewarded by gaining access to a large number of scholarships based on your interests, academic achievement, and other personal characteristics.

> **Did You Know?**
> Average undergraduate tuition (including room and board) at two-year institutions was $7,231 in 2005-06, according to the National Center for Education Statistics. Average tuition (including room and board) at four-year colleges and universities was $17,447 in 2005-06.

# ScholarshipHunter

http://scholarshiphunter.com

**What:** Scholarship Hunter provides information on scholarships, essay contests, and sweepstakes. Scholarships are categorized according to specific majors or by state of origin. Awards range from merit based to originality, an example being monetary awards for the best Duct Tape costumes. There are also sections that explain financial aid and federal student loans.

**Best Points:** This site contains a great section on essay contests, many offering serious money—such as the $10,000 Ayn Rand Essay Contest. You should also check out the sweepstakes section which lists a host of free contests to enter, with the chance to win money for school.

**What You Should Know:** Full access available. There is no mention of how often this site is updated—at least one scholarship listed was for the 2006-07 academic year, and some links were invalid.

# Scholarships for Hispanics

http://scholarshipsforhispanics.org

**What:** Sponsored by the National Hispanic Press Foundation, this database lists scholarships available to students of Hispanic origin. Sections of this site are also available in Spanish.

**Best Points:** Scholarship information includes academic and citizenship requirements, as well as the award's sponsors. Click on the scholarship to learn more details: description of the award, its website and contact name, the award's history, the number and dollar amounts of awards given, as well as important deadlines and criteria.

**What You Should Know:** Limited access available; free registration is required to use the scholarship database. You'll have to give basic information including your current year in school, GPA, and interest in particular fields of study. Your search can be categorized according to type of award, field of study, or citizen status, including non citizens.

# Scholarships.com

www.scholarships.com

**What:** Scholarships.com offers a free college scholarship search engine and financial aid resources for college-bound students and their parents. The search engine, which matches student profiles with its database of college scholarships, produces results including award summary and a custom application request letter. In addition, Scholarships.com offers 14 Fund Your Future Area of Study College Scholarships to high school seniors and undergraduate students.

**Best Points:** Many scholarships are listed by category, such as contests, ethnicity, grants, corporate sponsors, and largest dollar amount. Also check out Resources for the following useful sections: Common Financial Aid Questions, A High School Action Plan, Ace your College Interview, Choosing a Major, and Standardized Testing.

**What You Should Know:** Limited access available; free registration is required to be able to search scholarships. To register, you will be asked to give an email address and list other personal information such as GPA and mailing address.

# School Guides

www.schoolguides.com

**What:** Billed as "your comprehensive undergraduate resource," School Guides offers a basic college search engine, financial aid information, a college fair schedule, and test prep materials. The site is sponsored by School Guide Publications, a for-profit company that provides high schools with information on colleges and universities.

**Best Points:** You can search schools by name, state, major, or enrollment. Listings are relatively simple, including only contact information, tuition amounts, and enrollment numbers. The college fair schedule is useful; check the calendar to see if a fair is scheduled in your city. College assessment test material include basic information on the ACT and SAT.

**What You Should Know:** Full access available. If you would like to save your searches and archive them for future use, you will need to create an account with a username and password. However, most of the site is accessible for anonymous browsing.

# SchoolFinder.com

### www.schoolfinder.com

**What:** Visit this site to access information on more than 1,700 universities, colleges, and career colleges in Canada. School listings include information on admission requirements, costs, programs, and other topics. SchoolFinder.com is sponsored by EDge Interactive Publishing, a Canadian media company.

**Best Points:** You can search Canadian undergraduate and graduate schools, programs, careers, and scholarships by keyword. Many of the school listings include the option to take an E-tour, which brings up a pop-up window displaying pictures of the campus and more details about the school.

**What You Should Know:** Limited access available; free registration required for certain areas of this site. While you can research schools and read articles anonymously, you may want to consider creating an account to customize your searches; create your own school, career, and scholarship folders to save your research; receive email alerts when your college or scholarship application deadlines near; and use the Request Info section of the site to contact school representatives directly.

# SchoolsinCanada.com

### www.schoolsincanada.com

**What:** Sponsored by The EI Group (a for-profit career and educational resource company), this site offers information for international students who want to study at colleges and universities and in other educational settings in Canada. Information is also provided on the Canadian education system. The site is available in several foreign languages.

**FYI**

Approximately 5,000 American students attend Canadian colleges, with McGill University in Montreal boasting almost 1,600 American students.

**Best Points:** The school search option allows you to browse institutions by degree program, location, cost, enrollment size, and semester start. Each school listing offers a link to the school's website, the option to request more information, and details on the school such as size, application deadlines, and admission requirements.

**What You Should Know:** Full access available. This is a good starting point for research on Canadian colleges and universities.

## SchoolsintheUSA.com

### www.schoolsintheusa.com

**What:** Sponsored by The EI Group (a for-profit career and educational resource company), this site offers information on schools, college-prep advice, and a career center for students of all ages.

**Best Points:** A College Search Engine allows users to search by major, state, and tuition amount. Program profiles include details on the school, tuition costs, application deadlines, and admission requirements. Other useful resources include a College Planning section, information on financial aid, virtual tours of select colleges, and a Portfolio feature that allows users to assess their skills and interests.

**What You Should Know:** Full access available.

## Security on Campus, Inc.

### www.securityoncampus.org

**What:** This site was created by two parents whose daughter was tragically murdered at an otherwise "safe" college. Information is aimed at parents, high school seniors, and college students to make them aware of campus dangers and how to help prevent crime in the first place.

**Best Points:** Check out the Student section to watch videos (requires QuickTime Media Player) on the dangers of binge drinking and sexual assault. You can also read useful advice under Campus Safety Tips or research a particular school's crime statistics over the past three years.

**What You Should Know:** Full access available. This site may be a bit overwhelming with its scare tactics, but its goal is important: to educate prospective students, parents, and the campus community about the prevalence of crime on college and university campuses all over the country.

# Sloan Career Cornerstone Center

**www.careercornerstone.org**

**What:** The Sloan Career Cornerstone Center is a nonprofit resource for students interested in pursuing careers in science, technology, engineering, mathematics, computing, and health care.

## FYI

According to the National Academy of Engineering, the top 15 engineering achievements of the 20th century were:

1) Electrification
2) Invention of the Automobile
3) Invention of the Airplane
4) Safe and Abundant Water
5) Electronics
6) Radio and Television
7) Agricultural Mechanization
8) Computers
9) Telephone
10) Air Conditioning/Refrigeration
11) Highways
12) Spacecraft
13) Internet
14) Imaging
15) Household Appliances

Visit www.greatachievements.org for further information.

**Best Points:** Detailed information is provided for careers in these disciplines. The education information provided, which varies by discipline, will be especially useful for high school students interested in planning their college programs. For example, the education section (titled Preparation) for Electrical Engineering provides an overview of core courses, concentrations, and tips on choosing a graduate school, while the education section for Physics discusses what you can do with a bachelor's degree in physics, the benefits of pursuing an advanced degree in physics, and how off-campus experiences, mentors, and internships can benefit you when it comes time to enter the job world. Additionally, each discipline offers profiles of workers that include advice to students considering the field.

**What You Should Know:** Full access available. This website offers far more information than can be detailed here, and is an excellent place to learn more about education requirements and career options in science, technology, engineering, mathematics, computing, and health care.

## SmartMoney: College Preparation

**www.smartmoney.com/college**

**What:** This online publication provides information about affording a college education. College expense worksheets, investment information, and student loan advice are provided at this site. It was created as a joint venture between Dow Jones & Company, Inc. and Hearst SM Partnership.

**Best Points:** There is a lot of general information at this site about budgeting for college costs, applying for aid, seeking out often overlooked scholarships, and other topics. Check out the worksheet, How Much Aid Can You Expect? This resource allows you to plug in information about your financial situation to generate an estimate of what a college expects you to be able to pay. Other interesting resources at the site include 10 Things College Financial Aid Offices Won't Tell You and The College-Savings Superpage.

**What You Should Know:** Full access available. This is a great resource for college financial advice.

## Southern Association of Colleges and Schools—Commission on Colleges

**www.sacscoc.org**

**What:** This organization is one of six regional institutional accrediting associations in the United States. It accredits colleges and universities in Alabama, Florida, Georgia, Kentucky, Louisiana, Mississippi, North Carolina, South Carolina, Tennessee, Texas, Virginia, and Latin America.

**Best Points:** A basic database (found under Membership Directory) of accredited institutions is available at the site, allowing students to browse schools by name, state, and degree awarded. Contact information for each accredited school is provided.

**What You Should Know:** Full access available. Aside from the directory of accredited schools, this site is geared more toward members of the Commission than the general public.

# StaffordLoan.com

### www.staffordloan.com

**What:** Part of the Student Loan Network (a group of privately managed Internet sites created to inform students and parents about loan and financial aid options), this site provides basic information on eligibility and applying for Stafford Loans and other forms of financial assistance to attend college. The site also offers a $10,000 scholarship to high school seniors and college students.

**Best Points:** On the left side of the home page, you can access general information on financial aid options, how to apply for Stafford Loans and other sources of aid, and budgeting for college expenses.

**What You Should Know:** Full access available (although you will need to sign up your name and address to receive more information and a loan application by mail). While this is an informative resource, it is important to note that this is not a federal website. You may want to further research the Stafford Loan by visiting the U.S. Department of Education's website, http://studentaid.ed.gov.

# Statement of Purpose

### www.statementofpurpose.com

**What:** Nearly all college applications require a statement of purpose. Often students don't know how to begin their statement or what the college will be looking for in a "good" statement. This website provides all the answers to students looking for more information on writing statements of purpose.

**Best Points:** Advice on what a statement of purpose actually is, how to get started, and what colleges look for in a successful statement of purpose is provided. Students can also read sample statements and submit their own. In addition to help with the statement of purpose, this website also offers a blog and tips on writing letters of recommendation and scholarship essays; sample essays are provided, too.

**What You Should Know:** Full access available.

# Studentawards.com

**www.studentawards.com**

**What:** This free service allows high school, college, and graduate students to locate scholarships, grants, and other financial assistance for college in Canada. Some of these sources of funding are available only to members of Studentawards.com.

**Best Points:** Studentawards.com caters to individual students based on their planned major, grade point average, location preference, career goals, extracurricular activities, and other criteria. After filling in your credentials and preferences in a short personal profile, the search engine looks for available scholarships that match your interests and goals. Listings include descriptions of the available funding, application details, and deadlines.

**What You Should Know:** Limited access available; registration required for certain areas of this site. You will need to provide your name and address and detailed information about your personal interests in order to browse scholarships available.

# StudentJobs.gov

**www.studentjobs.gov**

**What:** This site, developed by the U.S. Office of Professional Management (OPM), lists funding resources and work opportunities with government agencies for students in high school, college, and graduate school. Information is listed under various categories: fellowships, internships, scholarships, grants, and cooperative education.

**Best Points:** The home page is a no-frills portal that directs you to a list of opportunities depending on your interest. For those looking for college scholarships, e-Scholar lists many options to pursue your education while serving in the armed forces. Other scholarship opportunities are offered by the National Aeronautics and Space Administration, the National Institutes of Health, and other government agencies. In addition, you can use the website's Resume Builder to get your resume in shape. This resume can then be used to apply for open positions. You must create an account to use the Resume Builder, but signing up is free and relatively easy. Another useful page on this website is the Agency

Information Gateway. This section allows you to browse different government agencies (listed alphabetically) and includes articles about what the agencies do and links to their websites.

**What You Should Know:** Limited access available; you will need to register to use the Resume Builder. This site has many listings, but it is not exhaustive. The OPM suggests that students with specific career goals go directly to government agency sites that fit their interest for a complete and more up-to-date listing of opportunities.

# Students.gov

**www.students.gov**

**What:** This U.S. government portal provides links to comprehensive education, career, and government resources on the Web.

**Best Points:** The site has the following main sections: Plan Your Education, Pay For Your Education, Campus Life, Career Development, and Military Service. Clicking on one of the section subheads will take you to a list of often-visited government and selected non-government sites. For example, clicking on the Prepare for College subsection (under Plan Your Education) brings up links to the Federal Student Aid-FAFSA4caster, the U.S. Department of Education, the Office of Postsecondary Education, and campus security statistics for more than 6,000 colleges and universities in the United States.

> ## Tips on Getting Into College
> According to the National Association for College Admission Counseling, academic "tip" factors that play a role in admissions include essay, class rank, and counselor and teacher recommendations. Evolving academic factors include a student's performance on state graduation exams and scores on SAT Subject Tests.

**What You Should Know:** Full access available. This site will save you time as you search for government information about college and other post-high school options.

# StudentsReview.com

**www.studentsreview.com**

**What:** With more than 67,000 reviews, this site allows students to get an insider look at what others are saying about a school. Reviews touch on the education quality, extracurricular activities, social life, faculty, and surround geographic area of a college and are used to rank schools nationwide. There are also sections where alumni rate college majors and provide tips on getting into college and comment on college life. StudentsReview.com was created by students at the Massachusetts Institute of Technology.

> **Did You Know?**
Between 1997 and 2007, the percentage of adults with a bachelor's degree increased from 24 to 29 percent, according to the National Center for Education Statistics.

**Best Points:** Randomly chosen student reviews were (surprisingly) well written and thought out. Instead of students just commenting that they "liked" their school, they described the particular reasons why. You can also read lists of the top-ranked schools (according to reviews compiled on the site) and compare schools against one another. There are also helpful summaries describing popular majors (such as What is Aerospace Engineering—Really?) and links to summer programs for high school students.

**What You Should Know:** Full access available. Though this site doesn't claim to be scientific, this is a good place to read candid and lengthy commentary about schools from the people that matter the most: the students themselves.

## Study Abroad: A Guide for Women

www.iie.org/Content/NavigationMenu/Research_and_Resources/
Publications3/Field_Papers1/Resources2/
StudyAbroadAGuideForWomen/Women.htm

**What:** This online publication was created by the Institute of International Education to promote studying and traveling abroad to women. Topics covered include where to find information about study abroad programs, important considerations to make when choosing a program, testing and application processes, selection and interviewing processes, and basic information about going abroad.

**Best Points:** Under Other Important Considerations, you can read about the importance of starting early when researching and applying to programs or scholarships and also how to overcome barriers you may face, such as those from your parents, spouse, or employer. Another helpful section is The Testing and Application Process, which includes advice on selecting good personal references and asking teachers to write letters of recommendations.

**What You Should Know:** Full access available. This publication, though slightly dated (created in the 1990s), offers useful tips that are applicable to both male and female students.

# Study in Canada

**www.studyincanada.com**

**What:** Study inCanada has been developed by EDge Interactive Publishing, a Canadian media company that aims to encourage students to study in Canada. This site, which is available in English, French, and Spanish, includes information on schools in every Canadian province.

**Best Points:** The school search engine provides tuition costs as well as requirements for specific levels of study such as bachelor's, master's, Ph.D., diploma, and certificate. You can also read about the benefits of a Canadian education and what you should know about Canada, Canadian culture, and the country's educational system before departure. E-tours of certain colleges are also available. There are limited scholarships available for international students who attend college in Canada, and they rarely cover the full cost of a program and are not always easy to find. This site provides information on scholarships for international students with exceptional skills and academic achievement.

**What You Should Know:** Full access available. This is a good site for U.S. students who are interested in studying abroad, but who are looking for a destination that is close to the United States. Be sure to read about the documentation and academic requirements before applying to Canadian schools.

# StudyAbroad.com

**www.studyabroad.com**

**What:** Sponsored by EducationDynamics, LLC (a for-profit company that offers education-related services to administrators, advisors, and students), this site helps students choose a study abroad program and prepare for their cultural exchange before they leave home. Visit this site to research study abroad opportunities aimed at students in high school, college, and graduate school.

**Best Points:** Students can locate schools that offer international study programs by searching under school subject, country, or city. Each search result features descriptions of programs, contact information, and links to helpful websites. Visitors can also read the Study Abroad Student Guide and Study Abroad Parent Guide, which are accessible at the site's home page. The guide includes tips on selecting a study abroad program, preparing for your trip, and adjusting to cultural changes once you've arrived.

**What You Should Know:** Full access available. This is a comprehensive site that is fun and easy to explore. One caveat: advertisements for programs are displayed all over the site. When reading information about programs, make sure you know whether you are reading an ad or general (more impartial) site content.

**Did You Know?**
College enrollment is expected to increase by 14 percent from fall 2007 to fall 2016, according to the National Center for Education Statistics.

## SuperCollege

www.supercollege.com

**What:** This website is a good source of general information on choosing a college, finding a scholarship, meeting admissions deadlines, and other important tasks faced by college-bound students. SuperCollege also includes resources for adult students and parents, a scholarship for high school seniors and college students, a scholarship and admissions newsletter, and a User Forum.

**Best Points:** Articles are informative and well organized and cover most of the hot topics regarding higher education. The scholarship database features more than 2.2 million awards worth more than $15 billion.

**What You Should Know:** Limited access available to all. You must register to use the scholarship search feature and receive the e-newsletters on the latest scholarship opportunities and admission policies. Though the site's founders use the site to promote and sell their books, users will find plenty of free information that would be helpful to anyone looking to go to college.

## Teen Ink: College Essays Written by Teens

http://teenink.com/College/Essays.html

**What:** Every college application requires an essay of some type, and often this is the most nerve-wracking part of the application process for students. This website provides more than 477 samples of real college-entrance essays. Students seeking ideas on how to focus their own essays will benefit from the example of others. Students who believe they've written a great essay themselves can also visit this website to submit their essay for online publication. This website is offered by *Teen Ink,* a national teen magazine that is "devoted entirely to teenage writing and art."

**Best Points:** There is an eclectic mix of college essays at this website, and will provide high school students with great examples as they craft their own essays.

**What You Should Know:** Limited access available. A fee is required to subscribe to the print magazine, but it is free to read the hundreds of essays.

> **Did You Know?**
> The number of college students who earn bachelor's degrees with a double or even a triple major has increased by 85 percent in the last decade, according to the U.S. Department of Education.

# Ten Steps to College With the Greenes

**www.pbs.org/tenstepstocollege**

**What:** Based on the expertise of America's college acceptance gurus and hosts of PBS's *Paying for College with the Greenes,* Howard and Matthew Greene, this website presents the 10 most important steps needed to get into college...and more. There are sections for students, parents, and educators.

**Best Points:** This website's 10-step program discusses the basics—from high school grades and activities to financial aid concerns. Unique to this site are the many checklists and assessment questionnaires available to make any student's college application process more organized. By filling out the Strengths Assessment or the Personal Writing Worksheet, for example, students can determine their best qualities and achievements—in preparation for the all-important personal essay. Also noteworthy are the Enrollment Diaries. In this section, students recount their experiences of making the most of their high school years, as well as their previous experience with the college application process. Students will also benefit from videos featuring advice from the admission directors of some of the nation's top schools, including Ivy League and Big Ten institutions. Topics range from making the most of standardized tests to finding the right school to meet your academic and personal needs.

**What You Should Know:** Full access available. This website is chock full of useful college resources, and is highly recommended.

## Thinking About Going to a Career College or Technical School?

www.ed.gov/students/prep/college/consumerinfo

**What:** This website, sponsored by the U.S. Department of Education, provides very useful information for students who are interested in attending a career college or technical school.

> **> Did You Know?**
> More than 40 percent of Americans believe that attending a career or technical college is the best alternative to attending a four-year college or university, according to the Career College Association. Only 17 percent of respondents favored community colleges as their next best option.

**Best Points:** Resources include advice on finding a school, choosing a school, locating funds to pay for school, as well as information on special considerations (such as accreditation and distance education). There is also an excellent list of questions to ask yourself when choosing a school.

**What You Should Know:** Full access available.

## Tomorrow's Doctors

www.tomorrowsdoctors.com

**What:** This portal site is brought to you by the Association of American Medical Colleges (AAMC). Included are links for those considering a medical career and more specific resources for those already writing prescriptions, including resources for residents and medical students.

**Best Points:** The Considering a Medical Career and Applying to Medical School sections have a lot of useful information for students. In the school section, you can learn about choosing and applying to a medical program and what schools look for in applicants. You can also browse financial planning advice and learn about different medical careers. At the top of all the site's pages, you can jump to other related AAMC sites to learn about the Medical College Admission Test (MCAT), research the role of minorities in medicine, or browse scholarship and financial aid options.

**What You Should Know:** Full access available. This is a great site to measure your interest and pre-paredness for a career in medicine. Whether you are just beginning to explore or have already taken the MCAT, this site will be highly informative.

> **Did You Know?**
> There are 126 accredited schools of medicine and 20 accredited schools of osteopathic medicine in the United States.

# Transitions/Facts on Tap

**www.factsontap.org**

**What:** Transitions and Facts on Tap are two prevention programs that were created by the Children of Alcoholics Foundation and the American Council for Drug Education, eaders in substance abuse prevention education. Transitions is geared toward college-bound high school students, and Facts on Tap focuses on reaching college students. The site offers hard facts about the prevalence and dangers of alcohol abuse and how to help yourself or someone you know. Each program site has information for students, parents, and education professionals.

**Best Points:** Transitions offers the following sections: Heading Off To College, Tips For Managing Your Time Now & In College, Making The Most Of The Campus Visit, What Is Alcohol Poisoning?, and Students In Recovery.

Facts on Tap has several interesting sections. Facts About Alcohol & Drugs separates facts from fiction about drinking/drug use in college and includes a quiz to test your knowledge about alcohol and potential abuse. There is also advice for students who have a family history of substance abuse and information for students in recovery.

**What You Should Know:** Full access available. These are good sites for students and anyone who wants to learn more about alcohol. Information is presented in a frank manner that should make you think twice before drinking heavily. However, in addition to presenting warnings and scary stories, these programs offer ideas for alternatives to parties and bars and provides suggestions on how to help yourself or others who might have a drinking problem.

## *Tribal College Journal*

www.tribalcollegejournal.org

**What:** This site provides information on the *Tribal College Journal*, a magazine published by the American Indian Higher Education Consortium. The publication presents news about tribal education for students, educators, and others interested in Native American issues.

**Best Points:** This is a good way to learn about the history and mission of tribal colleges, issues faced by the schools and its students, and ways to help fund and educate others about Native American higher education. The site offers a listing of past and present journal issues, including a table of contents and selected links to articles available for online reading.

**What You Should Know:** Limited access available. This site is somewhat limited in what you can read from the journal. Each issue offers only two or three articles online, but this is enough to gain a sense of the publication's mission and intended audience. If interested, you can subscribe to the journal at the website.

## U101 College Search: Links to Learning in the United States and Canada

http://u101.com

**What:** U101 is a directory of almost 4,000 colleges and universities in North America. Articles on college planning are also provided by outside content providers such as the Scholarship Experts.com, Accepted.com, and EssayEdge.com.

**Best Points:** The directory of colleges offers basic lists of and links to colleges and universities in the United States (including Guam and Puerto Rico), Canada, and the Caribbean.

**What You Should Know:** Full access available. This site is effective as a basic search tool for locating academic institutions.

## UCAN: Get the Facts For a Smart College Choice

www.ucan-network.org

**What:** Students interested in accessing information on private colleges and universities in the United States will find UCAN, which is sponsored by the National Association of Independent Colleges and Universities, to be a useful site. As of press time, the website featured nearly 500 profiles of private colleges and universities—with additional schools expected to be added shortly. The site offers limited search options (institution name, zip code, city, state), but the Association says that the search criteria may be expanded in the future.

**Best Points:** Each school entry features an overview of the institution and statistical information on up to 42 quantitative elements including the number of students who applied and were accepted, average ACT/SAT scores, enrollment, tuition, financial aid, faculty, campus safety, the number of female students, ethnic diversity, the percentage of freshmen who return for their sophomore year, the percentage of students who graduate in four years, and other categories. There are also up to 25 links per entry to school websites; these provide more information on topics such as career and placement services, internships, transfer or credit policies, accreditation, intercollegiate sports, study abroad, students with disabilities, and religious and spiritual life. The information is displayed via attractive bar and pie charts, and is also available in a printable PDF document.

**What You Should Know:** Full access available. Despite its basic search engine, UCAN is a great place to learn more about private colleges and universities.

# Undergraduate Mathematics Majors

**www.ams.org/employment/undergrad.html**

**What:** This site from the American Mathematics Society is a useful resource for students interested in pursuing a career in math. The site includes information on graduate programs and universities, semester and summer programs, issues in math, math clubs and conferences, and leads on part- and full-time jobs and internships.

**Best Points:** This site is just what it says it is, created for undergraduates who are majoring in math or considering the major. Resources on graduate programs (both here and abroad) and current employment trends are informative, many including detailed statistics and easy-to-read graphs. There is also general information on careers in mathematics, which should be useful for students who are still undecided about their major.

> **Did You Know?**
Students who major in mathematics can work in a wide variety of career fields, including statistics, business, computer science, accounting, education, actuarial science, physical sciences, and engineering.

**What You Should Know:** Full access available. Though the majority of this site is aimed at current or soon-to-be graduate students, students of all ages will find useful information.

# United Negro College Fund (UNCF)

**www.uncf.org**

**What:** This higher education assistance organization provides financial and technological assistance to deserving students at historically black colleges and universities.

**Best Points:** A general search option allows African-American students to search for scholarships by major, achievement level, and state. Students can apply for many UNCF scholarships online. Students can also browse unique scholarship options such as the UNCF/Merck Science Initiative, which benefits selected students pursuing biomedical studies and careers. Information on internships is also available.

**What You Should Know:** Full access available. This site offers many valuable opportunities for African-American students who have achieved educational excellence in high school and who are planning to attend college.

# U.S. Department of Education Database of Accredited Postsecondary Institutions and Programs

**www.ope.ed.gov/accreditation**

**What:** In the age of diploma mills, rising tuition, and growing competition for the best jobs, it has become increasingly important for students to attend schools that have a strong and proven reputation for providing a quality education. To assist students in identifying accredited schools, the U.S. Department of Education has created a website that allows users to locate all accredited programs (nationally and regionally) which are offered by approximately 6,900 universities and colleges in the United States and its territories.

**Best Points:** The search feature is very easy to use. Simply name an institution, and all accreditations will be listed along with links to accrediting bodies, as well as pertinent information regarding the school. You can also search by program accreditation, say, from the American Osteopathic Association. You can easily identify all institutions carrying that particular credit. Criteria can be tweaked—location, type of institution, and enrollment—to further narrow your search.

*(Photo courtesy of Dynamic Graphics)*

**What You Should Know:** Full access available. This is a good place to learn about accredited institutions.

## U.S. Department of Education

**www.ed.gov**

**What:** This award-winning site has been developed by the U.S. Department of Education to serve as a clearinghouse of information on all its programs and services. You can learn about the President's "No Child Left Behind" campaign to reform elementary and secondary education or browse educational and financial aid resources for high school and college students. The site has material geared toward the following audiences: Students, Teachers, Parents, and Administrators. Sections of this website are also available in Spanish.

**Best Points:** This website has a lot of information aimed at students of all ages. For the college-bound, check out the sections on financial aid and higher educational resources.

**What You Should Know:** Full access available. This is an excellent starting point for all students who are interested in learning more about college.

## U.S. Department of State: Travel Warnings and Consular Information Sheets

http://travel.state.gov/travel_warnings.html

**What:** This site offers updated information about the stability of countries and warnings to Americans traveling abroad.

**Best Points:** Each country listing includes a country description, entry/exit requirements, details on safety and security, crime statistics, medical coverage and insurance issues, road conditions, aviation safety and customs policies, criminal penalties, and U.S. embassy and consulate locations. In addition, each country listing shows the date the profile was last updated, so you will know how timely the information is that is presented.

**What You Should Know:** Full access available. Because this information comes straight from the source, this website is an essential must-read for students preparing to travel or study abroad.

## U.S. Network for Education Information (USNEI)

**www.ed.gov/about/offices/list/ous/international/usnei/ edlite-index.html**

**What:** The goal of USNEI is to "facilitate international educational mobility" by informing students about the differences between American and foreign systems of education. The site offers information for students, parents, teachers, and administrators.

### Useful Resource
Another great site to visit if you plan to study abroad is the *CIA World Factbook* (www.cia.gov/library/publications/ the-world-factbook), which provides detailed information (geography, people, communications, economy, transnational issues, transportation, etc.) about hundreds of foreign countries.

**Best Points:** The site is easy to navigate, with a large pull-down menu and side menu options to direct you to the page of your choice. One helpful topic includes how to apply for U.S. or foreign visas and permits and when they are required for work or travel. You can also read advice about what to do before going abroad, things to consider while traveling, and how to readjust to home after your travels.

**What You Should Know:** Full access available. Whether you are an American student hoping to study abroad or a foreign student thinking of visiting, studying, or teaching in the United States, this website has useful information and links to other online resources.

# *U.S. News & World Report:* Education

## www.usnews.com/sections/education

**What:** You can view select articles from the print version of *U.S. News & World Report* at this site, and you will also find college articles that are exclusive to the Web.

**Best Points:** Portions of the magazine's America's Best Colleges lists can be accessed for free at this site, or you can purchase the premium edition (either the online or print version). Schools are divided up into many categories on this list, including top liberal arts schools, highest graduation rates, and best values. The E-Learning & Technology section can help you find a distance education opportunity that is right for you. The site also answers FAQs about applications, such as "To how many colleges should I apply?" Additional features of note include educational blogs, information on careers, a scholarship database, a financial aid glossary, and a resource section for parents.

**What You Should Know:** Limited access available; registration required for certain areas of this site and use of some advanced features require a small fee. This site offers up-to-date resources and articles that will be very useful to aspiring college students and their parents.

# Upromise

## www.upromise.com

**What:** Upromise is a rewards program that offers money back for college savings after purchasing goods or services from more than 40,000 participating retail stores and services, such as JCPenney, Walmart, McDonald's, Nestle, and Eddie Bauer. Upromise also offers college loan services.

**Best Points:** Upromise is easy to use and keeps track of your purchases and resulting savings online for easy retrieval. Rewards are offered for anything from dining out at a participating restaurant (more than 8,000 nationwide) to using Kaplan Test Prep services. Money automatically adds up in your Upromise account, which you can then transfer into a 529 college saving plan each quarter.

**What You Should Know:** Registration required for all areas of this site. You will need to register your name, mailing address,

## Costly Colleges

George Washington University (DC) is the most expensive (including tuition, room, board, and other fees) major university in the United States, according to the *Washington Post*. The University has increased the amount of financial aid that it offers students as a means to reduce the effect of the tuition increase. Other expensive schools include Landmark College (VT), Sarah Lawrence College (NY), Kenyon College (OH), Trinity College (CT), and Hamilton College (NY).

phone number, and email to create an account. Then, to activate a Upromise account, you have to sign up one or more of your credit cards for savings. Regarding your credit privacy, Upromise "protects your credit card information with strict security precautions and uses information only for posting rebates to your account." Also note that you don't have to have a child to participate; you can sign up to save money for a grandchild or even for yourself.

# Virtual Family Medicine Interest Group (FMIG)

http://fmignet.aafp.org

**What:** This site, sponsored by the American Academy of Family Physicians, offers information for future and current medical students at all points in their education. Explore the discipline of family medicine, and browse resources to help you choose your career, find role models, develop leadership skills, survive the residency period, and more.

**Best Points:** The Medical School section is an excellent resource for students at any stage of their medical education. Read advice about what you should be doing and considering every month of each of your four years of med school. For students still in college who are considering pursuing a medical degree, check out the section on the basics of family practice to learn more about this area of medicine. Learn more about securing and surviving the medical residency by visiting the Residency section. Other useful resources include Hot Topics (which detail trends and developments in medical education), a Student Interest Discussion Board, and Strolling Through the Match (a 63-page booklet that aims to provide advice and guidance to "medical students, regardless of specialty interest or medical school").

**What You Should Know:** Full access available. Virtual FMIG is an essential, comprehensive resource for all students—whether they are just beginning to consider medical school or are wrapping up their degree.

## Wachovia: Education Loans

www.wachovia.com/personal/page/0,,325_496,00.html

**What:** This website provides information on the student loan division of Wachovia, a financial services company. The site is also available in Spanish.

**Best Points:** Visit this site to learn about the financial aid process, loan options, preparing for college expenses, and more. Information is relevant for high school, college, and graduate school students; parents; and current borrowers.

**What You Should Know:** Full access available.

## Wells Fargo: Student Loans & Banking

https://www.wellsfargo.com/student/
index.jhtml?_requestid=138462

**What:** Financial services giant Wells Fargo created this site to help students financially plan for college or graduate school. Included on this site are links to scholarship opportunities and tips on securing a student loan and filling out college applications. The site is also available in Spanish.

**Best Points:** Check out the CollegeSTEPS program, which allows you to sign up to receive e-postcards covering college preparation and financing issues. There is also useful information on student loans, loan consolidation, and college financial planning for younger children, as well as financial aid calculators.

**What You Should Know:** Limited access available. If you want to participate in CollegeSTEPS, you need to sign up your name and contact information, but the rest of the information on this site is available for anonymous browsing.

## Western Association of Schools and Colleges

www.wascweb.org

**What:** This is one of six regional accrediting institutions in the United States that accredits high schools, junior colleges, colleges, and universities. The association accredits institutions in California and Hawaii, the territories of Guam and American Samoa, the Federated States of Micronesia, the Republic of Palau, the Commonwealth of the Northern Marianas Islands, the

Pacific Basin, and American/international schools in areas of the Pacific and East Asia.

**Best Points:** The home page offers links to the main bodies of the organization, the Accrediting Commission for Schools (elementary, junior high, middle, high and adult schools), the Accrediting Commission for Community and Junior Colleges, and the Accrediting Commission for Senior Colleges and Universities. Each of these sites explains the process and purpose of accreditation and provides a directory of accredited institutions.

**What You Should Know:** Full access available. The directory of colleges is organized in alphabetical order, allowing you to search by name but not by location.

## What Can I Do With a Major in . . . ?

www.uncwil.edu/stuaff/career/Majors
http://career.utk.edu/students/majors.asp
www.wcu.edu/6679.asp
www.ncsu.edu/majors-careers
www.alvernia.edu/careerservices/wammies.htm

**What:** Choosing a major can be one of the most difficult decisions for high school students as they prepare for college. Most colleges and universities offer information to help students learn more about and choose a major. This information can often be located at a school's website by using a search phrase such as "What Can I Do With a Major in . . . ?" or something similar. The websites listed above provide good examples of the types of information available at these websites. For more sites, search on the aforementioned (or a similar) phrase or visit the websites of colleges that you are interested in and perform a keyword search using the phrase or visit the career services department website for more information.

**Best Points:** While each website has its own particular design and level of detail, most sites provide an overview of the major, a list of personal skills for students interested in the major, typical careers for the major, and a list of Web links for additional information.

**What You Should Know:** Full access available. Sites of this nature are an excellent complementary tool to help you learn more about college majors and career options.

# Where Shall I Go to Study Advertising?

http://ocean.otr.usm.edu/~w481504/wsig

**What:** This site was compiled by two college professors to assist college students in choosing an advertising or public relations program. The site has listings for nearly 195 U.S. colleges as well as recommended websites for students interested in pursing a career in advertising or public relations.

**Best Points:** Don't even waste your time with the other links; go straight to the main section, which presents a state-by-state listing of programs in advertising and public relations. Each school entry includes admission requirements, program size, tuition cost, contact information, and a direct link to the school's website.

**What You Should Know:** Full access available. Though the site is not visually appealing, it does present useful information to students who know they want to study public relations or advertising.

**Did You Know?**
Median annual earnings for advertising sales agents were $42,820 in 2007, according to the U.S. Department of Labor.

# Women's College Coalition

www.womenscolleges.org

**What:** Women who attend single-sex colleges participate more in class, tend to hold higher positions in their respective careers, and report higher academic and personal success than women who attend coed institutions. These and other interesting facts about the merits of single-sex education can be found at the website of the Women's College Coalition, an association of 58 women's colleges in the United States and Canada.

**Best Points:** The site features information on the benefits of attending a women's college, a fact-based analysis of the myths surrounding women's colleges, and contact information for its member schools.

**What You Should Know:** Full access available. This site will be valuable to female students who are weighing the pros and cons of attending an all-female college.

# WorldStudy.gov

**www.worldstudy.gov**

**What:** This site is sponsored by the National Security Education Program, a U.S. government program that promotes global education for American college and graduate students to areas not usually visited by students (such as Africa, Asia, Eastern and Central Europe, Latin America and the Caribbean, and the Middle East). The site also offers information on the Boren Scholarships and Fellowships, which help top undergraduate and graduate students pay for their study abroad experience.

**Best Points:** Much of the information presented is contributed by students who have participated in this program. Read material from the Feature Articles or Your Peers sections to learn about past Boren winners and view pictures from their experiences. These students even offer advice on helping to convince your parents that you should go abroad! Any additional questions you may have about scholarship eligibility or scope should be answered in the FAQs section.

**What You Should Know:** Full access available. Scholarship funds go directly to you, not to your college or university, which can allow you to structure your program to fit your education and career objectives. This is an excellent website for undergraduate or graduate students who have wanted to take the road less traveled when going abroad.

# Xap

**www.xap.com**

**What:** This is a comprehensive site for people interested in learning more about their college and career options. It is operated by the Xap Corporation.

**Best Points:** The site has five main sections: Apply, Go to College, Get Money, Prepare, and Plan a Career. Under Apply, students can search for information on admissions practices, academics, costs, financial aid, and student life at more than 500 colleges and universities. Many colleges also offer online applications in this section. The Go to College section offers a searchable database and campus tours of selected schools. Visit Get Money for a financial aid calculator, tips on saving and paying for college, and a searchable database of more than one million scholarships. The Prepare section features an application timeline and test prep tips, including an SAT, ACT, and GRE word and question of the day. Finally, the Plan a Career section will help you match your skills, interests, and personality traits with a career path.

**What You Should Know:** Limited access available. If you want to simply browse for information, registration is not required. However, if you want to apply for scholarships or fill out college applications online, you will need to create an account with Xap.

# Yahoo! Education

### http://education.yahoo.com

**What:** This site, dedicated to educational resources, is brought to you by Yahoo!, the convenient and easy-to-use Internet search engine.

**Best Points:** This site has a little of everything, including a search feature to research colleges, graduate schools, and distance education programs; education news and information; sample tests for the SAT, GRE, GMAT, and LSAT; and dictionary and encyclopedia references.

**What You Should Know:** Full access available. This is a good website to explore for general college information. The school summaries are brief but can be used to compare schools on a preliminary basis.

# YESICan

### www.yesican.gov/publications/tips.html

**What:** The White House Initiative on Educational Excellence for Hispanic Americans has created this website to educate Hispanic parents and their children about college options. The website has section for the following age groups: Early Childhood, Elementary School, High School, and College and Beyond. A Spanish-language version of the website is also available.

**Best Points:** The High School and College and Beyond sections will be most useful to readers of this book. The High School page has sections on Planning for College, Taking the Tests, Finding the Right College, Getting into College, and Paying for College. The College and Beyond page has sections on Succeeding in College, Making the Grade in College Classes, and Picking Your Major.

**What You Should Know:** Full access available. This is a well-organized, informative website for Hispanic students and their parents.

# Youth For Understanding (YFU)

**www.yfu.org**

**What:** This nonprofit educational organization runs or sponsors work and study abroad programs, opportunities to volunteer overseas, and scholarships to help send young adults abroad. The home page directs you to YFU programs in 60 countries.

**Best Points:** At the U.S. site, read about YFU study abroad programs. Applicants must be between the ages of 15 and 19, have a GPA of at least 3.0 for year and semester programs and 2.0 for summer programs, and be in good health (students with disabilities are encouraged to apply). Program options include nearly a year (10-11 months), a semester (4-6 months), or a summer (3-8 weeks). Many programs allow you to choose your academic focus to help you meet your educational goals. For detailed information on departure dates, application fees, deadlines, and more, visit the Program Details page. When you're ready to apply, click on How to Apply to download an application form.

**What You Should Know:** Full access available. In addition to reading about programs, check out the Scholarship pages to learn about how to apply for financial assistance to go abroad. Or perhaps you'd rather show off your country to a foreign student. If so, read about the benefits, application process, and students that take part in YFU's cultural exchange. To become a host family, you should get your parents' permission first, of course!

# Zinch

**www.zinch.com**

**What:** Students with less-than-perfect ACT or SAT scores might find Zinch to be a useful tool to help them get noticed by college admissions officers. The website is free to students; colleges pay a fee to access the profiles. The site's founders say that Zinch is not a social networking site and that it is not meant to replace traditional college applications, but to provide college recruiters with another method to find students with special abilities and talents. More than 570 colleges use the services of Zinch to locate creative and talented students who may not score well on standardized tests, but who would make excellent additions to their admissions classes. (Note: Scholarships are also offered to any student who creates a Zinch profile.)

**Best Points:** Zinch allows student to create online profiles that detail their unique hobbies and talents (such as poetry writing or filmmaking)—which do not appear on standardized tests or in academic transcripts. Students can upload their creative writing, artwork, videos of sports highlights, or recordings of their music for admissions officers to review. Colleges can then search the database of profiles to find students with particular interests.

**What You Should Know:** Limited access available; you must register (free) to use Zinch.

# Association Web Resources

Association, government, and corporate websites are great sources of information on college and careers. Unlike the College Resource Website listings (which feature reviews of entire websites), this section simply lists free online college-related publications and resources that are available at the organization's main professional development or career-based website.

Nearly 1,000 online resources and publications relating to college topics are offered by 366 professional associations and government agencies in this section. These resources will help students and educators learn more about college options as they relate to more than 400 careers—from accountants to zoologists.

The Web addresses we have provided for the publications and resources were the most direct and easiest path available at the time of our visit, but be aware that an address can sometimes change when the association's website is updated. To help you easily locate these resources on the Web, we have done the following:

✔ Placed the title of the publication or resource in bold.

✔ Occasionally listed a subsection name at the website in parentheses after the main Web address or after the name of an individual entry to help you locate especially hard-to-find resources.

Consider the following examples before you begin reading this section (see the next page):

**Example #1:**

**American Association of
Community Colleges (AACC)**

> Clicking on "About Community Colleges" at the home page of the AACC will take you to **Fast Facts** and other resources.

www.aacc.nche.edu (click on About Community Colleges)

**Fast Facts.** Contains a wealth of statistics on community colleges.

**Example #2**

**American
Phytopathological Society**

> Clicking on "Careers & Placement" at the home page of the American Phytopathological Society will take you to **Careers in Plant Pathology.**

www.apsnet.org

**Careers in Plant Pathology** (click on Careers & Placement).
Info on careers in plant pathology and educational paths.

# AACC International

www.aaccnet.org/membership/careersbrochure.asp

**Careers in Cereal Chemistry.** Details career opportunities (e.g., quality control and assurance, product development, research, and teaching) and educational requirements for students interested in studying cereal science.

**U.S. and Canadian Universities That Offer Graduate Education in Cereal Science.** Lists graduate programs that offer cereal science degrees as well as those that offer cereal science education as part of a degree in food science.

Additionally, the AACC International Foundation offers scholarships and fellowships to undergraduates and graduates studying cereal science. Visit the Foundation's website (www.aaccnet.org/foundation) for more information.

> **> Did You Know?**
> To work as an engineer, you will need to earn at least a bachelor of science degree in engineering. Many top jobs are only available to engineers who have earned a master's degree in engineering or a related field. Technician and technologist jobs usually require an associate degree.

# Accreditation Board for Engineering and Technology

www.abet.org/accredited_programs.shtml

**Accredited Applied Science Programs.**
**Accredited Computing Programs.**
**Accredited Engineering Programs.**
**Accredited Engineering Technology Programs.**

Lists accredited programs. Searchable by state, region, or academic discipline.

**Why Should I Choose an Accredited Program?** Lists the benefits of choosing an accredited program.

# Accreditation Commission for Acupuncture and Oriental Medicine

www.acaom.org

**Accredited & Candidate Schools.** Provides a list of accredited master's-level programs in acupuncture and Oriental medicine.

## Accreditation Council for Graduate Medical Education

www.acgme.org/adspublic

**List of ACGME Accredited Programs and Sponsoring Institutions.** A database of accredited medical graduate programs in more than 30 medical specialties. Searchable by state and program specialty.

## Accreditation Council for Pharmacy Education

www.acpe-accredit.org/students/programs.asp

**Accredited Professional Programs of Colleges and Schools of Pharmacy.** Provides a list of accredited pharmacy programs in the United States.

## Accrediting Bureau of Health Education Schools

www.abhes.org/areasofstudytemp.asp

**Accredited Programs.** Provides a list of accredited programs in medical assisting, medical laboratory technology, surgical technology.

## Acoustical Society of America (ASA)

www.asa.aip.org/map_education.html

**Directory of Graduate Education in Acoustics.** This online publication lists schools offering graduate programs in acoustical disciplines, such as acoustical oceanography, acoustical signal processing, animal bioacoustics, architectural acoustics, engineering acoustics, medical/bioacoustics, musical acoustics, nonlinear acoustics, physical acoustics, psychological acoustics, speech, ultrasonics, and underwater sound. You can search for programs by institution name or geographic region.

**Fellowships, Scholarships, Prizes, Grants and Student Awards Available from the ASA.** Lists available financial aid.

## Advanced Technology Environmental and Energy Center (ATEEC)

https://www.ateec.org/learning/student/careers.htm

**What Should I Study in High School to Prepare Myself for a Career in Environmental Technology?** Recommended courses, skills, and activities for high school students interested in environmental technology.

**Do Colleges Near Me Offer Programs in Environmental Technology?** Lists two- and four-year colleges and universities in the United States that offer educational programs in environmental technology, environmental science, and related disciplines.

# Advertising Educational Foundation

www.aef.com/industry/careers/6000

**Where to Study Advertising.** Provides a list of schools that offer advertising and/or joint advertising/public relations programs.

# Air and Waste Management Association (AWMA)

www.awma.org/enviro_edu/college_ed/index.html

**U.S. Colleges & Universities Offering Undergraduate Degrees in the Environmental Profession.** Lists undergraduate programs for students interested in the air, waste, and environmental fields.

**Colleges & Universities Offering Advanced Degrees in the Environmental Profession.** Lists North American colleges and universities offering graduate programs in environmental engineering, environmental science, air pollution meteorology, and environmental health.

**Environmental Careers Fact Sheet** (www.awma.org/ files_original/careersfactsheet07.pdf). Provides detailed information on career opportunities in the public, private, and non-profit sectors. Also lists required education training and suggested majors.

**Scholarships.** Lists scholarships offered by the AWMA.

# Aircraft Owners and Pilots Association

www.aopa.org

**Choosing Your Flight School.** Provides information on types of flight schools, choosing a school, and costs.

**Aviation Colleges: Why You Should Go and How to Select One.** Discusses the benefits of pursuing flight training in two- and four-year college settings. Includes information on financial aid, how to select a college, campus visits, and what to study.

**Collegiate Aviation Programs and Options.** Provides detailed information about educational offerings at two- and four-year colleges. Also includes information on accreditation.

**Find a Flight School.** Searchable database of flight schools in the United States.

**Directory of Aviation Colleges and Universities.** Database of two- and four-year U.S. colleges offering aviation training. Searchable by city, state, and type of training.

**Guide to Flight Careers** (www.aopa.org/path/careers.pdf). Details career opportunities and educational requirements for specific careers in the field.

# American Academy of Environmental Engineers

**www.aaee.net/Website/careers.htm**

**Careers.** Provides information on career possibilities and educational requirements for students interested in environmental engineering.

# American Academy of Forensic Sciences (AAFS)

**www.aafs.org**

**Accredited Schools.** Lists college programs that are accredited by the AAFS Forensic Science Education Programs Accreditation Commission.

**FYI**
You will need at least a bachelor's degree in a science-related discipline to work as a forensic scientist. Some positions require a graduate degree.

**Colleges & Universities.** Lists U.S. and international colleges and universities that offer undergraduate and graduate programs in the forensic sciences. Includes a separate list of forensic odontology programs.

**So You Want to Be a Forensic Scientist!** Details specialties (e.g., criminalistics, odontology, physical anthropology, toxicology), employment settings, and educational requirements for students interested in forensic science.

# American Academy of Nurse Practitioners (AANP)

**www.aanp.org/AANPCMS2/AboutAANP/Career+Resources**

**Foundation Scholarship & Grant Program.** Information on scholarships, grants, and other financial aid offered by the AANP Foundation (www.aanpfoundation.org).

# American Academy of Periodontology (AAP)

**www.perio.org/education/postdoctoral.html**

**Profiles of Postdoctoral Programs.** Lists postdoctoral periodontal programs in the United States, the U.S. military, and Canada. Each program listing includes information on application deadlines, length of program, degrees offered, prerequisites, accreditation status, tuition, faculty, and other useful categories.

**Steps in the Application Process.** Presents tips and advice for students applying to postdoctoral periodontal programs.

**Tips for Getting Accepted.** Offers advice on improving your postdoctoral program application and interview tips.

Additionally, the AAP Foundation offers a variety of financial aid options to periodontology students. Visit www.perio.org/foundation/scholars.html for more information.

# American Academy of Physician Assistants

**www.aapa.org**

**What is a PA?** Provides information on the career of physician assistant (PA), educational requirements, the prerequisites for applying to a PA program, and the difference between a physician and a physician assistant.

**PA Educational Programs.** Lists physician assistant programs in the United States that are accredited by the Accreditation Review Commission on Education for the Physician Assistant (www.arc-pa.org).

**Central Application Service for Physician Assistants.** Link to an online service that allows students to apply to multiple physician assistant programs with one application. Visit https://portal.caspaonline.org for more information.

> **> Did You Know?**
> The majority of physician assistants have bachelor's or master's degrees, according to the Academy of Physician Assistants.

# American Agricultural Economics Association

**www.aaea.org** (click on Careers & Education)

**Careers in Agricultural Economics.** Lists recommended high school and college courses and careers students can land with a degree in agricultural economics.

**Colleges & Universities Offering Coursework in Agricultural Economics.** Lists U.S. bachelor's, graduate, and post-graduate educational programs in agricultural economics.

# American Alliance for Health, Physical Education, Recreation and Dance

**www.aahperd.org**

**Graduate Bulletin.** Annual directory of U.S. graduate and doctoral programs in more than 150 disciplines in the health, physical education, recreation, dance, and sports fields. Searchable by degree and field.

**Scholarships and Awards.** Information on a scholarship for undergraduate and graduate student members.

# American Anthropological Association

**www.aaanet.org/profdev/careers/Careers.cfm**

**Careers in Anthropology—Anthropology: Education for the 21st Century.** Details the career of anthropologist, educational options, and personal skills developed by studying anthropology in college.

**FYI**
According to the AATA, art therapists are employed in hospitals and clinics; halfway houses; schools, colleges, and universities; out-patient mental health agencies; correctional facilities; elder care facilities; art studios; and in private practice.

# American Art Therapy Association (AATA)

www.arttherapy.org

**Approved Graduate Degree Programs.** Lists more than 30 AATA-approved graduate programs in art therapy. Includes types of degrees awarded and contact information.

**Frequently Asked Questions About Art Therapy.** Provides an overview of the career, typical employment settings, educational requirements, and the employment outlook for the field.

# American Association for Clinical Chemistry

www.comacc.org/Pages/default.aspx

**Graduate and Postdoctoral Training Programs in Clinical Chemistry.** Lists U.S. and Canadian programs accredited by the Commission on Accreditation in Clinical Chemistry. Each program listing includes information on level of training available, duration of training, and faculty research interests.

# American Association for Paralegal Education (AAfPE)

www.aafpe.org (click on Find a School)

**Choosing a Paralegal Program.** Details types of paralegal educational programs in the United States.

**Evaluating Paralegal Programs.** Lists questions to ask when evaluating paralegal programs (e.g., What is the reputation of the institution and the paralegal program?, What services are offered to students?, and What are the graduation requirements?), and methods for finding a paralegal program.

**AAfPE Member Directory.** Lists contact information for AAfPE member schools. You can search this list alphabetically, by state, by type of degree granted, and by other criteria.

# American Association for Respiratory Care (AARC)

**www.aarc.org/career**

**Be an RT.** In addition to extensive career information, provides a list of respiratory care programs accredited by the Commission on Accreditation of Allied Health Education Programs and the Committee on Accreditation for Respiratory Care. The list is searchable by state and bachelor's degree only or by all types of degrees.

Additionally, the AARC Foundation (www.arcfoundation.org/awards) offers a number of scholarships, awards, and grants to undergraduate and graduate students who are studying respiratory care.

# American Association of Colleges of Nursing

**www.aacn.nche.edu/Students/index.htm**

**Your Nursing Career: A Look at the Facts.** Details the changing job market and educational requirements as well as new nursing specialties such as certified registered nurse anesthetists and clinical nurse specialists.

**Scholarships and Financial Aid Resources for Nursing Students.** Offers links to associations and government agencies that provide financial assistance to nursing students.

**List of AACN-Member Schools.** Lists more than 600 AACN-member schools (listed by state).

**Nursing Education Programs.** Provides detailed overviews of undergraduate nursing programs, programs for RNs, doctoral programs, and accelerated programs.

**Good Earnings! Good Career Outlook!**
Registered nurses earned average annual salaries of $60,010 in 2007, according to the U.S. Department of Labor. Salaries ranged from less than $42,020 to more than $87,310. Additionally, the U.S. Department of Labor predicts that the employment of registered nurses will grow much faster than the average for all careers through 2016.

# American Association of Colleges of Osteopathic Medicine (AACOM)

www.aacom.org/InfoFor/applicants/Pages/default.aspx

**Becoming an Osteopathic Physician.** Provides an overview of the types of students who find success in osteopathic medical school. Details are provided on general admissions requirements, an overview of the four-year curriculum, board examinations and licensure, and websites for potential medical students.

**Osteopathic Medical School Directory.** Lists osteopathic medical schools in the United States. Includes information on accreditation, curriculum, facilities, tuition, special programs, and supplemental requirements. Also features a useful comparative feature that allows users to compare schools by geographic region, pre-requisites, number of students enrolled, application deadlines, and tuition.

**Osteopathic Medical College Information Book.** Comprehensive information on osteopathic careers, college admission requirements, financial aid, board examinations, and osteopathic colleges. This resource is available for a small fee.

> ## FYI
> According to the AACOM, approximately 25 percent of students enrolled in osteopathic medical schools are classified as "nontraditional students." This group consists of those who have worked in another career such as business executives or managers, administrators, professional musicians, allied health care providers, and newspaper reporters.

**Financial Aid.** Details information on more than 150 scholarships available to osteopathic medicine students.

**Fast Facts About Osteopathic Medical Education** (click on About AACOM). Provides statistical information about osteopathic education applicants and acceptance rates.

# American Association of Colleges of Pharmacy (AACP)

www.aacp.org

**Frequently Asked Questions about Pharmacy Admissions.** Answers questions such as What can I do with a pharmacy degree?, Do I need a bachelor's degree before I apply to pharmacy school?, and Can I enroll in a pharmacy school right after high school?

**Pharm.D. Degree.** An overview of degree requirements, length of study, major areas of study, and post-professional education.

**Pharmacy School Admission Requirements.** Features two-page descriptions of admission requirements for every Pharm.D. program in the United States.

**Pharmacy College Admissions Test: PCAT.** Information for prospective test-takers.

**PharmCAS.** Link to The Pharmacy College Application Service online application.

**Pharmacy Colleges and Schools: Contact Information.** Lists AACP-accredited pharmacy schools in the United States and Canadian and international schools of pharmacy.

**Graduate Programs.** Lists graduate schools of pharmacy in the United States.

**Financial Aid.** Information on loans, grants, and scholarships available to pharmacy students.

**Pharmacy: Prescription for a Rewarding Career.** Details educational requirements and career options.

*Employment of pharmacists is expected to grow much faster than the average through 2016. (Photo courtesy of Photos.com)*

# American Association of Colleges of Podiatric Medicine (AACPMAS)

www.aacpm.org

**College Links.** Lists colleges of podiatric medicine.

**Residency Training** (click on Career Zone). Provides information on residency training for new podiatric physicians.

**FAQs.** Includes answers to these and other questions: What is a Doctor of Podiatric Medicine?, What does the curriculum consist of at colleges of podiatric medicine?, When can I apply to colleges of podiatric medicine?, What are the selection procedures for admission?, How much will podiatry school cost?, What do I as a pre-health student need to know about financing my professional education?, and Is residency training required?

**Admissions Requirements** (click on Apply to Colleges). Details prerequisites, admissions procedures, and admissions tests.

**Statistics.** Contains statistics on applicants and students at schools of podiatric medicine.

**Apply Online** (click on Apply to Colleges). Allows prospective podiatric students to apply electronically to "eight colleges of podiatric medicine and over 200 affiliated teaching hospitals and other types of institutions which offer graduate or postdoctoral training in podiatric medicine."

## The Most Popular Associate Degrees

1. Liberal Arts and Sciences, General Studies, and Humanities
2. Health Professions and Related Sciences
3. Business, Management, and Marketing
4. Computer and Information Sciences
5. Engineering-Related Technologies
6. Visual and Performing Arts
7. Security and Protective Services
8. Multi/Interdisciplinary Studies
9. Personal and Culinary Services
10. Mechanics and Repairers
11. Education
12. Family and Consumer Sciences
13. Social Sciences and History
14. Agriculture/Natural Resources
15. Public Admin./Social Services

Source: National Center for Education Statistics

# American Association of Community Colleges

**www.aacc.nche.edu** (click on About Community Colleges)

**Fast Facts.** Contains a wealth of statistics on community colleges.

**Trends and Statistics.** Provides information on demographics, financial aid, enrollment, and staffing at community colleges.

**Community College Finder.** Features a U.S. map that allows users to scroll around the country to see the number of community colleges in each state. Once you select a state, you can browse statistics and a listing of colleges and contact information.

# American Association of Endodontists

www.aae.org/dentalpro/BecomeAnEndo

**Accredited Programs.** Lists educational programs in the United States and Canada. Programs listed by state.

# American Association of
# Family and Consumer Sciences (AAFCS)

www.aafcs.org/education/accreditation.html

**Accredited Universities.** Lists AAFCS-accredited family and consumer science programs in the United States. Organized by region.

# American Association of Immunologists

www.aai.org

**Graduate Programs.** Lists U.S. and Canadian graduate programs in immunology, microbiology, and related fields.

# American Association of Law Libraries

www.aallnet.org/committee/rllc/resources/education.asp

**Education for a Career in Law Librarianship.** Provides answers to FAQs about the field such as How Can I Learn about Law Librarianship as a Career?, What are the Academic Qualifications for a Law Librarian?, How do I Evaluate Library and Information Science Programs for a Career in Law Librarianship?, What are the Admission Requirements for Graduate Schools of Library and Information Science?, and How Can I Finance a Degree in Library and Information Science?

The following resource is available by visiting www.aallnet.org/committee/rllc/resources/lawlib-state.asp:

**ALA-Accredited Graduate Programs in Library Science with Law Library Classes or Joint MLS/JD Classes.** Provides a list of programs in the United States.

Additionally, information on educational scholarships is available at www.aallnet.org/services/scholarships.asp.

# American Association of Legal Nurse Consultants

www.aalnc.org/about/Whatis.cfm

**What is an LNC?** Includes information on the career of legal nurse consultant (LNC), work settings, and a list of criteria that should be considered when choosing a legal nurse consulting education program.

# American Association of Naturopathic Physicians

**www.naturopathic.org**

**Education.** Lists educational requirements and accredited North American colleges and universities that offer training in naturopathic medicine.

# American Association of Nurse Anesthetists (AANA)

**www.aana.com**

**Accredited Programs** (click on Becoming a CRNA). Lists nurse anesthesia programs accredited by the Council on Accreditation of Nurse Anesthesia Educational Programs. The list is searchable by state.

**About the Profession** (click on Becoming a CRNA). In addition to useful career information (including a video and answers to frequently asked questions), provides information on the components of a nurse anesthesia education program and admission requirements.

**Student Scholarship Information** (click on AANA Foundation). Information on scholarship opportunities for nurse anesthesia students.

# American Association of Orthodontists

**www.braces.org/studentsteachers**

**Orthodontic Careers.** Lists career options (orthodontist, orthodontic technician/assistant, laboratory technician, administrative staff), educational requirements, and graduate orthodontic schools in the United States and Canada.

# American Association of School Librarians (AASL)

**www.ala.org/ala/aasl/aasleducation/educationcareers.cfm**

**School Library Media Education Programs.** Lists U.S. school library media education programs approved by the National Council for Accreditation of Teacher Education and the AASL.

# American Association of Zoo Keepers

www.aazk.org

**Zoo Keeping as a Career.** Provides information on careers and educational paths.

# American Astronomical Society

www.aas.org/education/careers.php

**A New Universe to Explore: Careers in Astronomy.** Includes detailed career information and tips on how to prepare for a career in astronomy in high school, college, and graduate school.

> **> FYI**
> High school students who are interested in astronomy should take math through pre-calculus as well as chemistry and physics.

# American Bar Association (ABA)

www.abanet.org/education.html

**ABA-Approved Law Schools.** Lists U.S. law schools approved by the ABA. Organized alphabetically or by public or private status.

**Frequently Asked Questions.** Answers to questions about accreditation and law school including How should I prepare for the LSAT?, When should I apply to law school?, and When should I apply for financial aid?

**Preparation for a Legal Education.** Discusses personal skills that students need for success in law school.

# American Board of Funeral Service Education

www.abfse.org

**Directory of Accredited Programs in Funeral Service.** Provides a link to the 56 degree programs accredited by the American Board of Funeral Service Education. The list is searchable by state.

**Frequently Asked Questions.** Provides answers to questions about careers, earnings, and the course work that comprises the funeral service educational curriculum.

**Scholarship Information.** Details scholarships available to students pursuing education in the funeral services.

# American Board of Genetic Counseling (ABGC)

www.abgc.net/genetics/abgc/accred/tr-prog1.shtml

**Genetic Counseling as a Career** (click on Careers). Provides an overview of the career and details educational requirements and typical college courses.

**Graduate Programs in Genetic Counseling.** Lists ABGC-accredited graduate counseling training programs in the United States and Canada.

# American Camping Association

www.acacamps.org

**Careers in the Camp Community** (click on Community/Student). Provides information on job descriptions, educational requirements, work settings, earnings, and job openings.

A chemist and technician (foreground) work to create enzymes that produce ethanol in a more cost-effective manner. (Photo courtesy of Scott Bauer, USDA)

# American Chemical Society (ACS)

www.chemistry.org

Click on the Education link (and then on Students/College Planning) at the ACS's home page to access the following resources:

**Earning a Chemistry Degree.** This resource details the types of undergraduate chemistry degrees, typical courses, and what you will do during the lab part of your education.

**Earning a Degree in Chemical Technology.** Provides information on educational requirements and programs, financial aid, and internships.

**Starting at a Community College.** Touts the benefits of starting your education at a community colleges and provides tips on getting the most out of a community college education and transferring to a four-year college.

**Find an ACS-Approved Chemistry Program.** Directory of approved chemistry, biochemistry, chemical physics, chemical education, environmental chemistry, materials, and polymers programs in the United States. Searchable by state, alphabetical order, and degree level offered.

**Financial Aid.** The ACS offers scholarship programs to minority and women students who are interested in pursuing careers in chemistry, biochemistry, or chemical engineering. Scholarships are based on merit and financial need. Details on the awards, eligibility requirements, and online application forms are provided. This program is only open to African-American, Hispanic/Latino, or American Indian high school seniors and college students.

Click on the Education link (and then on Students/Graduate Education) at the ACS's home page to access the following resources:

**Planning for Graduate Work in Chemistry.** Information on applying to and being successful in a chemistry graduate program. (Planning for Graduate Work in Chemistry: A Resource for Students Considering Advanced Study, a downloadable guide, is also available.)

**ACS Directory of Graduate Research.** Lists chemistry and related degree programs in the United States and Canada—searchable by name, city, region, section, degrees offered, and specialization. School listings include information on the program, current enrollment, and faculty.

Click on the Careers link at the ACS's home page to access the following resource:

**Career Descriptions.** Provides descriptions of 30 chemistry-related career paths (including biochemistry, forensic chemistry, and pulp and paper chemistry). Job descriptions, educational requirements, and earnings and outlook information is provided for each career.

# American Chiropractic Association

**www.amerchiro.org** (click on Students)

**Education Requirements** (click on Chiropractic Education/ Careers). Details educational requirements for chiropractic students.

**CCE-Accredited Colleges** (click on Chiropractic

Education/Careers). Lists U.S. and foreign chiropractic colleges accredited by the Council on Chiropractic Education.

**Scholarships.** Offers information on financial aid offered by the Association.

## American College of Nurse-Midwives (ACNM)

**www.midwife.org/become_midwife.cfm**

**Frequently Asked Questions for Prospective Students.** Answers career- and education-related questions including What type of degree will I receive upon graduation?, What are the minimum requirements to get into a nurse-midwifery or midwifery education program?, and What type of degree will I receive upon graduation?

**Find a Midwifery Education Program.** Lists contact information for ACNM-accredited educational programs.

**Financial Aid.** Provides information on financing your education.

## American Congress on Surveying and Mapping (ACSM)

**www.acsm.net/student.html**

> **Did You Know?**
> Salaries for surveyors ranged from less than $28,590 to $83,510 or more in 2007, according to the U.S. Department of Labor. The median salary was $51,630.

**College and University Listings** (click on Education and Certification). Lists surveying and geomatics educational programs accredited by the Accreditation Board for Engineering and Technology.

**Careers in Cartography and Geographic Information Science.** Provides information on cartography and geographic information systems careers, suggested high school courses, options in higher education, and lists of colleges that offer training.

**ACSM Scholarships.** Information on scholarships offered by the ACSM.

## American Council for Construction Education (ACCE)

**www.acce-hq.org**

**Accredited Programs.** An alphabetical listing of ACCE-accredited associate and bachelor's degree construction programs.

# American Council for Pharmacy Education (ACPE)

**www.acpe-accredit.org/students/programs.asp**

**Accredited Professional Programs of Colleges and Schools of Pharmacy.** Lists ACPE-accredited pharmacy schools by state. Includes an overview of accreditation status and types of degrees awarded.

# American Council of Hypnotist Examiners

**www.hypnotistexaminers.org**

**Approved Schools.** A list of approved hypnotherapy schools in the U.S. and around the world.

# American Council on Education (ACE)

**www.acenet.edu**

**Frequently Asked Questions** (click on Online Resources). Provides answers to a variety of education-related questions, including How many institutions of higher education are there in the United States and how many students are enrolled?, How much student loan debt does the average student accumulate?, and What percentage of undergraduates receive financial aid and how much do they get?

> **Did You Know?**
> Women make up 58 percent of college students, according to the *Chronicle of Higher Education*—an increase of 18 percent since 1966.

***Higher Education and National Affairs*** (click on News Room). Online newsletter that offers information on changing trends and public policy in colleges and universities across the country.

**General Educational Development (GED) Testing Service** (click on Programs and Services). Offers information for students and education professionals interested in learning more about the GED.

## American Counseling Association

**www.counseling.org/Students**

**Choosing a Graduate Program.** Includes criteria to consider—such as faculty makeup, student diversity, educational philosophy, training levels, accreditation, and location—when choosing a graduate counseling program.

**Directory of Accredited Programs.** Lists U.S. and Canadian graduate-level counseling programs accredited by the Council for Accreditation of Counseling and Related Educational Programs.

**Ross Trust Graduate Student Scholarship Competition.** Information on the scholarship program offered by the Association.

*Approximately 115,000 chefs and cooks are employed in the United States. (Photo courtesy of Photos.com)*

## American Culinary Federation

**www.acfchefs.org** (click on Education)

**Accreditation.** Lists college and university culinary programs accredited by the Accrediting Commission of the American Culinary Federation. The list is searchable by state.

**Apprenticeship Programs.** Offers students information on apprenticeship training and how to apply to programs.

**Scholarships.** Provides information on financial aid for high school students, college students, and professional chefs.

## American Dance Therapy Association (ADTA)

**www.adta.org** (click on Resources/ Students)

**Considering a Career in Dance/Movement Therapy?** Answers frequently asked questions about the field such as What is dance/movement therapy?, What do dance/movement therapists do?, and What undergraduate preparation should one have? Also provides advice from dance/movement therapy students.

**Educational Opportunities in Dance/Movement Therapy.**
Features a list of accredited dance therapy graduate programs.

# American Dental Association (ADA)

**www.ada.org/public/education**

**Definitions of Dentistry.** Includes definitions of dentistry specialty areas and dental degrees.

**Be a Dentist—Career Resources for High School and College Students.** Includes information on the career, preparing for a dental education, applying to dental school and financing your dental education, as well as an overview of the dental school program.

**Dentistry Fact Sheet.** Answers a variety of questions about the dental profession, including What's unique about dentistry?, How can I prepare for a career in dentistry?, and What are the future opportunities for dentistry?

> **Consider Specializing**
> The nine dental specialties approved by the ADA are Dental Public Health, Oral and Maxillofacial Pathology, Oral and Maxillofacial Radiology, Endodontics, Orthodontics and Dentofacial Orthopedics, Oral and Maxillofacial Surgery, Pediatric Dentistry, Periodontics, and Prosthodontics.

**Something to Smile About—Careers in the Dental Profession.** Provides a wealth of educational and career information for aspiring dentists, dental hygienist, dental assistants, and dental lab technicians.

**Dental Schools: DDS/DMD Programs.** Lists Commission on Dental Accreditation-accredited dental schools in the United States.

**Dental Schools: Advanced Programs.** Database of advanced specialty or postdoctoral general dentistry programs in the United States. Searchable by state and discipline (e.g., endodontics, oral and maxillofacial pathology, pediatric dentistry).

**Dental Schools: Dental Assisting, Hygiene, Lab Technology Programs.** Database of dental assisting, hygiene, and lab technology programs in the United States. Searchable by state and discipline.

**Scholarships.** Link to scholarship information at the ADA Foundation.

Many of these resources are also available in Spanish.

# American Dental Education Association

**www.adea.org**

**Official Guide to Dental Schools** (click on About Dental Education/Careers in Dental Education). Provides advice on career options in dentistry, choosing and applying to dental school, and financing your dental education.

**Scholarships, Awards, and Fellowships** (click on About Dental Education). An overview of financial aid options for students interested in dental careers.

# American Dental Hygienists' Association (ADHA)

**www.adha.org**

See the Education & Careers section for the following resources:

**Earning a Dental Hygiene Education.** Details general admission requirements and prerequisites, types of educational programs, and course work required for those interested in studying dental hygiene at the college level.

**Dental Hygiene Programs.** Lists certificate, associate, bachelor's, and master's degree programs in dental hygiene by state.

**Scholarships.** Features information on ADHA scholarships available to college students studying dental hygiene.

# American Dietetic Association

**www.eatright.org** (click on Careers & Students)

**RD and DTR Information Sheets.** Provides career information, educational requirements (including suggested course work), and financial aid options for registered dietitians (RDs) and dietetic technicians, registered (DTRs).

**Education Flowcharts: Where Do I Start?** Provides detailed educational pathways for high school students, career changers, and international students planning to become RDs or DTRs.

**Accredited Education Programs.** Lists college and university dietetic education programs accredited by the Commission on Accreditation for Dietetics Education.

**Career FAQs.** Includes answers to the following questions: What do I need to do to become a registered dietitian?, Is there a ranking of dietetics education programs?, Is there a list of courses I need to take?, and Will getting my master's degree in nutrition meet the requirements to become a registered dietitian?

**Scholarships and Financial Aid.** Details information on financial aid that is available to students pursuing undergraduate or graduate degrees in dietetics or nutrition.

# American Geological Institute (AGI)

**www.earthscienceworld.org/careers**

**Guide to Geoscience Departments.** Provides links to geoscience departments in the United States and Canada. Can be searched alphabetically and by state, type of institution (public or private), and degree level. Each institution listing provides information on admissions procedures, degrees, tuition and other costs, research facilities and support, faculty experience, and department specialties.

**Careers in the Geosciences.** Provides detailed information on careers in the geosciences and a basic overview of suggested high school courses and postsecondary education options.

**Geoscience Career Frequently Asked Questions.** Includes answers to the following questions: What area of studies should I pursue to work as a geoscientist?, How much education do I need? Can I get a job with a bachelor's degree?, What classes should I take?, and Should I focus my education toward being a generalist in my field, or should I consider being a specialist early in my career?

**Stats.** Provides information on geoscience enrollments and geoscience degrees granted in the United States.

**Minority Participation Program Geoscience Student Scholarships.** Offers more information on financial aid for minority geoscience students at the college level.

# American Health Information Management Association (AHIMA)

**www.ahima.org/careers**

**Accredited and Approved Health Information Management Programs.** Lists AHIMA-accredited health information educational programs. You can search for programs by institution name, program level, state, or distance learning programs.

**Recruitment Tool Box.** Provides a variety of resources on health information management careers and education. Where the Future Clicks: Your Health Information Management Career details career options and salaries for students at various degree levels, key professional credentials, and ways to learn more. Careers in Health Information Management provides information on careers, suggested high school courses, educational paths, financial aid, and certification.

**Information on scholarships** for undergraduates pursuing degrees in health information administration and health information technology can be obtained by visiting the website (www.ahima.org/fore) of the Foundation of Research and Education, AHIMA's sister organization.

## Did You Know?

People who major in history work not only as historians and teachers but as curators, archivists, museum directors, writers, tour guides, elected officials, advertising workers, editors, and in virtually any other career that requires critical thinking. Some students pursue an undergraduate degree in history to prepare for advanced studies in library science, religion, government, political science, law, business, education, or other areas. One excellent publication on careers in the field is *Careers For Students of History,* available from the American Historical Association for a small fee.

# American Historical Association

**www.historians.org**

**Careers for Students of History** (click on Jobs & Careers). Online version of a detailed print publication that lists educational requirements for a variety of history career paths (such as those in museums, publishing, and historic preservation), features profiles of historians, and details recent trends in the field.

**Directory of History Departments and Organizations in the United States and Canada** (click on Publications). Contains information on more than 845 colleges, universities, historical and governmental organizations, and other resources for history majors. The list is searchable by institution name, state/province, and U.S. degree level.

# American Horticultural Therapy Association

**www.ahta.org/education**

**Education and Training in Horticultural Therapy.** Provides information on educational avenues for horticultural therapy (HT) students and lists U.S. and Canadian certificate, bachelor's, and master's degree programs in HT. Also covers colleges that offer distance education programs in HT.

# American Hotel & Lodging Association (AHLA)

**www.ahla.com**

**Hospitality Schools and Programs** (click on Information Center). Searchable database that lists U.S. and foreign colleges and universities that offer associate, bachelor's, and graduate degrees in hospitality or related areas.

**Scholarships.** Information on scholarships and other financial aid is available at the AHLA Foundation's website, www.ahlef.org.

# American Indian College Fund (AICF)

**www.collegefund.org**

**Tribal College Map** (click on Tribal Colleges). Lists more than 30 tribal colleges in the United States serving approximately 26,000 students.

**Students and Alumni** (click on Scholarships & Students). Includes personal profiles of American Indian students currently attending or who have recently graduated from tribal schools.

**Online Guides** (click on Scholarships & Students). Four informative, full-color guides that cover topics such as choosing a tribal college, paying for education, managing money, and selecting a career path.

**Scholarships Available** (click on Scholarships & Students). Information on financial aid for high school through graduate school students offered by the AICF. The majority of financial assistance is available only to students of American Indian descent who are enrolled in a tribal school. However, the Fund has recently introduced an additional scholarship option based on merit and financial need aimed at American Indian students attending selected four-year colleges and universities. Visit its website or contact bskenadore@collegefund.org for more details.

## American Indian Higher Education Consortium

www.aihec.org

**Tribal Colleges: An Introduction** (click on Tribal Colleges/TCU Students). Provides answers to the following questions: What are Tribal Colleges?, What Makes Tribal Colleges Unique?, Who Goes to Tribal Colleges?, and What Resources are Available to Tribal Colleges?

**How Many Students Do Tribal Colleges Serve?** (click on Tribal Colleges/TCU Students). Offers an overview of trends in student populations.

**Who Goes to Tribal Colleges?** (click on Tribal Colleges/TCU Students). Provides an overview of the student bodies of tribal colleges and financial resources of students.

**Tribal Colleges and Universities Map** (click on Tribal Colleges). Presents a U.S. map with contact information for member colleges.

## American Indian Science and Engineering Society

www.aises.org

**National American Indian Science and Engineering Fair** (click on K-12 Programs). An annual fair for K-12 students who are interested in pursuing education and careers in science and engineering.

**Scholarships and Internships** (click on Programs). Provides a list of scholarships for undergraduate and graduate students and internships at government agencies.

## American Institute for Conservation of Historic and Artistic Works

http://aic.stanford.edu/education/becoming

**Conservation Training in the United States.** Details career options, educational paths, apprenticeships, internships, and graduate programs and provides lists of national and regional conservation associations and colleges that offer conservation training programs.

**Undergraduate Prerequisites for Admission into a Conservation Training Program.** Details required course work in science (such as general and organic chemistry), the humanities (such as art history, anthropology, and archaeology), studio art, and languages that is required to prepare for graduate training in conservation science.

**FYI**

*Conservation workers* help preserve artistic and cultural artifacts for museums, libraries, archives, laboratories, universities, government agencies, private conservation enterprises, and other employers. You will need a master's degree to work in the field.

# American Institute for Foreign Study

**www.aifs.org**

**College Study Abroad.** Directory of semester-, summer-, and year-long study abroad programs. Searchable by field of study/specific subject. Section also includes information on study abroad scholarships.

**Students On Location.** Features student accounts and photographs of their study abroad experiences. In come cases, you can even email students with your own questions about studying abroad.

The site also provides information on study abroad options and summer programs at U.S. campuses for high school students.

# American Institute of Architects (AIA)

**www.aia.org/ed_arched**

**The Architect's Journey: Exploring a Future in Architecture.** Offers an overview of career options and educational requirements for the field.

**Summer Architecture Education Programs for High School Students.** Offers a list of more than 50 colleges and universities that offer architectural-related summer programs.

**AIA/AAF Minority/Disadvantaged Scholarship Program.** Provides a link to financial aid for high school seniors and college freshmen offered by the American Architectural Foundation.

**ACE Mentor Program.** Offers a link to a mentorship program offered by the ACE Mentor Program of America, Inc.

# American Institute of Architecture Students

www.aias.org/student_resources/student_resources.php

### Questions to Ask When Choosing an Architecture School.
Offers a list of questions to ask regarding accreditation, degree options, and curriculum, as well as questions students should ask themselves such as How much are you able or willing to pay for your education? and Are you certain that you want to be an architect or would like a program that is broad-based in the first two years, allowing you to experience various options?

> **Did You Know?**
> More than 125 colleges and universities in the United States and Canada offer professional degrees in architecture, according to the Association of Collegiate Schools of Architecture.

### Student Grants, Fellowships and Scholarships. Provides information on financial aid for undergraduate and graduate students, including those from minority or disadvantaged backgrounds.

# American Institute of Biological Sciences (AIBS)

www.aibs.org

**Careers in Biology** (click on Education Office). Provides information on educational requirements for biological specialties. For example, students who earn an associate degree in biological science can work as veterinary technicians or medical assistants, while biology teachers need at least an undergraduate degree in biology and a teaching certificate.

**Frequently Asked Questions about Careers in Biology** (click on Education Office). Answers questions such as What do biologists do?, How can I prepare for a career in biology?, Where are the best college and university biology programs?, and What is the job outlook for the future?

**Student Chapters** (click on Organization). Information on chapters for college students interested in the biological sciences.

# American Institute of Chemical Engineers (AIChE)

**www.aiche.org/Students/Careers/highschoolresources.aspx**

**Careers in Chemical Engineering: Frequently Asked Questions: Laying the Foundation.** Chemical engineers answer student questions about educational preparation for a career in this field. Sample questions include: What courses did you study in college and did you acquire any degrees beyond biochemical engineering?, How well did your high school studies prepare you for college?, How well did college prepare you for being a chemical engineer?, and Is there any personal advice you would give someone entering this field?

**Accredited Chemical Engineering Programs.** Lists college and university chemical engineering programs accredited by AIChE and the Accreditation Board for Engineering and Technology.

**Students Website** (www.aiche.org/Students). Provides information on student chapters and conferences, chemical engineering tools, and scholarships.

# American Institute of Graphic Arts

**www.aiga.org**

**Design Programs** (click on Education). Lists design programs in the United States.

**Graphic Design: A Career Guide** (click on Careers). Detailed information on graphic design careers, what goes on in design school, and how to select a design program. Also features profiles of designers at work in a wide variety of employment settings.

**Worldstudio AIGA Scholarships** (click on Education). Information on financial aid for students who are minorities and/or from economically disadvantaged backgrounds. Scholarships are available to high school seniors who plan to attend college and current undergraduate and graduate students.

# American Institute of Physics

**www.aip.org** (click on Statistical Research Center)

**Statistical Research Center.** Provides a wealth of employment and educational statistics pertaining to physicists.

**Career Guidance for High School and Undergraduate Students.** Offers detailed information on personal and technical skills for physics graduates, earnings, tips on resume writing and interviewing, and other resources.

**What Universities Offer a Degree in Physics in My State?** Lists of physics programs in the United States.

# American Intellectual Property Law Association

**www.aipla.org** (click on Student Center)

**Careers in IP Law Brochure.** Provides an overview of intellectual property specialties and information on choosing a, applying to, and paying for law school.

**Foundation/Scholarships.** Provides information on financial aid for law students (including minorities) provided by the American Intellectual Property Law Education Foundation.

## FYI
*Kinesiotherapists* are health care professionals who use therapeutic exercise and education to help patients with disease, injury, and other disorders. They typically have bachelor's degrees in kinesiology, physical education, exercise science, or health science.

# American Kinesiotherapy Association (AKTA)

**www.akta.org** (click on Education)

**Accredited Programs.** Features a list of educational programs that are accredited by the Commission on Accreditation of Allied Health Education Programs

**Scholarship.** Financial award offered to undergraduate or graduate kinesiotherapy students by the AKTA.

# American Library Association (ALA)

**www.ala.org** (click on Education & Careers)

**Directory of ALA-Accredited Master's Programs in Library and Information Studies** (click on Education & Degrees). Lists ALA-accredited colleges and universities that offer library and information science programs in the United States and Canada. Searchable by state, province, and institution name. Each program entry lists contact information and degrees offered. There is also a list of schools that offer distance education opportunities.

**Scholarships for ALA-Accredited Master's Programs.**
Information on financial aid for graduate-level students.

Visit www.ala.org/ala/hrdr/educprofdev/
educationcontinuous.cfm to access the following resources:

**Financial Assistance for Library and Information Studies.**
Annual directory (in PDF format) of awards for undergraduate
and graduate study in library and information studies.

**Directory of Library Technician Programs by State.** Includes
certificate, associate, and bachelor's degree programs.

# American Massage Therapy Association

www.amtamassage.org/students.html

**Becoming a Professional Massage Therapist.** Offers an
overview of work settings and education paths to enter the field.

**Massage School Profile Search.** A database of U.S. and international massage therapy schools. Searchable by name, city, state,
and country.

**Hints for Choosing the Right Massage Training Program.**
Offers a list of 10 suggestions to help students choose a quality
training program.

# American Mathematical Society

www.ams.org/employment/undergrad.html

**Guide to Master's Programs.** Offers a list of master's degree
programs in mathematics—searchable by state and program type.

**Resources for Undergraduates in Mathematics.** Provides
information on what students can do with a mathematics major
and details available scholarships and internships.

# American Meteorological Society (AMS)

www.ametsoc.org/amsstudentinfo

**A Career Guide for the Atmospheric Sciences.** Interesting publication that details career options, employment settings, and earnings for people interested in the atmospheric sciences. The
Getting an Education section provides an overview of educational

opportunities for students interested in studying the atmospheric sciences, including information on suggested curriculum, internships, scholarships, and institutions offering training in this field.

**Challenges of Our Changing Atmosphere: Careers in Atmospheric Research and Applied Meteorology.** Provides answers to the following questions: What is a meteorologist?, What do meteorologists do?, Where do meteorologists work?, and What kind of education do I need to be a meteorologist?

**Curricula in the Atmospheric, Oceanic, Hydrologic, and Related Sciences.** Lists colleges and universities offering study in the atmospheric sciences alphabetically, by degree offered, and by state. Each college description lists contact information, faculty, undergraduate and graduate courses offered, and ethnicity and gender profiles.

**AMS Scholarships and Fellowships.** Details financial aid opportunities for undergraduates and graduates.

## FYI
Music therapists work in medical and psychiatric hospitals, rehabilitative facilities, outpatient clinics, nursing homes, hospice programs, day care treatment centers, drug and alcohol abuse programs, geriatric care centers, correctional facilities, schools, and in private practice. You must have at least a bachelor's degree in music therapy to practice in the field.

# American Music Therapy Association (AMTA)

**www.musictherapy.org/career_ind.html**

**A Career in Music Therapy.** Details career options, the approved curriculum for the baccalaureate degree in music therapy, educational paths, and employment opportunities for aspiring music therapists.

**Schools Offering Music Therapy.** Lists AMTA-approved baccalaureate programs in music therapy; schools are listed by state. Some listed schools also offer graduate degrees in music therapy.

The AMTA also offers **membership for students** who are declared music therapy majors.

# American Musicological Society

**www.ams-net.org**

**Graduate Programs in Musicology.** Provides links to graduate programs in the United States and around the world.

# American Occupational Therapy Association

**www.aota.org/Students.aspx**

Click on For Prospective Students to access the following resources:

**A Career in Occupational Therapy: A Rewarding Choice in Health Care.** Includes information on careers, educational requirements, and employment settings.

**FAQs About OT Education.** Answers to commonly asked questions, including What is the difference between a postbaccalaureate degree and a baccalaureate degree for becoming an occupational therapist?; I've been accepted by two programs. How should I decide if I want to enter the postbaccalaureate or the baccalaureate program?; and How do I know which program is the best or has a higher ranking?

**Why I Choose Occupational Therapy.** Seven workers in the field detail why they entered the field.

Click on Schools to access the following resources:

**Entry-Level OT Programs.** Lists occupational therapy baccalaureate and master's programs accredited by the Accreditation Council for Occupational Therapy Education (ACOTE).

**Educational Prep**

If you wish to receive the professional credential, occupational therapist, registered, you will need to earn at least a master's degree in occupational therapy.

**Postprofessional OT Programs.** Lists ACOTE-accredited master's and doctorate occupational therapy programs by state. Degrees offered, major fields of study, areas of concentration, distance degree options, admission requirements, and types of available financial aid are listed for each institution.

**Entry-Level OTA Programs.** Lists occupational therapy assistant programs accredited by ACOTE.

Click on Financial Aid to access the following resources:

**Scholarships** (click on Financial Aid). Presents information on scholarships offered by the American Occupational Therapy Association and other organizations.

## American Optometric Association

**www.aoanet.org** (click on Students & Educators)

**Why Choose Optometry?** Offers information on the career, educational requirements, and a list of accredited schools and colleges of optometry in the United States and Canada.

## American Osteopathic Association (AOA)

**www.osteopathic.org/index.cfm?PageID=ost_main**

**Osteopathic Medical Education.** Offers tips on preparing for college admission and details the osteopathic curriculum and postdoctoral training. Also lists AOA-accredited osteopathic colleges in the United States.

**What is a D.O.?** Details the differences between osteopathic physicians (DOs) and allopathic physicians, including differences in educational training. (Also available in Spanish)

**Becoming a D.O.** (click on What is a D.O.?). Provides an overview of educational requirements (including typical classes) and personal qualities necessary to become an osteopathic physician.

*A physical therapist tracks the progress of a patient. (Photo courtesy of Photos.com)*

## American Physical Therapy Association

**www.apta.org/Education**

Click on Student Resources to access the following resources:

**Who are PTs & PTAs?** Provides statistical information (such as current annual income, entry-level education, highest earned academic degree) on physical therapists and physical therapist assistants.

**Where Can I Go To School?** Lists educational programs accredited by the Commission on Accreditation in Physical Therapy Education. Searchable by state and program type.

**PT/PTA Education FAQs.** Providers answers to questions such as What types of physical therapy degrees are there?, What should I consider when looking at schools/programs?, How can I help my chances of getting into a program?, and Where can I find financial aid information?

**APTA Student Membership.** Information on membership for college students.

**Scholarship/Financial Aid Info.** Features information on financial aid available from the American Physical Therapy Association. Includes awards for minorities.

Click on Post-Professional Degree Programs for the following resource:

**Directory of Postprofessional Education Programs for Physical Therapists.** Lists master's and doctoral physical therapy programs.

# American Physiological Association

**www.the-aps.org/careers/careers1/midhigh.htm**

**Careers in Physiology.** Information on career and educational paths for aspiring physiologists.

**Becoming a Physiologist** (click on Career Decisions). Details career paths for students who major in physiology.

**Selecting an Undergraduate Major/College** (click on Career Decisions). Tips on selecting an undergraduate major and school.

**Minority Resources.** Links to information on financial aid opportunities, profiles of minority physiologists and scientists, and colleges with predominantly minority populations.

> **FYI**
> *Physiology* is a branch of biology that deals with the study of the functions of life. To work in top positions, you will need to earn a Ph.D. in physiology or a medical degree.

**Student Membership.** Available to undergraduate students.

# American Phytopathological Society

**www.apsnet.org/careers**

**University Plant Pathology Programs.** Lists U.S. colleges and universities that offer plant pathology education programs.

**Careers in Plant Pathology.** Info on careers in plant pathology and educational paths.

# American Planning Association (APA)

**www.planning.org/careers/index.htm**

**What is Planning?** According to the APA, the goal of planning "is to further the welfare of people and their communities by creating convenient, equitable, healthful, efficient, and attractive environments for present and future generations."

**How Are Planners Educated?** Details the three main degrees that are awarded in the field.

**Planning Schools and Accreditation.** Lists undergraduate and graduate U.S. and Canadian planning programs accredited by the PAB.

**Ten Tips for Selecting a Planning Program.** Advice on choosing a planning educational program.

**Scholarship for Students.** Offers information on planning scholarships for undergraduate and graduate students offered by the APA and other organizations.

The Association also offers **membership** to college students.

# American Podiatric Medical Association

**www.apma.org** (click on Careers in Podiatric Medicine)

**Podiatric Medicine: A Career That Fits Your Future.** Video that provides information on careers in podiatric medicine.

**Podiatric Medical Colleges.** Provide contact information on the eight colleges of podiatric medicine in the United States.

# American Political Science Association

**www.apsanet.org**

**What is Political Science?** (click on About APSA). Brief overview of the discipline.

**Department Sponsored Graduate Student Memberships** (click on Membership). Information on membership for graduate students.

# American Polygraph Association

**www.polygraph.org/content/apa-accredited-polygraph-schools**

**Accredited Polygraph Schools.** Lists schools in the United States, Canada, Mexico, Israel, and Slovenia that are accredited by the American Polygraph Association.

# American Psychiatric Nurses Association (APNA)

**www.apna.org**

**About Psychiatric-Mental Health Nurses** (click on About APNA). Provides answers to the following questions: What do psychiatric-mental health nurses do?, How can I become a psychiatric-mental health nurse?, Why do psychiatric-mental health nurses obtain a master's or doctoral degree?, and How do I find a good program for psychiatric nursing?

**Graduate Programs by State** (click on Resource Center). Lists psychiatric nursing graduate programs in the United States.

**Janssen Scholarship** (click on Awards). Offers information on the APNA-Janssen Student Scholarship Program for undergraduate and graduate nursing students.

# American Psychological Association (APA)

**www.apa.org/students** (click on Publications/Brochures)

**Psychology: Scientific Problem Solvers: Careers in Psychology for the 21st Century.** Provides a description of the field, information on specialties (such as clinical, cognitive and perceptual, developmental, and engineering psychology), an overview of employment prospects for psychology students by level of education, recommended high school classes, typical college educational paths, and information on accreditation, and financial aid.

**FAQs on Graduate Education** (www.apa.org/ed/graduate/faqs.html). Answers questions such as Which is the "best" program in psychology?, How do I determine which program is best suited for me?, and Should I apply to a master's or doctoral degree program?

**A Guide to Getting Into Graduate School.** Tips on preparing for and applying to graduate school.

**Accredited Doctoral Programs.** Lists APA-accredited doctoral programs by specialty.

**Psychology Education and Careers: Guidebook for High School Students of Color.** Details career options for psychology majors by degree, the achievements of psychologists of color, and what minorities should do in high school to prepare for college study and the career.

**Psychology Education and Careers: Guidebook for College Students of Color.** Topics include notable psychologists of color, tips for minority community college students, researching graduate school, and psychology subfields.

**Psychology Education and Careers: Guidebook for College Students of Color Applying to Graduate and Professional Programs.** Advice for students of color who are interested in attending graduate school.

**Directory of Selected Scholarship, Fellowship, and Other Financial Aid Opportunities for Women and Ethnic Minorities in Psychology and Related Fields.** Online directory of financial aid resources.

# American Public Transportation Association

www.apta.com/links/univ.cfm

**Educational Institution Transportation Program Links Index.** Lists transportation programs in the United States and other countries.

# American School Counselor Association

www.schoolcounselor.org (click on School Counselors & Members/Careers-Roles)

**School Counseling Training.** Provides links to colleges and universities that offer certificate, master's degree, Ph.D., Ed.D. or Psy.D. programs in school counseling, counselor education, or counseling psychology.

# American Society for Biochemistry and Molecular Biology

www.asbmb.org

**Unlocking Life's Secrets: Career Opportunities in Biochemistry and Molecular Biology** (click on Professional Development/Graduate & Post Doctoral Interests). Details career options, suggested high school courses, and undergraduate and graduate educational paths for students interested in biochemistry and molecular biology.

*A nutritional biochemist extracts lipids from blood plasma to test for carotenoids. (Photo courtesy of Stephen Ausmus, USDA)*

**Becoming a Graduate Student** (click on Professional Development/Graduate & Post Doctoral Interests). Offers tips on preparing for, applying to, and paying for graduate school.

**Funding Opportunities for Graduate Students/Funding Opportunities for Postdocs** (click on Professional Development/Graduate & Post Doctoral Interests). Information on financial aid.

**ASBMB-Recommended Biochemistry Undergraduate Degree Requirements** (click on Professional Development). Recommended course work and skill requirements for undergraduate biochemistry and molecular biology students.

# American Society for Clinical Laboratory Science

www.ascls.org/jobs/careers.asp

**What is a Clinical Laboratory Science Professional?** Provides an overview of the career.

**Educational Requirements.** Offers details on typical high school courses and college educational paths for clinical laboratory science professionals.

**Locate an Accredited Education Program.** Database of accredited programs searchable by institution name, state, and program type (Clinical Assistant, Cytogenetic Technologist, Clinical Laboratory Scientist/Medical Technologist, Clinical Laboratory Technician/Medical Laboratory Technician, Diagnostic Molecular Scientist, Histotechnician, Histotechnologist, Pathologists' Assistant, Phlebotomy).

**Directory of Online CLT or CLS Programs.** Provides information on online clinical laboratory technician and clinical laboratory science educational programs.

**Scholarships.** Provides links to financial aid for clinical laboratory science professionals.

# American Society for Clinical Pathology (ASCP)

**www.ascp.org**

Click on Pathologists/Pathology Careers to access the following resources:

**The Pathologist.** Offers an overview of the career, educational requirements, and sources of additional information.

**Pathologists' Assistant.** Offers an overview of the career, educational requirements, and sources of additional information.

**Careers in Pathology and Medical Laboratory Science.** Detailed information on the careers of pathologists' assistant, medical technologist, medical laboratory technician, histotechnician, histotechnologist, cytotechnologist, phlebotomy technician, and donor phlebotomy technician. Includes advice on suggested personal skills, educational paths, and contact information for educational program accrediting agencies.

Other resources:

**Scholarships** (click on Students/Laboratory Science Students). An overview of scholarships available to undergraduates from the Society.

# American Society for Engineering Education

**www.asee.org/publications**

**Profiles of Engineering and Engineering Technology Colleges.** Directory of nearly 360 U.S. and Canadian schools offering undergraduate and graduate engineering and engineering technology training. Information includes types of degrees offered, degree requirements, areas of faculty expertise, and financial aid.

Additionally, **Engineering, Go For It!,** a useful print publication, is available for a small fee from the Society.

# American Society for Indexing

www.asindexing.org/site/courses.shtml

**Meetings and Courses.** Provides information on college courses and programs in indexing.

# American Society for Information Science and Technology

www.asis.org/careers.html

**Information Science Schools.** Lists colleges and universities (web links only) that offer information science programs.

**Education Programs.** Provides information on colleges and universities that offers classes or degree programs in information architecture.

# American Society for Investigative Pathology

www.asip.org

**Pathology as a Career in Medicine** (click on Career Development Resources). Provides detailed information on career options in pathology, undergraduate and graduate medical education in pathology, and a directory of pathology training programs.

**Directory of Pathology Training Programs** (click on Career Development Resources/Students, Residents & Post Docs). Lists graduate programs in pathology in the United States and Canada.

**The Road to Becoming a Biomedical Physician Scientist in Pathology and Laboratory Medicine** (click on Career Development Resources/Biomedical Physician Scientist Careers). Provides an overview of career options in the field and reasons for pursuing these career paths, advice on choosing a training program, and other resources.

## Earnings for Microbiologists

Microbiologists earned salaries that ranged from less than $37,180 to $104,390 or more in 2007, according to the U.S. Department of Labor. The average salary was $60,680.

# American Society for Microbiology

**www.asm.org**

**Careers in the Microbiological Sciences** (click on Education/ Middle and High School Students). Lists career info and suggested high school and college courses for aspiring microbiologists.

## American Society for Nutrition

**www.asns.org**

**Graduate Program Directory** (click on Education and Professional Development). Directory (Web links only) of nutritional science graduate programs in the United States and Canada.

## American Society for Pharmacology and Experimental Therapeutics

**www.aspet.org**

**Undergraduate & Graduate Pharmacology Training Programs** (click on Training Programs). Links to pharmacology departments in the United States and Canada.

## American Society for Photogrammetry & Remote Sensing

**www.asprs.org**

**Career Brochure** (click on Students). Describes careers in photogrammetry and remote sensing, suggested high school classes, college educational paths, and employment options.

**Awards & Scholarships** (click on Students). Provides information on a wealth of financial aid resources for undergraduate and graduate students.

# American Society of Agricultural and Biological Engineers

www.asabe.org/pr/careerpromo.html

**International Academic Programs Agricultural, Food, or Biological Engineering Departments.** Lists (websites only) educational programs.

**Educational Programs in Agricultural Engineering and Related Fields.** Lists programs in the United States, Canada, and Ireland. Information includes accreditation status and type of degree awarded.

**Discover Careers in Biological and Agricultural Engineering.** Details career options and information on educational programs for students interested in biological and agricultural engineering.

**Scholarships/Grants.** Information on financial aid available from the Society.

## American Society of Agronomy (ASA)

https://www.agronomy.org/awards

**Awards, Scholarships, & Fellows.** Information on undergraduate and graduate financial aid opportunities from the ASA and other organizations.

**Students of Agronomy, Soils and Environmental Sciences** (https://www.agronomy.org/students). Membership organization for undergraduate students.

## American Society of Anesthesiologists

www.asahq.org/residentCareer.htm

**College Student/General Overview.** Brief description of the career, including an overview of educational paths for aspiring anesthesiologists.

**College Student/Undergraduate Studies.** Brief section on suggested college courses and sources of additional information for students interested in anesthesiology.

**Frequently Asked Questions.** Answers to frequently asked questions about anesthesiology careers and education, including What are some good classes that I can take in both high school and college that will help me on this career path?, Why did you choose this career?, and What qualities should a person possess to be successful in this career?

**Frequently Asked Questions for Anesthesiologist Assistants.** Answers to frequently asked questions such as Who are anesthesiologist assistants (AAs)?, What are the differences between AAs and physician assistants?, What are the differences between nurse anesthetists and AAs?, Where are AA education programs located?, What is the length of the AA education program?, and What types of students enter AA education programs?

## American Society of Animal Science

www.asas.org/career.htm

**Career Information.** Details career options, undergraduate requirements, typical curriculum, and graduate education.

> **Did You Know?**
> Employment for civil engineers is expected to grow much faster than the average for all careers through 2016, according to the U.S. Department of Labor. Approximately 256,000 civil engineers are employed in the United States.

## American Society of Civil Engineers (ASCE)

www.asce.org/kids

**Civil Engineering: Careers.** Presents information on civil engineering careers, suggested high school coursework, choosing the right college, tailoring an undergraduate academic program to your interests, financial aid, and study beyond a bachelor's degree.

**College Civil Engineering and Civil Engineering Technology Programs** (click on Colleges and Universities). Lists (Web links only) two- and four-year college-programs in the United States.

## American Society of Cytopathology

www.cytopathology.org

**Cytotechnology Programs** (click on Professional Networking & Development). Lists cytotechnology educational programs in the United States that are accredited or approved by the Commission on Accreditation of Allied Health Education Programs.

# American Society of Electroneurodiagnostic Technologists (ASET)

## www.aset.org

**FAQs** (click on Resources). Provides answers to the following questions: What are the skills I will need to be successful in this profession?, How do I prepare to enter the profession?, and Do I need a license to work as an EN technologist?

> **FYI**
> *Electroneurodiagnostic technologists* are health care workers who operate equipment that measures and records the electrical activity of the brain.

**List of Electroneurodiagnostic (EN) Technology Schools** (click on Education). Lists U.S. and Canadian colleges that offer programs in EN technology. Presents information on program length and type of degree awarded.

**List of Polysomnographic Technology Schools** (click on Education). Lists U.S. academic institutions that offer polysomnographic technology education. Presents information on program length and type of degree awarded.

**Scholarships** (click on Education). Offers information on educational grants and scholarships for college students from the ASET Foundation.

# American Society of Exercise Physiologists

## www.asep.org/services/ACCREDITEDprograms

**Exercise Physiology Accredited Academic Programs.** Lists programs in the United States.

# American Society of Ichthyologists and Herpetologists

## www.asih.org

**Careers in Ichthyology** (www.asih.org/ichjobs). Detailed information on the career, educational preparation, employment opportunities, and U.S. and Canadian colleges and universities offering graduate programs in ichthyology.

**Careers in Herpetology** (www.asih.org/herpjobs). Detailed information on the career, informal and formal educational preparation, employment opportunities, and U.S. colleges and universities offering herpetology programs.

## American Society of Interior Designers

**www.asid.org**

Click on Education for the following resources:

**Selecting a School or Program.** Information on choosing a design program, checking accreditation, and online education.

**Choosing a Design Career.** Covers areas of specialization, necessary skills, the importance of design education, and typical career paths.

## American Society of Landscape Architects (ASLA)

**www.asla.org**

**Be a Landscape Architect!** (click on Career Resources/Career Discovery). Details job responsibilities, educational paths, employment settings, and earnings for landscape architects.

> **> Did You Know?**
> You will need at least a bachelor's degree in landscape architecture to enter the field. Sixty-one colleges and universities offer 79 undergraduate and graduate programs in landscape architecture.

**Want to Be a Landscape Architect?** (click on Career Resources/Career Discovery). Provides information on educational requirements, how to choose a school, and employment.

**Accredited Programs in Landscape Architecture** (click on Career Resources/Accredited Programs). Lists Landscape Architectural Accreditation Board-accredited U.S. colleges and university programs in landscape architecture. Also lists Canadian programs accredited by the Canadian Society of Landscape Architects Accreditation Council.

**Putting a New Spin on the Earth.** A 20-minute video about the career of landscape architecture.

**ACE Mentor Program of America.** This program, which is sponsored by the ASLA, introduces high school students to career opportunities in landscape architecture and related professions. Visit www.acementor.org for more information.

# American Society of Limnology and Oceanography

www.aslo.org/career.html

**Aquatic Sciences Careers.** In addition to detailed career information, provides useful educational information on high school and college course work, extracurricular activities, and graduate school.

**Career Link Program.** Free service for college students interested in contacting potential graduate and post-graduate mentors and employers.

> **> Did You Know?**
> *Limnology,* according to the American Society of Limnology and Oceanography, is the "study of inland waters — lakes (both freshwater and saline), reservoirs, rivers, streams, wetlands, and groundwater."

# American Society of Mechanical Engineers

www.asme.org/Communities/Students

**Ementoring for Student Members.** Advice for student members.

**Engineering Camps.** List of engineering summer camp programs for pre-college students in the United States and Canada.

**Worldwide Mechanical Engineering Department Websites.** Offers links to more than 600 mechanical engineering and related department websites at colleges and universities.

**Financial Aid.** Information on financial aid for high school students, undergraduates, and graduate students.

# American Society of Newspaper Editors (ASNE)

www.asne.org/index.cfm?id=2

**Preparing for a Career in Newspapers.** Answers the following questions: Should I major in journalism?, Should I choose an accredited J-school?, How important are internships?, and Is a graduate degree worth the time and effort?

**Start Your Journalism Career in High School.** ASNE sister site (http://highschooljournalism.org) that provides comprehensive information on journalism careers and preparation for study in the field. The Students section includes job descriptions, a journalism skills test, a list of summer programs for high school students, a searchable database of accredited and unaccredited journalism schools in the United States, a scholarship database (searchable by state, minority background, and organization), and profiles of successful journalists. The website also has sections for teachers, guidance counselors, and editors.

## American Society of Radiologic Technologists (ASRT)

https://www.asrt.org/Content/CareerCenter/_careercenter.aspx

**Careers in Radiologic Technology.** Provide information on career options and educational requirements for radiologic technologists.

**Educational Programs.** A list of accredited educational programs in magnetic resonance imaging, nuclear medicine technology, radiation therapy, radiography, and sonography.

**Scholarships.** Provides information on financial aid offered by the ASRT Education and Research Foundation for high school seniors, undergraduate students, and professionals.

## American Society of Safety Engineers (ASSE)

www.asse.org/foundation

**Career Guide to the Safety Profession.** Includes information on high school preparation, community and technical colleges, four-year colleges and universities, and graduate study in safety science.

**ASSE Foundation Scholarship Program.** Information on undergraduate and graduate scholarships offered by the ASSE.

> **> Did You Know?**
> Famous sociology majors include novelist Saul Bellow, civil rights activist Martin Luther King, Jr., U.S. President Ronald Reagan, actor Robin Williams, and basketball star Alonzo Mourning.

## American Sociological Association

www.asanet.org

**Guide to Graduate Departments of Sociology.** Alphabetical list of more than 200 U.S. and international institutions with graduate sociology departments. (Note: this resource is available for a small fee.)

**Careers in Clinical Sociology.** Includes info on educational preparation for the career and career paths.

**Careers in Sociology.** Includes the following sections: What Can I Do With a B.A. in Sociology?, What Can I Do With an

M.A. or Ph.D. in Sociology?, Career Preparation: Making the Most of an Undergraduate Major, Linking to Other Majors and Minors, and Graduate Training in Sociology.

**Majoring in Sociology: A Guide for Students.** Offers advice to high school students interested in studying sociology in college as well as career paths for sociology majors.

**The Sociology Major: As Preparation for Careers in Business and Organizations.** A detailed examination of nonacademic career options for sociology majors at the undergraduate and graduate level.

> ## Career Paths
> Typical career paths for those with a B.A. in sociology include options in business, social service, journalism, politics, public relations, government, and public administration. Those with graduate degrees work as professors, researchers, applied sociologists, and in other fields.

**What Can I Do with a Bachelor's Degree in Sociology?** Provides information on what types of jobs students can get with a degree in sociology.

**Statistics on the Profession for Students and Faculty.** Provides a wealth of statistics on the field, including the annual number of sociology degrees awarded by degree level.

**Navigating the Sociology Major.** Provides answers to the following questions: What courses should I take?, Should I strive to be an expert or a generalist?, How many sociology courses should I take?, and How should I select (or avoid) professors? Tips are also provided for landing a job after graduation.

# American Speech-Language-Hearing Association

www.asha.org/students

**Strategies for Entry Into Graduate Schools in Communications Sciences and Disorders.** Useful information on the application process, the Graduate Record Examination, and admission requirements.

**Find Academic Programs.** Lists U.S. audiology and speech-language master's and doctoral programs. Searchable by Academic Institution Name and Program Characteristics (area of study, location, financial support, minority focus, etc.)

**Get Financial Aid.** Information on scholarships, grants, and other financial aid offered by the American Speech-Language-Hearing Foundation and other organizations.

**What is an Audiologist?** Provides an overview of the nature of the work, typical job settings, educational requirements, earnings, work conditions, and employment outlook.

**What is a Speech-Language Pathologist?** Offers an overview of the nature of the work, typical job settings, educational requirements, earnings, work conditions, and employment outlook.

**What is a Speech, Language and Hearing Scientist?** Provides an overview of the nature of the work, typical job settings, educational requirements, earnings, work conditions, and employment outlook.

**Career Profiles.** Features profiles of 19 workers who are employed in academic/research settings. Includes detailed information on educational paths and challenges.

**Student Profiles.** Presents profiles of eight students who became audiologists and speech-language pathologists.

# American Statistical Association

www.amstat.org/careers

**How Do I Become A Statistician?** Details educational paths for aspiring statisticians.

**Frequently Asked Career Questions.** Answers the following questions: I have/will have a degree in math, but do not want to be a teacher. What else can I do?; What fields and industries employ statisticians?; What internships are available for college students?; and What are the best schools for studying statistics?

**Careers in Statistics: Possibilities and Opportunities** (click on What is Statistics). A PowerPoint presentation that provides detailed information on the career.

**Careers in Statistics** (click on Other Resources). Provides information on employment areas, educational paths (high school and college), and employment outlook.

**Schools Offering Degrees in Statistics.** Lists U.S. and Canadian colleges offering programs in statistics.

# American Therapeutic Recreation Association

**www.atra-tr.org/careersinrt.htm**

**Career/Education Information.** Provides information on career and educational requirements for recreation therapists.

**Therapeutic Recreation Programs in Universities or Colleges: Academic Curriculum Directory.** Lists associate's, bachelor's, master's, and doctoral degree therapeutic recreation (TR) programs in the United States. Program information includes TR faculty, degrees offered, and distance education options.

**Frequently Asked Questions About Recreational Therapy.** Provides answers to FAQs such as What do recreational therapists do?; What clients do recreational therapists serve?; How are recreational therapy services different from other therapies?; What are a recreational therapist's education, qualifications, & credentials?; and Where is recreational therapy headed in the future?

# American Translators Association (ATA)

**www.atanet.org/careers/ T_I_programs.php**

**ATA Institutional Members Offering Translation/ Interpreting Courses.** Provides contact information for U.S. and Canadian colleges that offer courses in the field.

# American Veterinary Medical Association (AVMA)

**www.avma.org**

Click on Careers to access the following resources:

**A Career in Veterinary Technology.** Information on careers, education, and professional associations. Also available in Spanish.

## FYI

According to the Modern Language Association of America, the most popular foreign languages studied in college in 2006 were Spanish, French, German, American Sign Language, and Italian. While the study of Spanish, French, and German continues to increase, other foreign languages—such as Arabic, Chinese, and Korean— are growing in popularity. Since 2002, the study of Arabic has increased by nearly 127 percent; Chinese, by 51 percent; and Korean, by 37.1 percent.

**The Road to Becoming a Veterinarian** (click on Today's Veterinarian). Information on undergraduate course work and applying to veterinary school. Also available in Spanish.

Click on Education to access the following resources:

**Veterinary Colleges Accredited by the AVMA.** Lists U.S. and foreign veterinary schools accredited by the AVMA Council on Education.

**Veterinary Technology Programs.** Lists U.S. and Canadian veterinary technology programs accredited by the Committee on Veterinary Technician Education and Activities.

**Distance Learning Programs in Veterinary Technology Accredited by the AVMA Committee on Veterinary Technician Education and Activities.** Listed alphabetically with web links.

# American Youth Policy Forum

www.aypf.org/publications/higherlearning.pdf

**Higher Learning = Higher Earnings: What You Need to Know About College and Careers.** This online publication, created for middle and high school students, details the pros (higher earnings and higher job satisfaction) and cons (student debt) of attending college. It also discusses alternatives to four-year colleges, such as community college and technical programs.

# American Zoo and Aquarium Association

www.aza.org/ForEveryone/Careers

**Types of Jobs in Zoos and Aquariums.** Details educational requirements and career options in the field.

# Animation World Network

http://schools.awn.com

**Animation School Database.** Database of more than 900 schools that offer courses and programs in animation and related fields. Searchable by name, location, courses/programs, and degree level. Information provided for each school includes degrees and programs offered, number of students enrolled, and availability of financial aid.

# ARCHcareers

http://archcareers.org

ARCHcareers is sponsored by the American Institute of Architecture Students and the American Institute of Architects.

**Architecture Education.** Provides information on accredited programs, types of degrees, selecting a school, and preparing for college.

> **> Did You Know?**
> Employment for architects is expected to grow faster than the average for all careers through 2016, according to the U.S. Department of Labor. You will need a bachelor's or master's degree in architecture to enter the field.

**Internship & Experience.** Provides information on internships and other ways to get experience in the field.

# ASM Materials Education Foundation

http://asmcommunity.asminternational.org/portal/site/www
(click on Education Foundation)

**National Merit Scholarships.** Information on scholarships available to high school students interested in materials science and engineering.

**Undergraduate Scholarship Program.** Provides information on scholarships offered by the Foundation.

Visit www.asminternational.org/Content/NavigationMenu/
ASMFoundation/MaterialsEngineeringasaCareer/
Materials_Engineering_Career.htm to access the following resource:

**Materials Engineering as a Career.** Provides an overview of career options in materials engineering and a list of U.S. and Canadian colleges and universities offering materials science/ engineering programs.

# AspiringDocs.org

www.aspiringdocs.org

This website, which is sponsored by the Association of American Medical Colleges, offers the following resources:

**What You Need to Know.** Answers FAQs about medical careers and education including How do I know if medicine is the right

**Did You Know?**
Mean annual earnings for physicians were about $155,150 in 2007, according to the U.S. Department of Labor (USDL). The USDL reports the following mean earnings in 2007 by physician specialty: surgeons, $191,410; internists, $167,270; obstetricians and gynecologists, $183,600; family and general practitioners, $153,640; and pediatricians, $145,210.

career for me? What kind of person makes a good doctor?; What courses do I need to take to be prepared for medical school?; Where can I get more information about medical schools and their admission requirements?; How does the application process work for medical school?; and How do I apply for financial aid?

**Timeline for Applications & Admission.** Useful chart to help college students plan for medical school.

**Ask the Experts.** In this section, students can submit questions about medical school to industry experts.

**Meet the Experts Podcasts.** Downloadable audio advice from industry experts about medical school.

## Associated Colleges of the Midwest

www.acm.edu/admiss

**Pre-College Planner.** Offers a self-assessment test and information on financial aid, how to choose colleges that match your education and career goals, and the application process. Also available in Spanish.

**Campus Visits.** Tips for students on what to do before and during campus visits. Includes questions to ask college students during the visit, questions to ask yourself if you attend a class or take a tour, and questions to ask during an interview or information session.

**Writing a College Application Essay.** Tips for writing a top-flight application essay.

**Questions to Ask Colleges About Financial Aid.** Information on types of financial aid, common financial aid terms, sources of additional information, and questions to ask college financial aid officers, such as What kind of financial aid does the college offer?, What costs for a student are taken into account by a financial aid office?, and What is the average student loan indebtedness of the college's graduates?

**Going to a College Fair.** What to do before and at a college fair.

**ACM College Admission Offices.** Lists the 13 ACM members.

The website also provides information on study abroad and exchange programs.

# Associated General Contractors (AGC) of America

**www.agc.org** (click on Career Development/College)

**Endorsed Master's Degree Program.** List construction management programs that have been endorsed by the AGC.

**Scholarships** (click on College). Information on undergraduate and graduate scholarships and other financial aid options provided by the AGC Foundation.

# Associated Schools of Construction (ASC)

**www.ascweb.org**

**Members** (click on Regional Directory). Lists ASC-member colleges and universities in the United States and other countries that offer construction education programs.

# Association for Career and Technical Education (ACTE)

**www.acteonline.org/career_tech/faq.cfm**

**Frequently Asked Questions.** Provides answers to questions about career and technical education, including What subject areas are covered by career and technical education?, Is career and technical education only for students who are not college bound?, and How many career and technical programs are there in the U.S.?

**Did You Know?**
Approximately 9,400 postsecondary institutions—including community colleges, technical institutes, skill centers and other public and private two- and four-year colleges—offer technical programs, according to the ACTE.

**GetCareerSkills.com.** Resource from the Association for Career and Technical Education that offers videos and publications that profile careers in fashion, business, auto service, aviation, and cosmetology. Information on community and technical colleges that provide training in these areas is often provided.

# Association for Education and Rehabilitation of the Blind and Visually Impaired

**www.aerbvi.org**

**College and University Programs** (click on Continuing Education). Lists colleges and universities in the United States, Canada, and other countries that offer undergraduate and graduate training in the "education and rehabilitation of people who are visually impaired, deaf/blind, or have multiple disabilities." Information includes area of study, degree levels, and instruction options.

**Careers in the Vision Field.** Provides information on careers (including teacher of students with visual impairments, orientation and mobility specialists, vision rehabilitation therapists, rehabilitation counselors, and low vision therapists), an overview of educational requirements, and a list of university programs offering training in these specialties.

**Awards & Scholarships.** Information on financial aid for legally blind college students who are studying for a career in the field of services to persons who are blind or visually impaired.

# Association for Gerontology in Higher Education

**www.aghe.org**

**Careers in Aging: Consider the Possibilities** (www. careersinaging.com/careersinaging). Provides answers to commonly asked questions about the field, including What is gerontology? Geriatrics?, Why study aging and older persons?, How do you become a professional in aging?, How do you select a program in aging?, and How can you find out more about the field of aging?

**Database on Gerontology in Higher Education** (click on Resources). Fee-based service for students looking for information on academic programs in gerontology. Search criteria include educational level, geographic region, credential awarded, and discipline (e.g., education, mental health, psychology, social work). (Note: A print edition is also available.)

In addition, the Association offers **www.experienceinaging.com,** a clearinghouse for internships and fellowships.

# Association for Healthcare Documentation Integrity (AHDI)

www.ahdionline.org/scriptcontent/visitorcenter.cfm

**Approved Schools.** Provides a short list of approved educational programs.

**AHDI Answers Frequently Asked Questions About Medical Transcription.** Provides an overview of the work of medical transcriptionists, required personal skills, typical education requirements and paths, and other information.

**Choosing an MT School.** Offers advice on what to look for in a medical transcription school and how to evaluate program advertising.

# Association for the Advancement of Cost Engineering (AACE)

www.aacei.org/education

**Education Programs Related to Cost Engineering.** Lists colleges and universities in the United States and Canada that offer courses in cost engineering.

**Scholarship Competition.** Information on undergraduate scholarships provided by the AACE.

# Association for the Advancement of Medical Instrumentation

www.aami.org/resources/BMET

**Biomedical Education Links.** Lists two- and four-year biomedical education programs in the United States. Searchable by state.

**Biomedical Job Descriptions.** Provides an overview of nine specialties in the field, as well as educational requirements for each career.

**What is a BMET?** Covers job duties and educational requirements for biomedical engineering technologists and biomedical equipment technicians.

**The Career Opportunity of a Lifetime: Servicing Technology That Saves Lives.** Provides an overview of job duties, necessary personal skills, educational and training requirements, typical earnings, and advancement opportunities for biomedical engineering technologist and biomedical equipment technicians.

# Association of American Geographers

**www.aag.org/Careers/Intro.html**

**Tips for Teens** (click on Explore). Offers advice on preparing for a career in geography.

**Educational Opportunities Database** (click on Preparation). Searchable database of educational and training programs in geography and related geographic technologies. Searchable by country, U.S. zip code, or program specialty.

**Careers in Geography** (www.aag.org, click on Jobs/Careers). Answers the following questions: What is geography?, How do you know if you want to be a geographer?, and What will it take to get a good job? Also features an Interactive Map of Geography Departments in the United States and Canada.

# Association of American Veterinary Medical Colleges

**www.aavmc.org**

Click on Students & Admissions to access the following resources:

**Schools & Colleges.** Provides a list of veterinary medicine programs and schools in the United States.

**Admissions Data.** Lists information on applicants and historical tuition costs for veterinary school.

**Externships.** Provides information on externships, which provide students with hands-on, real-world experiences in veterinary medicine.

**Career Center.** Features two main sections: Roles of Veterinarians and Becoming a Veterinarian.

**Scholarships & Awards.** Provides information on financial aid for veterinary medicine students offered by other organizations and the federal government.

Click on Applying to Veterinary School to access the following resources:

**Applicant Responsibilities.** Offers advice and helpful hints for those applying to veterinary school.

**About the Veterinary Medical College Application Service.** Offers information on this centralized application system.

# Association of Collegiate Schools of Architecture

https://www.acsa-arch.org/students/studentsguide.aspx

**High School Preparation.** Discusses suggested courses and extracurricular activities for high school students interested in architecture.

**Architectural Programs.** Useful section that provides information on school accreditation, types of architectural degrees, and typical architectural curricula.

**Selecting a School.** Offers advice on program choices, questions (on accreditation, degree and curriculum options, and scholarships) to ask schools, and questions (e.g., How far from home do I want to be? Do I thrive best in a small school environment or large?) to ask yourself.

**Resources.** Lists U.S. architectural schools accredited by the National Architectural Accrediting Board and information on accredited Canadian schools of architecture.

# Association of Collegiate Schools of Planning

www.acsp.org/Guide/guide_index.htm

**Choosing a Career in Urban and Regional Planning.** Provides information on career options, profiles of planners, details on educational requirements, and a list of accredited training programs.

**Guide to Graduate and Undergraduate Education in Urban and Regional Planning.** Comprehensive information on planning programs in the United States.

# Association of Community Health Nursing Educators

www.achne.org

**Master's Programs in Community/Public Health Nursing.** Provides a list of master's programs in the U.S. and Canada.

# Association of Environmental & Engineering Geologists

www.aegweb.org

**Academic Programs & University Links.** Provides a list of colleges with "exceptional geology, hydrogeology, geological engineering, and other geoscience-related programs."

**Summer Field Camp.** Provides information on geology-related summer camps for high school students. Camps are located throughout the U.S. and the world.

**Scholarships/Grants.** Provides information on financial aid for undergraduate and graduate students from the AEG Foundation.

# Association of Environmental and Resource Economists (AERE)

www.aere.org/grad/gradprog.htm

**Graduate Programs in Environmental and Resource Economics.** Results from a 1997 survey of U.S. and Canadian AERE member institutions regarding graduate programs in environmental and resource economics. Survey results include school name, contact information, and details on financial aid, specializations, faculty, and job placement programs.

# Association of Environmental Engineering and Science Professors (AEESP)

www.aeesp.org

**Education.** Lists baccalaureate, master's, and doctoral environmental engineering and science degree programs offered by institutions with AEESP faculty members.

# Association of Jesuit Colleges and Universities

www.ajcunet.edu/welcome/students.asp

**Jesuit Institutions.** Information on the 28 Roman Catholic Jesuit colleges and universities in the United States.

**Jesuit College Search.** Directory of Jesuit colleges and universities searchable by academic major, geographical region, and size of institution. This section also includes a database of Admissions

Information for member schools. Listings include details on location, setting (urban, suburban, rural), enrollment, admission and financial aid deadlines, and tuition/room and board.

**Distance Education.** Information on distance education options at Jesuit colleges. This section also offers links to international Jesuit academic institutions.

The following resources can be accessed by clicking on About AJCU/AJCU Publications:

**Degree Programs.** List of degree programs available at Jesuit institutions.

**AJCU Shared Study Abroad Programs** (click on contact information for study abroad opportunities at international Jesuit institutions.)

## Association of Medical Illustrators (AMI)

www.ami.org

**Medical Illustrator as a Career** (click on About AMI). Provides information on the career, necessary skills, educational requirements (including suggested medical science and art and theory courses), and salary information.

> **Did You Know?**
> There are only four accredited graduate medical illustration programs in the United States and one in Canada.

**Accredited Graduate Programs** (click on Education). Lists AMI-accredited U.S. and Canadian graduate programs in medical illustration.

**Scholarships** (click on Education). Information on AMI scholarships for graduate students.

## Association of Military Colleges and Schools of the United States (AMCSUS)

www.amcsus.org

**Directory of Schools.** Searchable database of military schools; searchable by type of institution, state, gender, and school name.

**Why Choose a Military School?** Details the benefits of attending a military school (college preparatory, two-year college, and college and university).

**Frequently Asked Questions.** Provides answers to FAQs such as What is a military school?, How do I begin the process of selecting the right school?, How can I afford an independent military school?, How do I begin the application process?, and What is the military service obligation?

**Admissions.** Offers information on how to apply and financing options.

## Association of Perioperative Registered Nurses

www.aorn.org

**Consider a Career in the OR as a Perioperative Nurse** (click on Career Center/Career Development). Describes job duties, personal skills, salaries, and educational requirements for perioperative nurses.

**Perioperative Nursing Course Directory** (click on Education/Education Resources). Database of perioperative nursing programs in the United States. Searchable by state, program type, institution type, and mode of learning.

**Scholarship** (click on AORN Foundation). Lists undergraduate and graduate scholarships offered by the Association.

## Association of Presbyterian Colleges and Universities (APCU)

www.apcu.net

**Member Schools/Colleges by Region.** Lists APCU-member schools in the United States. Searchable by region.

**Choosing a College.** Provides the following sections Finding a College, The Campus Visit, What About Rankings, Reasons to Choose a College, About Presbyterian Colleges, Private Colleges, College Myths, Important Things to Keep in Mind, and Scholarships for Presbyterian Students.

The Association offers a free print *Directory of Schools, Colleges and Universities,* which presents information on the more than 60 APCU-member institutions. Each school entry includes a general overview of the institution and information on enrollment, tuition, student/faculty ratio, degrees offered, application deadlines, and athletics.

# Association of Professional Genealogists

**www.apgen.org**

**Becoming a Professional Geneaologist** (click on Publications). Lists career options, educational pathways, and personal skills for professional genealogists.

**Information on college-level courses and bachelor's degrees** from a handful of U.S. schools can be found in the Publications & Resources section.

# Association of Schools and Colleges of Optometry

**www.opted.org**

**Optometry: A Career Guide** (click on About Optometric Education/Student and Advisor resources). Comprehensive information on careers, the optometry curriculum, admission requirements, financing an optometric education, and types of practice.

**Frequently Asked Questions.** Information on careers, admissions, the Optometry Admissions Test, and post-optometry school options. Questions include What is a Doctor of Optometry?, Where can I go to school to study optometry?, How do I know which is the best school or college of optometry for me?, What undergraduate courses should I take to help prepare me for optometry school?, What type of education is required to become a Doctor of Optometry?, What do I have to do to apply for admission to optometry school?, How much will optometry school cost?, and What happens after I graduate from optometry school?

> **Educational Requirements**
> You will need a doctorate in optometry to practice in the field. There are 18 colleges of optometry in the United States. The Association recommends the following undergraduate curriculum to prepare for the field: one year of biology, chemistry, organic chemistry, general physics, and microbiology; English; college mathematics; and other social science and humanities courses.

**Student Profile and Prerequisites** (click on About Optometric Education/Student and Advisor Information). Statistics on optometry applicants, admitted students, enrollments, and graduates.

**Member Schools & Colleges** (click on About ASCO). Lists member schools of optometry in the United States.

**Frequently Asked Questions About the Optometry Admission Test (OAT)** (click on About Optometric Education/OAT). Answers FAQS about the field such as What is the OAT?, What subjects does the OAT cover?, and When should I take the OAT? Also provides online applications to optometry graduate schools.

## Association of Schools of Public Health (ASPH)

**www.asph.org** (click on Member Schools)

**Information for Prospective Students.** Includes information on public health degrees, answers to frequently asked questions (e.g., What undergraduate major should I choose?, What are the areas of public health that I can get a degree in?, and What are the average GPA/GRE scores of accepted students?), and information on careers and financial aid.

**Member Schools.** Lists colleges and universities with public health education programs accredited by the Council on Education of Public Health. Includes information on school type, schedule, tuition, demographics, and program areas.

**Search for a Program.** Public health programs database searchable by program area and type of degree.

**Distance Learning Programs Available at Accredited Schools of Public Health.** Lists ASPH-member schools that offer distance education options.

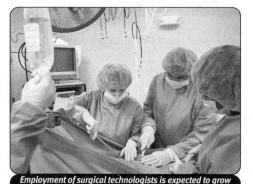

*Employment of surgical technologists is expected to grow much faster than the average through 2016. (Photo courtesy of Photos.com)*

## Association of Surgical Technologists

**www.ast.org**

**Surgical Technology: A Growing Career** (click on Professionals/About the Profession). Details career information, educational requirements, types of educational program accreditation, and typical surgical technology curriculum.

**Scholarships** (click on Students). Offers information on financial aid.

**Find a School** (click on Students). Lists accredited surgical technology programs in the United States.

# Association of Theological Schools in the United States and Canada (ATS)

www.ats.edu

**Member Schools.** Listings of accredited schools, organized by name, geographical location, or degree offered. The latter search option allows students to search by different degree options, such as a Doctorate of Philosophy (Ph.D.), Master of Church Music (M.C.M.), or Master of Theology (M.Th.).

**Fact Book on Theological Education** (click on Resources). Interesting facts on enrollment, tuition, schools, degrees awarded, and other subjects.

# Association of Universities and Colleges of Canada

www.aucc.ca

**Canadian Universities.** Directory of Canadian schools searchable by province, program, language of institution, and degree level. Includes subsections aimed at educating students and parents about the Canadian educational system, how to choose and apply to schools, paying for school, and study abroad opportunities.

**Information for Students** (click on Canadian Universities). Provides a variety of resources including Canada's Universities Present a Wealth of Options, Choosing Your University, An Overview of Graduate Studies in Canada, Scholarship Tips For Students, and Quality Assurance at Canada's Universities.

**Reality Check** (click on Publications and Resources/Resources for Researchers). A series of fact-based essays that dispel myths about Canadian colleges.

**Higher Education Scholarships.** Provides information on scholarship programs administered by the Association. Includes an FAQ section that answers common financial aid questions.

The AUCC website is available in French- and English-language versions.

# Association of University Programs in Health Administration (AUPHA)

www.aupha.org

**Find a Program.** Database of AUPHA-member colleges and universities that offer bachelor's and master's degrees in health administration. Searchable by school name, city, state, and country.

Click on the Resources for Students section to access the following resources:

**Reasons to Pursue a Career in Healthcare Management.** Provides a list of reasons (excellent earning potential, career flexibility, etc.) to pursue a career in the field.

**What Education is Required?** Details educational requirements for health administration students at the baccalaureate and master's level.

**What is the Typical Program of Study?** A brief description of a typical health administration curriculum.

**Scholarships and Fellowships.** Financial aid information from the AUPHA for graduate students in health administration.

# Association of Women Surgeons

www.womensurgeons.org/aws_library/pub_resources.htm

**Career Development Resource.** Comprehensive surgeon-written resource for aspiring and new surgeons. Provides information on 14 surgical specialties (including training and residency requirements), professional organizations, and private practice, academic, government, and other career options.

# Association of Writers and Writing Programs

http://guide.awpwriter.org

**AWP's Official Guide to Writing Programs.** Searchable databases of undergraduate and graduate programs in creative writing. The graduate program database is searchable by type of degree, institution name, location (U.S. or international), type of program, and concentrations of study (creative nonfiction, criticism and theory, fiction, playwriting, poetry, professional writing, screenwriting, and writing for children).

## Association to Advance Collegiate Schools of Business (AACSB)

www.aacsb.edu/accreditation/accreditedmembers.asp

**Accredited Schools.** Lists U.S. and international accounting and business schools accredited by the AACSB. Each listing includes information on number of degrees awarded, faculty, tuition, and types of programs offered.

## Automotive Careers Today

www.autocareerstoday.net

**Explore Auto Careers.** Offers information on a variety of careers at automotive dealerships—some of which require postsecondary training.

**Find Training.** Database of automotive training programs in the United States. Searchable by state and program type (dealership administration, sales and leasing, service, body shop, parts).

The site is also available in Spanish.

> **> Did You Know?**
> There are many nontechnical career options in the automotive industry. They include those in dealership administration (general manager, bookkeeper, and director of marketing), sales and leasing (finance and insurance manager, sales manager, Internet sales specialist), and parts (parts manager, parts counter sales).

## AvScholars: Student Gateway to Aviation

www.avscholars.com

**Careers in Aviation.** Provides information on aviation careers (pilot, mechanic, manufacturing engineer, airport manager, etc.) and exploring your career interests.

**Aviation Colleges.** Offers information about types of aviation degree programs, choosing a training program, and applying for financial aid.

**Paying for School.** Provides comprehensive information about financial aid for aviation students.

Also available: glossaries of aviation, college admission, financial aid, and investment terms, as well as college preparation, financial preparation, and scholarship tracking checklists.

# Be an Actuary: A Career Without Boundaries

**www.beanactuary.org**

This site was created by the Casualty Actuarial Society (CAS) and the Society of Actuaries (SOA) to provide high school students, college students, and career changers with more information about actuarial careers. The site offers the following resources:

## Top Traits for Actuaries

According to BeAnActuary.org, successful actuaries need to have "specialized math knowledge; keen analytical, project management, and problem solving skills; good business sense; solid communication skills; and strong computer skills." They also need to be creative, self-motivated, independent, ambitious, and work well with others.

**A Career Choice Worth Exploring.** Features career and educational information. (Note: a video with the same title is also available.)

**Preparing for an Actuarial Career While in High School.** Lists suggested high school courses and activities for aspiring actuaries.

**Preparing for an Actuarial Career While in College.** Presents an overview of college curricula and suggested classes and extracurricular activities.

**Actuarial College Listing.** Links to a list at the SOA website.

**FAQs.** Provides answers to frequently asked questions about education and careers such as What courses should I take in college?, What degrees are appropriate to an actuarial career?, Does it help me to have a graduate degree?, Where are most of the actuarial jobs in North America located?, and What is the outlook for the actuarial job market over the next few years?

**Scholarships.** Information on scholarships (available to high school and college students) offered by the CAS, the SOA, and other actuarial organizations. Includes information on financial aid for minorities.

# Biomedical Engineering Society

**www.bmes.org**

**Planning a Career in Biomedical Engineering** (click on Careers). Offers information on the career, specialty areas, work activities, employment settings, and educational requirements.

# Biophysical Society

www.biophysics.org

Click on Career Center to access the following resources:

**Careers in Biophysics.** Details career specialties, suggested high school courses, and undergraduate and graduate study for people interested in biophysics.

> ## FYI
>
> Recommended high school courses for aspiring biophysicists include physics, biology, English, chemistry, and mathematics. Suggested activities include science fairs, assembling electronics, and photography.

**Graduate Programs in Biophysics.** Lists U.S. and international graduate biophysical educational programs.

# Botanical Society of America

www.botany.org/bsa/careers

**Careers in Botany.** Information on career options, high school preparation, college programs of study, and employment settings.

# BookJobs.com

www.bookjobs.com

BookJobs.com is sponsored by the Association of American Publishers.

**Internships** (click on Jobs in Publishing). Lists internships that are available at U.S. publishers.

**Publishing Programs/Education** (click on About Publishing). Provides links to certificate and degree programs in the United States.

# Careers in Court Reporting and Broadcast Captioning

www.bestfuture.com

This site is sponsored by the National Court Reporters Association.

**Court Reporting Schools.** Provides information on certified schools and other programs.

**Questions To Ask Your Prospective Court Reporting School.** A list of 20 questions to ask a prospective court reporting school to ensure it offers a top quality program.

**Frequently Asked Questions.** Provides answers to FAQs such as What do court reporters do in the legal field? and Where can I learn to become a court reporter or broadcast captioner?

## Careers in Interior Design

**www.careersininteriordesign.com**

This site is sponsored by several U.S. and Canadian interior design associations.

**Education** (click on Stages of a Career). Details educational requirements for entry into the field.

**FAQs.** Provides answers to questions such as How can I find a reputable interior design school?, How can I decide on the best interior design school for me?, and Where can I find a list of accredited interior design programs?

## Careers in Supply Chain Management

**www.careersinsupplychain.org** (click on Building Expertise)

**University Education.** Provides an overview of postsecondary supply chain management courses.

**University Listing.** Provides link to colleges and universities that offer logistics-related courses.

## Careers Outside the Box: Survey Research: A Fun, Exciting, Rewarding Career

**www.casro.org/careers**

**What Qualifications/Education Do I Need?** Offers information on educational requirements for survey workers.

**College Degree Programs in Survey Research.** Provides a list of undergraduate and graduate programs in survey and marketing research.

## Child Life Council

**www.childlife.org**

Click on Students & Educators to access the following resources:

**Choosing an Academic Program.** Detailed advice for students on selecting a college program.

**Curriculum Recommendations.** Recommended theoretical and applied areas of study for child life students.

**Academic Program Directory.** Provides list of U.S. colleges and universities that offer degrees/curricula in child life.

**Choosing a Student Internship Site.** Detailed advice for students on selecting an internship site.

# CollisionCareers.org

http://collisioncareers.org

**Find Out How You Can Begin Your Career in the Collision Industry.** Offers information on vehicle collision repair training, earnings, and employment.

# Commission on Accreditation for Health Informatics and Information Management Education

www.cahiim.org/directory

**Program Directory.** Database of health informatics and information education programs at the master's, baccalaureate, and associate degree levels. Searchable by program level, program name, U.S. state, and availability of distance learning.

# Commission on Accreditation of Allied Health Education Programs (CAAHEP)

www.caahep.org

**Find An Accredited Program.** Database of nearly 2,000 Commission-accredited U.S. and Canadian educational programs for the following careers: anesthesiologist assistant, cardiovascular technologist, cytotechnologist, diagnostic medical sonographer, electroneurodiagnostic technologist, emergency medical technician/paramedic, exercise physiologist, exercise science professional, kinesiotherapist, medical assistant, medical illustrator, orthotic and prosthetic technician, orthotist/prosthetist, perfusionist, personal fitness trainer, physical assistant, polysomnographic technologist, respiratory therapy, specialist in blood bank technology, surgical assistant, and surgical technologist. Searchable by profession name, state, and whether the program is accredited, newly accredited, recently withdrawn from accreditation, or offered online or via distance education.

**Profession Description and Certification Information** (click on For Students). Career information and educational requirements for the careers listed on page 191.

## Commission on Opticianry Accreditation (COA)

www.coaccreditation.com

**Essentials.** Includes Essentials for 2-Year Opticianry Degree Program and Essentials for a Ophthalmic Laboratory Program. These documents list curriculum and admission requirements for opticianry and ophthalmic laboratory programs.

**Accredited Programs.** Lists COA-accredited two-year opticianry degrees and ophthalmic laboratory technology programs in the United States.

> **> Did You Know?**
> A college degree is required for 50 percent of careers in the construction industry, according to ConstructMyFuture.com.

## ConstructMyFuture.com

www.constructmyfuture.com/Students

**Overview.** Provides a description of job duties, work settings, and educational requirements for more than 40 careers in the construction industry-from drafters to industrial engineers to general/operational managers.

**Schools.** Database of construction schools, searchable by state/province and industry segment.

**Scholarships.** Provides information on financial aid offered by ConstructMy Future and other organizations.

## Council for Higher Education Accreditation

www.chea.org

**Database of Institutions and Programs Accredited by Recognized U.S. Accrediting Organizations** (click on Databases and Directories). Directory of approximately 7,000 institutions that are "accredited by participating or recognized organizations of the Council for Higher Education Accreditation or are recognized by the United States Department of Education." Searchable by institution name, U.S. state or territory, country, program type, and accredited agency.

**Degree Mills and Accreditation Mills.** Offers information to help students avoid "degree mills, dubious providers of educational offerings or operations that offer certificates and degrees that may be considered bogus, and accreditation mills, dubious providers of accreditation and quality assurance that may offer a certification of quality of institutions without a proper basis."

# Council for Interior Design Accreditation

www.accredit-id.org/accreditedprograms.php

**Accredited Programs.** Lists associate's and baccalaureate interior design programs in the United States that are accredited by the Council.

# Council for the Advancement of Science Writing

www.casw.org/booklet.htm

**A Guide To Careers in Science Writing.** Provides answers to the following questions: What do science writers do?, How do I know if I should become a science writer?, and How do I get started in science writing?

## FYI

*Science writers* report on developments in science and medicine to the general public. They are employed by publishing companies, newspapers and magazines, scientific research companies, colleges and universities, and hospitals.

# Council of Colleges of Acupuncture and Oriental Medicine

www.ccaom.org

**Member Colleges.** List of acupuncture and Oriental Medicine training programs that have been approved by the Accreditation Commission for Acupuncture and Oriental Medicine.

# Council of Graduate Schools

**www.cgsnet.org**

**Resources for Students** (click on Programs and Awards). Useful section for students interested in attending graduate school. Section titles include Sources for Fellowships and Financial Aid, Sources of Information on Graduate Programs and Graduate School, and Graduate Student Organizations.

**Preparing Future Faculty Program** (click on Programs and Awards). You can read a description of the program's initiatives and browse the schools that meet established quality criteria. Advanced degree programs are organized by the following subject areas: biological and life sciences, chemistry, communications, computer science, English, history, mathematics, physics, political science, psychology, and sociology. School listings include contact information and Web addresses.

The Council also offers **Graduate School and You,** which provides information on topics such as choosing a graduate school, financing a graduate education, sources of information on graduate programs and graduate school, timetable for applying to graduate school, and caring for yourself while in graduate school. It is available for a small fee.

# Council of Logistics Management

**www.clm1.org**

**University Listings** (click on Publications and Resources/ Outside Resources). Lists U.S. and international colleges and universities that offer logistics-related course work.

**Careers in Supply Chain Management Website** (click on Career Center). Sister site that provides information on career options, work settings, educational requirements, and earnings.

# Council on Chiropractic Education

**www.cce-usa.org**

**Doctor of Chiropractic Programs.** Provides contact information for accredited doctor of chiropractic education programs.

# Council on Forensic Science Education

www.criminology.fsu.edu/COFSE/default.html

**Member Colleges and Universities.** Provides a list of colleges that offer undergraduate and graduate training in forensic science.

# Council on Rehabilitation Education (CORE)

www.core-rehab.org

**Programs Approved for Core's Undergraduate Rehabilitation Registry** (click on Undergraduate Education). Lists U.S. college and university undergraduate degree programs in rehabilitation education.

**CORE-Recognized Master's Programs in Rehabilitation Counselor Education** (click on Programs Recognized). Lists U.S. college and university master's degree programs in rehabilitation education.

# Council on Social Work Education (CSWE)

www.cswe.org

**Frequently Asked Questions.** Information for prospective and current social work students. Answers are provided for the following questions: How do I become a social worker?; What is the value of studying social work instead of a related field such as sociology, psychology, counseling, or human services?; Why should I attend a program accredited by CSWE?; and Where are the social work programs near me?

**Database of Accredited Programs** (click on Membership). Directory of undergraduate and graduate social work programs in the United States. Searchable by state, institution name, and dean/director name.

# Dietary Managers Association (DMA)

www.dmaonline.org/DMA_Students_Home.php

**DMA-Approved Programs (Schools).** Lists U.S. college and university dietary education programs approved by the DMA. Also includes information about online programs.

# Directors Guild of America

**www.dga.org**

**Film Schools** (click on Site Map). Links to colleges, universities, institutes, and foundations that offer film programs.

# Discovery Education: College & Career Resources

**http://school.discoveryeducation.com/foodscience/college_resources.html**

**Careers in Food Science.** A multimedia resource kit that provides information on careers in food science and technology. Information on typical college classes, financial aid, and salaries, as well as profiles of workers in the field and a list of colleges that offer food science programs, is also provided.

# Distance Education and Training Council (DETC)

**www.detc.org**

**FAQ (click About Us).** Provides answers to frequently asked questions about distance education, such as What is distance education?, What does accreditation mean?, and Is DETC accreditation equal to "regional" accreditation?

**Accredited Institutions.** Lists DETC-accredited high schools, postsecondary schools, and military schools. List is searchable by institution name, educational level, state, country, and subject taught.

At the Council's home page, click on Publications to access the following resources:

**Is Distance Education for You?** Outlines the benefits of pursuing distance education.

**A Student's Guide to Transfer Credit.** A resource guide for students who are transferring to another school to continue their education.

**Using Your Distance Education to Earn an Academic Degree.** Advice from an American Council on Education official on transferring distance education credits to a traditional college or university.

# Dow Jones Newspaper Fund

**https://djnewspaperfund.dowjones.com**

**Search Journalism Schools.** A searchable database of journalism programs by U.S. state and territory.

Click on Programs to access the following resources:

**College Internships.** Information on annual summer internships in business reporting, news, online, and sports copy editing offered by the Fund.

**High School Journalism Workshops.** Details on summer workshops offered by the Fund for students who face challenges to become journalists. Held at colleges throughout the United States.

**Other High School Journalism Workshops.** List of non-Fund-sponsored workshops that are offered by colleges, state and regional scholastic press associations and private firms.

**Scholarship Listings.** Offers information on financial aid, internships and job fairs and job postings for high school students, college students, and practicing journalists.

In addition, the Fund offers *The Journalist's Road to Success,* a very useful online publication for aspiring journalism students. (Note: also available in Spanish.) Noteworthy sections include:

> **Did You Know?**
> The most popular U.S. newspapers (by circulation) are *USA Today, Wall Street Journal, The New York Times, Los Angeles Times, Chicago Tribune, Washington Post, New York Daily News,* and *New York Post.*

**Choosing the Right College.** Offers advice on choosing a journalism program, attending a two- or four-year college, and picking a major. Includes a list of typical journalism and mass communications courses offered at U.S. colleges and universities.

**Journalism/Mass Communications Schools.** Lists nearly 400 U.S. schools by state.

**Internships: Don't Leave School Without One.** Discusses the benefits of landing an internship while in college.

**Jobs, Scholarships, Internships & Groups.** Provides information on financial aid for journalism and mass communications students.

An ecologist (r) and technician gather samples of small invertebrates in a wetland. (Photo courtesy of Peggy Greb, USDA)

# Ecological Society of America

www.esa.org/
education_diversity/explore.php

**Careers in Ecology (high school version).** Presents an overview of the career, work settings, and suggested high school activities.

**Careers in Ecology (undergraduate version).** Includes information on careers, suggested courses, and ways students can gain experience (e.g., work as a teaching assistant in a biology or ecology course, get an internship, or volunteer) in the field during college.

**Focus on Ecologists.** Provides profiles of nearly 100 ecologists, who discuss the educational and career challenges they faced as they worked to enter the field.

## Educational Foundation for Women in Accounting

www.efwa.org/scholarships.htm

**Scholarships.** Provides information on undergraduate and postgraduate scholarships for female accounting students.

## Educational Theatre Association (ETA)

www.edta.org/thespian_resources

Click on College Prep for the following resources:

**Choosing a Theatre Training Program/Choices.** Comprehensive information for high school students interested in attending an undergraduate theatre program. Contents include a discussion of the merits of pursuing a bachelor of arts versus a bachelor of fine Arts and questions to ask yourself (e.g., What do I want to get out of college theatre training? and What size program do I prefer?) and school representatives (e.g., What is your philosophy of training in theatre? and Where are your recent graduates now, and what are they doing?). The section also includes specialized questions for acting students, theatre education majors, and playwriting students.

**The Portfolio.** Information for students who are interested in working behind the scenes in design and production. Includes advice on preparing a resume and portfolio for a college representative and choosing a tech theatre program.

**The Audition.** Advice on preparing for an audition at the college and professional level.

**College Links.** Features links to nearly 250 U.S. and international college, university, and conservatory theatre programs that are listed in the *Dramatics College Theatre Directory.* (A print edition of this resource is also available for a small fee.)

**Thespian Scholarships.** Information for high school seniors interested in applying for ETA scholarships.

# Engineering Your Future

www.futuresinengineering.com

**Career Track.** Provides a list of recommended high school classes and activities for engineering-bound students.

# Engineer Your Life: Dream Big. Love What You Do

www.engineeryourlife.org

Sponsored by the National Science Foundation and Northrop Grumman Foundation, this website that introduces high school girls to engineering offers the following useful resources in its Making It Happen section:

## Best Undergraduate Engineering Programs

*U.S. News & World Report* asked engineering deans and faculty to name the best programs. They ranked the following schools with engineering programs at the bachelor's or master's level as the best: Harvey Mudd College (CA), Rose-Hulman Institute of Technology (IN), Cooper Union (NY), California-Polytechnic-San Luis Obispo, and the United States Military Academy (NY).

**Being an Engineering Student.** Presents profiles of three female engineering students and offers an overview of a typical engineering program.

**Preparing for College.** Lists recommended high school courses for aspiring engineers.

**Taking a Test Drive.** Details exploration activities such as high school engineering clubs, internships, and information interviews.

**Looking at Programs.** Offers advice on researching and contacting college engineering programs.

**Scholarships and Financial Aid.** Provides tips on finding financial aid.

# EngineerGirl

**www.engineergirl.org**

**Becoming an Engineer.** Provides information on college planning, scholarships, and mentoring.

**Careers.** Offers information on more than 60 engineering careers (including answers to frequently asked questions and details on work settings and earnings) and educational requirements.

# Entomological Society of America

**www.entsoc.org/resources/education/index.htm**

**Interviews with Entomologists.** Entomologists discuss the challenges and rewards of a career in entomology (includes advice on educational preparation).

**College and University Entomology Programs.** Lists U.S. and Canadian colleges that offer courses in entomology or entomology-related degrees and courses (including online options).

**Discover Entomology Brochure.** Provides information on the career, academic preparation, and colleges and universities that offer entomology-related programs.

**Scholarships from ESA and the Entomological Foundation.** Provides information on financial aid for undergraduate and graduate students.

> **Did You Know?**
> Two-thirds of teens surveyed in 2007 by Junior Achievement reported that they would like to start their own business someday.

# EntrepreneurU

**www.entrepreneurU.org**

**Entrepreneur U Database.** Database of community college, college, and university entrepreneurship programs in the United States.

**Scholarships/Awards/Grants.** Provides information on a variety of financial aid resources for entrepreneurism students.

# Episcopal Church USA

www.episcopalchurch.org/ministry

**Frequently Asked Questions.** Answers a variety of questions about the ordained ministry and Episcopal Church USA programs, including How does one become an ordained priest or deacon? and How much does it cost to go to an Episcopal seminary?

**Theological Education for All.** Includes information on the General Ordination Examination (which is taken by candidates for ordained ministry), statistics about seminaries and education for the priesthood, and resources for financial aid. Also includes a list of Episcopal Church USA seminaries in the United States.

# ExploreHealthCareers.org

http://explorehealthcareers.org

ExploreHealthCareers has been created with the cooperation of national foundations, professional associations, health career advisors, educational institutions, and college students. It has two goals: encourage minority students to pursue careers in the health care industry and encourage students to consider working in medically underserved communities. Useful sections include:

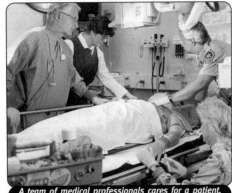

A team of medical professionals cares for a patient. (Photo courtesy of Dynamic Graphics)

**Paying for School** (click on Getting Started). Provides information on the types of financial aid, how to obtain financial aid, and how to avoid scholarship scams.

**Student Profiles** (click on Profiles). Q&As with students in health care programs.

Click on Career Explorer to access the following resources:

**Healthcare Fields.** Provides information on job duties, work settings, and educational requirements for dozens of health care careers in more than 20 specialties (including arts and humanities, dentistry, nursing, physical therapy, and veterinary medicine).

**Find a Health Career.** Database of fast-growing health careers, searchable by minimum salary and number of years of college training to enter the field.

**Find Funding Opportunities.** Searchable database of financial aid resources for students pursuing health care education.

**Find Pre-Health Enrichment Programs.** Database of information on internships and summer study programs for students (including minorities). Searchable by field of study, academic level (high school, college, etc.), state, and keyword.

# Federal Aviation Administration (FAA)

**www.faa.gov/pilots/become**

**Become a Pilot.** Provides an overview of "FAA-approved" and "non-approved" aviation schools, answers to frequently asked questions about the career, and advice on choosing an aviation school.

**Pilot School Locator.** A database of U.S. and international schools that offer pilot training. Searchable by name, U.S. city and state, country, and other criteria.

Visit www.faa.gov/jobs/job_opportunities/airtraffic_controllers to access the following resources:

**How to Become an Air Traffic Control Specialist.** Offers advice on entering the field.

**Approved Air Traffic Controller Schools.** Lists U.S. training schools for air traffic controllers.

At the FAA's home page, click on Education & Research to access the following resources:

**Aviation Schools & Universities.** Includes the following sections: Air Traffic Controller Schools, Aviation Schools Online, Maintenance School Locator, and Pilot Schools Locator.

**Scholarships & Grants** (www.faa.gov/education_research/ education/student_resources/scholarships_grants/index.cfm). Information on aviation-related financial aid offered by the government and private associations.

# Federal Trade Commission (FCC)

www.ftc.gov/bcp/consumer.shtm

Click on Education, Scholarships, & Job Placement/Education to access the following resources:

**Choosing a Career or Vocational School.** Advice on choosing a career or vocational school. Includes information on filing a complaint if you are unhappy with the quality of training or instruction that you receive.

**Student Loans: Avoiding Deceptive Offers.** Tips on obtaining legitimate loans for college.

**Diploma Mills: Degrees of Deception.** Detailed information on diploma mills and how to avoid them (also available in Spanish).

**Six Signs that Your Scholarship Is Sunk-Poster.** Details the obvious signs of scholarship scams. Also available as a bookmark.

> **Scholarship Scam "Lines"**
> According to the FCC, be wary of scholarship offers that say the following: "The scholarship is guaranteed or your money back," "You can't get this information anywhere else," and "I just need your credit card or bank account number to hold this scholarship."

Click on Education, Scholarships, & Job Placement/Scholarships to access the following resources:

**Scholarship Scams.** Microsite that provides detailed information on scholarship scams.

**Ouch!...Students Getting Stung Trying to Find $$$ for College.** Presents advice on avoiding scholarship scams, including avoiding "tell-tale lines" and getting the most out of financial aid seminars.

**Free Grants: Don't Take Them For Grant-ed.** Tips to avoid being taken advantage of by scam "free grant" programs.

# Fiber Optic Association (FOA)

www.thefoa.org/foa_aprv.htm

**FOA-Approved Training Programs.** Lists U.S. and Canadian schools that offer courses in fiber optics technology.

## FYI

*Fire protection engineers,* according to the SFPE, use engineering and science to "protect people, property, information, and organizational operations from the effects of fire and explosion."

# Fire Protection Engineering

**www.careersinfireprotectionengineering.com**

**Colleges.** Lists U.S. and international colleges and universities that offer course and programs in fire protection engineering and technology.

**Preparing for College.** Provides information on types of college programs, course descriptions, scholarships, and distance learning.

# Forensic Sciences Foundation

**www.forensicsciencesfoundation.org**

**Career Paths.** Offers information on career options in forensic science, necessary personal skills, and education requirements.

# Foundation for Independent Higher Education (FIHE)

**www.fihe.org** (click on College Search)

**College Search.** Lists approximately 670 private U.S. colleges and universities that are FIHE members. Searchable by state.

**Tips to Help You Search For a College.** Includes printable College Comparison and Financial Aid Checklists and short articles on federal financial programs and campus visits.

**Why Independent Colleges & Universities?** Details the benefits of attending this type of institution.

**Dispelling the Myths and Highlighting the Strengths: The Six "Rs" of Private College.** Details reasons why it's a good idea to attend a private college.

# GenEdNet: Your Genetics Education Resource

**www.genednet.org**

This website is sponsored by the American Society of Human Genetics.

**Training and Careers in Human Genetics** (click on Careers and Beyond). Describes career options (such as research geneticist, laboratory geneticist, genetic counselor, and clinical geneticist) and educational requirements for students interested in human genetics.

**Graduate School Training Programs Guide** (click on Graduate/Postdoc Training). Lists graduate and postgraduate institutions in the United States and Canada that offer human genetics programs. Each program listing includes information on degree granted, training available, areas of concentration, faculty status, accreditation, application deadlines, and financial aid offered.

# General Aviation Manufacturers Association

**www.gama.aero/resources/AVEducation**

**Annual Awards & Scholarships.** Provides information on financial aid for high school seniors and college students who are pursuing careers in aviation.

# GetRealGetReady: Real Estate + Real Future

**www.irem.org/getrealgetready**

This site is sponsored by the Institute of Real Estate Management.

**Careers In Real Estate Management.** Eleven-page brochure that provides information on career options and educational requirements.

**Real Estate College Degree Search** (click on Get Help). Database of postsecondary real estate programs in the United States, searchable by state and classroom environment (regular or online).

# GetTech.org

**www.gettech.org**

This site is sponsored by the National Association of Manufacturers and several government agencies.

**GetTech Careers.** Features career overviews and educational requirements for more than 40 careers in the following fields: New Manufacturing, Biotechnology & Chemistry, Information Technology, Health & Medicine, Engineering & Industrial Technology, and Arts & Design.

# Golf Course Superintendents Association of America (GCSAA)

**www.gcsaa.org** (click on Students)

**Picture This: A Career as a GCSAA Golf Course Superintendent.** Provides information on the career and educational information, including a sample college curriculum and degree requirements.

**Internship Handbook.** Provides comprehensive information on internships for students.

**Choosing a Program.** Offers advice on selecting a postsecondary golf course management training program.

**College Guide.** Searchable database of golf course management training programs in the United States.

**Scholarships.** Provides information on financial aid for high school seniors and college students from the Environmental Institute for Golf and other providers.

# Group for the Advancement of Doctoral Education

**www.gadephd.org**

**Membership by University/State.** Lists social work doctoral programs in the United States, Canada, and Israel.

# Health Physics Society (HPS)

**http://hps.org/publicinformation/opportunities.html**

**Health Physics Academic Programs in the United States.** Online version of the *Health Physics Education Reference Book,* which lists two-year, four-year, and graduate programs in health physics. Each school listing includes information on type of program, degrees granted, enrollment, financial assistance, research facilities, and faculty.

**Health Physics Academic Programs Around the World.** Online version of the *CRPPH-Sponsored Survey of University-Level Education Programmes in Radiation Protection,* which lists undergraduate and graduate health physics programs in the United States and other countries. The survey was first published in 1997.

# High School Journalism

www.highschooljournalism.org

This comprehensive website provides information on journalism careers and education. Click on the Students section to access the following resources:

**Journalism Schools.** A searchable database of accredited and unaccredited journalism schools in the United States.

**Scholarship Information.** Provides information on financial aid for high school seniors and college students who are interested in pursuing careers in journalism. Searchable by U.S. state and minority status.

**Summer Programs.** Provides information on summer journalism programs for high school students. Listed by state.

# Hillel: The Foundation for Jewish Campus Life

www.hillel.org/students

**Hillel's Guide to Jewish Life on Campus.** Presents detailed overviews and contact information for Jewish student life at 500 colleges and universities in the United States and abroad. Topics covered include the number of Jewish students attending the university, the number of Jewish organizations on campus, types of religious services

> **Did You Know?**
Hillel is the largest Jewish campus organization in the world. It seeks to encourage Jewish students on campus to explore and celebrate their Jewish identity.

offered, Kosher food, available Jewish studies programs or classes, and a general overview of Jewish campus life.

*Hillel Campus Report.* Free monthly enewsletter that highlights Jewish life on campus.

**Scholarships and Financial Aid Resources** (click on On Campus). Information on organizations that provide financial aid to Jewish students.

# Hispanic Association of Colleges and Universities

www.hacu.net

**Members.** Lists member schools.

Click on Student Resources to access the following resources:

**College Search.** Database of U.S. college programs searchable by state, major, and school type. Sponsored by CollegeView.com.

**National Internship Program.** Provides information on the Association's internship programs.

**Scholarship Program/Other Scholarship Resources.** Information on scholarship opportunities from the Association and other Hispanic-promoting organizations.

# Human Factors and Ergonomics Society

www.hfes.org

Click on Information for Students for the following resources:

**Directory of Human Factors/Ergonomics Graduate Programs in the United States and Canada.** Lists human factors/ergonomics graduate programs. Includes information on admission requirements, tuition and fees, financial assistance, curriculum, degree requirements, and faculty.

**Human Factors/Ergonomics Undergraduate Programs.** Lists programs in the United States.

**How to Find a Job in Industry.** Includes information on the top three elements for job success in the field: educational achievements, internship experience, and networking. The educational achievements section provides a detailed look at the benefits of pursuing a graduate degree, recommended courses outside the major, and creating a career "road map."

# Idaho Fish and Game

http://fishandgame.idaho.gov/apps/employment/career.cfm

**Planning a Career in Fish and Wildlife Management and Related Fields of Natural Resource Conservation.** Provides information and advice on high school and college preparation, planning your major, graduate training, and career options.

# Industrial Designers Society of America (IDSA)

**www.idsa.org**

**ID Programs** (click on About ID). Lists undergraduate and graduate industrial design programs in the United States and Canada that have been accredited by the National Association of Schools of Art and Design. Includes contact information and type of degree offered.

**Undergraduate/Graduate Scholarships** (click on Resources). Information on financial aid provided by the IDSA.

**Student Mentor Directory** (click on About ID). This directory contains the names of 350 IDSA members who have offered to serve as mentors to industrial design students and young workers in the field.

**Did You Know?**
Median annual earnings for industrial designers were $56,550 in 2007, according to the U.S. Department of Labor. Employment is expected to grow about as fast as the average for all careers through 2016.

# Institute for Operations Research and the Management Sciences

**www.informs.org** (click on Education/Student Union)

**Is a Career in OR/MS Right for You?** (click on Career Center/Career Booklet). Answers FAQs such as What exactly is operations research/management science?, What sorts of skills do operations researchers need?, and Where can you get the preparation you need?

**Operations Research/Management Sciences Educational Programs.** Lists U.S. and international educational programs.

# Institute for Supply Management

**www.ism.ws**

Click on Education, Seminars, and Conferences/Scholastic Opportunities to access the following resources:

**Colleges and Universities Offering Purchasing/Supply Management Courses.** Lists U.S. schools that offer classes, programs, and degrees related to supply management.

**Scholarships Offered by Affiliates, Groups, and Forums.** Provides information on outside providers that offers financial aid to high school and college students.

**R. Gene Richter Scholarship Program for Undergraduate Students.** A scholarship program for college seniors.

Additional resources:

**Careers in Purchasing and Supply Management** (click on Membership/Careers). Features information on educational requirements and career paths in the field.

**Career Q&A** (click on Membership/Students and Educators/Students). Answers questions such as What non-academic skills are important to your organization?, What experience in part-time jobs or internships do you consider useful?, What extracurricular activities in college do you value?, and How important is an MBA in supply management?

# Institute of Electrical and Electronics Engineers Computer Society

**www.computer.org**

**Careers in Computer Science and Computer Engineering** (click on Career Development & Information/College & Career Information). Information for students interested in majoring in computer science in college, including educational requirements and college curriculum, suggested extracurricular activities, and information on scholarships.

# Institute of Electrical and Electronics Engineers

**www.ieee.org/organizations/eab/precollege/careerprep**

**Getting Started.** Provides a list of suggested coursework and personal skills for high school students interested in careers in electrical, electronics, and computer engineering. Also includes information on student competitions.

**Pre-University Careers Guide.** Provides a variety of resources, including links to engineering websites and lists of recommended classes and personal skills for those interested in electrical and electronics engineering.

# Institute of Food Technologists (IFT)

**www.ift.org** (click on Education)

**Approved Undergraduate Programs.** Lists U.S. and international colleges that have food science/technology departments or programs that meet the IFT Undergraduate Education Standards for Degrees in Food Science.

**Graduate Program Directory.** Provides a list of more than 40 universities in the United States and Canada that offer food science graduate programs. Information includes entrance requirements, type of programs, and costs and financial aid.

> ## Educational Requirements
> To enter this field, you will need at least a bachelor's degree in food technology, food science, or food engineering. Forty-five college programs have been approved by the Institute of Food Technologists.

**Culinary Schools.** List of U.S. and international culinary schools. (Note: These programs have not been approved by the IFT Committee on Higher Education).

**IFT Scholarships.** Provides information on more than 100 scholarships available to high school seniors and undergraduate and graduate students.

# Institute of Industrial Engineers

**www.iienet.org**

**Accreditation** (click on Education). Provides link to a list of U.S. and international bachelor's degree programs in industrial engineering that are accredited by the Accreditation Board for Engineering and Technology.

**Scholarships and Fellowships** (click on Community/Student Center). Lists undergraduate and graduate scholarships and other financial aid offered by the Institute.

# Institute of Internal Auditors

www.theiia.org/guidance/academic-relations/iaaaf/iaep-schools

**Internal Auditing Education Partnership: List of Participating Schools.** Lists endorsed graduate internal auditing schools in the United States, China, France, Italy, Malaysia, the Netherlands, South Africa, Thailand, and the United Kingdom.

# Institute of Real Estate Management (IREM)

www.irem.org

**Careers in Real Estate Management** (www.irem.org/pdfs/ iremfoundation/cinfo1.pdf). Provides information on career options, suggested college courses, business administration degrees, and financial aid.

**GetRealGetReady.org.** IREM sister site that offers comprehensive information on careers, educational training, and scholarships. A real estate college degree search database is also available.

**Scholarships and Grants** (click on Education). Information on financial aid for undergraduates and graduate students studying real estate management.

# Institute of Transportation Engineers

www.ite.org/career/index.asp

**The Transportation Profession.** Details career options and educational requirements for aspiring transportation engineers.

# Instrumentation, Systems, and Automation Society

www.isa.org (click on Careers)

**Education: What You Will Need.** Details educational requirements for careers in engineering, design, sales engineering, management, and other automation and control careers.

**Steps You Can Take Now.** Presents ways high school students can prepare for study and careers in the field.

**Educational Institutions.** Lists U.S. and international two- and four-year colleges accredited by the Accreditation Board for Engineering and Technology.

**Scholarships.** Lists undergraduate and graduate scholarships offered by the Society.

# Interior Design Educators Council

**www.idec.org**

**Interior Design and Related Undergraduate Programs** (click on Students/Undergraduate Student). Lists programs in the United States

# International Association of Administrative Professionals

**www.iaap-hq.org/researchtrends/research_trends.htm**

**What Type of Educational Degree is Most Valuable to Administrative Professionals?** Tips for students and career changers who are interested in exploring education options for administrative support workers.

**Should You Go Back to School?** Lists questions to ask yourself if you are thinking of going back to school.

# International City/County Management Association

**http://icma.org/nextgen/?bcr=2**

**Local Government Management: It's the Career for You!**Provides answers to FAQs such as What does a local government manager do?, What courses will best prepare me for a career in local government management?, and What other qualifications are needed?

**Find Internships & Fellowships.** Provides a list of internships and fellowships for college students.

# International Council on Hotel, Restaurant & Institutional Education

**www.chrie.org** (click on About I-CHRIE/Accreditation)

**ACPHA-Accredited Institutions.** Lists bachelor's degree programs in hospitality management accredited by the Accreditation Commission for Programs in Hospitality Administration.

**CAHM-Accredited Institutions.** Lists associate degree programs in hospitality management accredited by the Commission for Accreditation of Hospitality Management Programs.

# International Facility Management Association (IFMA) Foundation

www.ifmafoundation.org/scholarships/degree.cfm

**Recognized Degree Programs.** Lists IFMA-approved baccalaureate and graduate degree programs in facility management in the United States, The Netherlands, United Kingdom, Austria, and Hong Kong.

# International Game Developers Association

www.igda.org/breakingin

**Breaking In: Preparing For Your Career in Games.** The Career Paths section provides an overview of the many careers available to students interested in game development. Developer Profiles presents nearly 50 useful interviews with workers in the field who discuss their career paths and recommend skills and educational paths for aspiring game developers. The Resources section features a list of degree-granting programs and courses in game development at U.S. and international colleges and universities.

# International Society of Women Airline Pilots

www.iswap.org

**Tips on Becoming an Airline Pilot in the United States** (click on Resources/Tips). Features information for aspiring women pilots on military and civilian training, as well as recommendations for breaking into the field.

**Scholarship.** Information on financial aid offered by the Society.

# Joint Commission on Allied Health Personnel in Ophthalmology (JCAHPO)

www.jcahpo.org

**Training Programs** (click on Education). Lists accredited programs for aspiring ophthalmic medical technicians/technologists and clinical medical assistants in the United States, Canada, and throughout the world.

**My Eye Career . . . A Guide to New Careers in Ophthalmic Assisting** (click on JCAHPO Store/Free Publications). Information on careers, educational requirements, and certification.

# Joint Review Committee on Educational Programs in Nuclear Medicine Technology

www.jrcnmt.org

**Accredited Programs.**
Directory of accredited nuclear medicine technology programs in the United States. Each listing includes information on entrance requirements, program length, and type of program.

> **> Did You Know?**
> Approximately 16 million nuclear medicine imaging and therapeutic procedures are performed annually in the United States, according to the Society of Nuclear Medicine.

# Junior Engineering Technical Society

www.jets.org

*The Pre-Engineering Times* (click on News/Newsletter). Monthly newsletter (from September to May) that offers information on engineering careers (such as forensics technology, fire investigation, and sports engineering) colleges and universities, and industry trends.

**Explore Engineering** (click on What We Do/Explore). Useful resource to help people learn about career options in engineering. Sections include Find Your Dream Job (which provides information on more than 40 engineering specialties); Extreme Engineer Profiles (which introduces readers to actual engineers in a variety of specialties); Why Engineering? (which provides 10 excellent reasons to enter the field); and Make It Happen (which offers information on recommended high school classes, tips on choosing between a career in engineering or engineering technology,

## FYI

Some of the most popular engineering disciplines include aerospace, agricultural, architectural, bio/biomedical, chemical, civil, computer software, electrical, environmental, industrial, manufacturing, mechanical, metallurgy and materials, mineral and mining, nuclear, ocean, and transportation engineering.

and a link to a list of accredited engineering schools).

**Experience Engineering** (click on What We Do/Experience). Information on competitions and challenges for aspiring engineers.

**The Uninitiates' Introduction to Engineering Program** (click on What We Do/UNITE). Summer college-based program for aspiring engineering students.

**Next Generation Scholarship Fund** (click on What We Do/Scholarship). Scholarship that is available to high school seniors who plan to "pursue an engineering career in a field related to electric power generation (for example, chemical engineering, electrical engineering, nuclear engineering, mechanical engineering, or materials engineering)."

## Law School Admission Council (LSAC)

**www.lsac.org**

Click on Thinking About Law School to access the following resources:

**Getting Started.** Answers FAQs about the field such as How do I prepare for a law school education?, What does a legal education cover?, How can I find out about law schools?, and How do I choose a law school?

**LSAT/LSDAS Checklist.** A checklist of tasks for students preparing to study law. Helps students plan for and take the Law School Admissions Test.

**Think About Law School.** Provides an overview of legal education, typical law school curricula, and choosing a school.

**Official Guide to ABA-Approved Law Schools.** Lists U.S. and Canadian law schools approved by the American Bar Association. Searchable by tuition, geographic region, employment of graduates, undergraduate GPA, and other criteria. Comprehensive information on enrollment, curriculum, faculty, library and physical facilities, admissions, financial aid, and student activities is provided for each institution.

**The Juris Doctor Degree.** Provides an overview of the degree, including typical curriculum and extracurricular activities.

**Preparing for Law School.** Offers advice on getting ready to attend law school, including recommendations regarding undergraduate preparation.

Click on Choosing a Law School to access the following resources:

**Assessing Yourself Realistically.** Tips on choosing a law school that matches your personality, interests, and professional goals.

**Resources for the Prelaw Candidate.** A detailed bibliography of useful books categorized under the following categories: Law School and Legal Education, Legal Profession, Biography, Jurisprudence and Legal Issues, and Financing Law School.

Other useful resources in this section include Evaluating Law Schools, Ranking Law Schools, Links Related to Legal Education, and Canadian Law Schools.

Click on Applying to Law School to access the following resources:

**The Law School Admission Process: What to Expect.** Offers advice for students planning to apply to law school.

**The Admission Process.** Sections include Rolling Admission, Applying to More Than One School, The Preliminary Review of an Application, and Waiting Lists.

Click on Financing Law School to access the following resources:

**Financing a Legal Education Video/Brochure.** Features advice from law students about the application process.

**Financial Aid Options.** An overview of types of financial aid and related resources for law school students.

Also available from the LSAC:

**Official Guide to Canadian Law Schools.** Comprehensive guide to legal education in Canada.

# LibraryCareers.org

### www.librarycareers.org

LibraryCareers.org is sponsored by the American Library Association.

**Oh, The Places You Will Go.** Details the types of work settings (academic, public, school, and public libraries) and career options (library assistants, librarians, library directors, etc.) for library professionals.

**What You Need to Know.** Provides an overview of educational and career requirements for various library careers and advice on choosing a library school.

**Getting a Little Help Along the Way.** Provides information on professional associations, scholarships and other types of financial aid, and finding a job.

# LifeWorks: Explore Health and Medical Science Careers

### http://science.education.nih.gov/LifeWorks.nsf/feature

LifeWorks is sponsored by the National Institutes of Health.

**Prepare for College Early.** Offers specialized information for students in grades eight through 12.

**Explore Careers.** Provides comprehensive coverage of more than 100 careers in the health and medical sciences—ranging from art therapist and chemical technician to oral and maxillofacial surgeon and speech-language pathologist. Users can search for careers that match their interests via an alphabetical list, by education required, interest area (artistic, conventional, enterprising, investigative, realistic, and social), or by median salary. Includes information on educational requirements (recommended high school courses and college degree requirements).

**Career Finder.** Self-assessment test that helps match student interests with careers.

# Linguistic Society of America

### www.lsadc.org

**Directory of Programs and Departments** (click on Resources). Alphabetical list of colleges and university linguistics programs in the United States and Canada. Includes information on available degrees, department emphasis, and special resources and facilities.

**Guide to Choosing a Graduate School** (click on Resources/ Student Resources). Offers advice on choosing a linguistics program.

**FAQ: Why Major in Linguistics?** (click on Resources/Student Resources). Answers questions such as What is linguistics?, What will I study as a linguistics major?, and What opportunities will I have with a linguistics degree?

# LongTermCareEducation.com

**www.longtermcareeducation.com**

**Colleges Offering Coursework in Long Term Care Education** (click on Learn About the Field/College Coursework). Features a list of bachelor's and master's degree programs in nursing home administration.

**Explore a Career in Long Term Care Administration.** Provides information on career options as life care community administrators, nursing home administrators, and assisted living/residential care facility administrators.

# Lutheran Educational Conference of North America

**www.lutherancolleges.org** (click on For Students)

**Our Colleges.** Lists Lutheran colleges in the United States and Canada.

**Why a Lutheran College?** Provides statistically based reasons why attending a Lutheran college is a good choice.

**College Fairs.** Lists Lutheran college fairs.

**Profiles.** Features profiles of students and faculty at Lutheran colleges.

**Planning for College.** Sections include Questions to Ask, Your Personal Essay, The Right Classes, Recommended Reading, Will I Be Challenged?, and Will I Make Friends?

**Career Preparation.** Sections include What is a Liberal Arts Education?, Employers Seek Liberal Arts Skills, and Long Live the Liberal Arts!

# Make a Difference: Discover a Career in Healthcare Management!

www.healthmanagementcareers.com

**Make a Difference: Discover a Career in Health Care Management.** This website from the American College of Healthcare Executives provides an overview of career options in the field. The Getting Started section offers information on undergraduate and graduate options for aspiring health care executives, advice on what types of health care administration degrees to pursue, and links to accredited programs.

# Marine Science Institute

www.sfbaymsi.org/career.htm

**Career Planning in Marine Science.** Discusses education and research career options for students interested in studying marine science. Includes information on educational requirements, personal skills, and employment prospects.

# MassageTherapy.com

www.massagetherapy.com/careers

**Your Massage & Bodywork Career.** Provides information on career options and educational requirements for massage therapists.

**Choosing the Right Program.** Provides helpful advice on picking a massage therapy education program including information on financial aid.

**Schools and Training Programs.** Directory of massage therapy training programs by U.S. state. A search criteria for distance education is also featured.

# Measuring the World Around Us: A High-Tech Career in Professional Surveying

www.surveyingcareer.com

**Becoming a Surveyor.** Covers educational requirements and includes links to accredited surveying training programs.

# Medical Library Association

www.mlanet.org/career/
career_explore.html

**Tip Sheet for Teens.** Offers advice to high school students on what they can do to prepare for college and a career as a medical librarian.

**Tip Sheet for College Students.** Details educational paths, suggested courses, scholarships, and graduate school options for those interested in the field.

**Medical Librarianship: A Career Beyond the Cutting Edge and Medical Librarians: Part of the Health Care Team!** Offers detailed information on the career of medical librarian, including work settings, job duties, minimum educational requirements, and earnings. (These two publications are also available in Spanish-language versions.)

**Mentoring.** Online feature that allows students to receive advice from professional medical librarians.

**Library Schools.** Lists American Library Association-accredited health sciences librarianship educational programs in the United States and Canada.

**Tip Sheet for Graduate Students and Career Changers.** Provides advice for entering the field.

**Scholarship and Grants** (www.mlanet.org/students). Provides information on financial aid for graduate students—including those from minority backgrounds.

> ## FYI
>
> *Medical librarians* link people to health information. They work in libraries and information resource centers at colleges and universities, hospitals, corporations, government agencies, and other places where health information is disseminated. According to Salary.com, medical librarians earned salaries that ranged from less than $39,049 to $64,198 or more in 2008.

# MENC: The National Association for Music Education

www.menc.org (click on Career Center)

**Careers in Music.** Nicely presented online brochure that details career opportunities, personal skills, and recommended precollege and college training for the following areas: music education, instrumental performance, vocal performance, conducting, composing, music for worship, music business, instrument making and repair, music publishing, music communications, the recording industry, the television and radio industry, music technology, music librarianship, music therapy, and performing arts medicine.

**What it Takes To Be a Music Major.** Provides personal and creative qualities that are intrinsic to success as a music major. Also provides a list of recommended experiences for high school students planning to study music in college.

## The Minerals, Metals & Materials Society (TMS)

www.crc4mse.org/resources/colleges.html

**Materials Science & Engineering: College Programs.** Lists ceramics, materials, and metallurgical programs in the United States and Canada.

Information on **undergraduate and graduate scholarships** and other awards offered by the TMS can be accessed by visiting www.tms.org/Students/AwardsPrograms/Scholarships.html.

## Music Library Association

www.musiclibraryassoc.org/employmentanded/index.shtml

**Music Librarianship: Is It For You?** Details career and educational information for aspiring music librarians.

**Directory of Library School Offerings in Music Librarianship.** Lists programs in the United States and Canada. Includes an overview of the program, degrees offered, and information on distance learning.

## National Academy of Elder Law Attorneys

www.naela.org

**Law School Programs** (click on Professionals/Law Students). Lists U.S. law schools that offer programs or classes in elder law.

# National Accrediting Agency for Clinical Laboratory Sciences (NAACLS)

www.naacls.org/student-center

**Find a Program.** Directory of NAACLS-accredited programs searchable by type, program name, state, and zip code. Accredited programs include clinical assistant, cytogenetic technologist, clinical laboratory scientist/medical technologist, clinical laboratory technician/medical laboratory technician, diagnostic molecular scientist, histotechnician, histotechnologist, pathologists' assistant, and phlebotomist.

**Scholarships.** The website has links to scholarships offered by other science-related organizations.

# National Aeronautics and Space Administration

www.nasa.gov/astronauts/recruit.html

**Astronaut Selection and Training.** Provides information on astronaut selection, including educational and training requirements.

# National Association for Business Economics

www.nabe.com/publib/careers02.pdf

**Careers in Business Economics.** Comprehensive publication on careers in business economics. Includes detailed information on educational requirements and pathways, including a recommended course of study for a master's degree in business economics. (Note: You must register at the website to download this publication.)

# National Association for Drama Therapy (NADT)

www.nadt.org

**NADT-Approved Drama Therapy Master Degree Programs** (click on Education). Lists programs in the United States and Canada. Also includes a list of schools that offer alternative training opportunities.

> **> Did You Know?**
> Drama therapists are employed in schools, hospitals, mental health facilities, community centers, substance abuse treatment centers, nursing homes, corporations, after-school settings, shelters, adolescent group homes, medical schools, theaters, and in private practice.

# National Association for Law Placement (NALP)

### www.nalplawschoolsonline.org

**Directory of Law Schools.** Database of law schools in the United States. Searchable by law school name, city, state, region, fields of study, areas of practice, and other categories.

# National Association of Advisors for the Health Professions (NAAHP)

### www.naahp.org

**Abstracts On-line.** Online abstracts from its journal, *The Advisor,* are informative and well organized. You can browse articles in categories such as medical profession trends, concerns for students with learning disabilities, choosing a career, MCAT testing, and more. Though this site is aimed at health advisors, the information is just as applicable to the student interested in learning more about the health professions and college preparation.

**Finding an Advisor.** Information on how college students interested in careers in medicine can benefit by using a health professions advisor. Provides answers to the following questions: Who are health professions advisors?, How can a health professions advisor help you?, Who can be aided by a health professions advisor?, and How can you find a health professions advisor?

# National Association of Chain Drug Stores (NACDS)

### www.nacds.org

**Pharmacy: Your Prescription for Success in the Health Care Industry** (click on Pharmacy/Consider Pharmacy as a Career). Features the following sections: What It Means to Be a Pharmacist, Learn More About a Career in Pharmacy, Pharmacy School Admission Requirements, Pharmacy College Application Service, U.S. Schools and Colleges of Pharmacy, and Careers in Pharmacy: Berlex 2003 Student Guide Book.

**Scholarships and Student Resources** (click on Pharmacy/Scholarships). Provides information on the NACDS Foundation Pharmacy Student Scholarship Program, other financial aid, and internships.

# National Association of Clinical Nurse Specialists

www.nacns.org/cnsdirectory.shtml

**Directory of U.S. Clinical Nurse Specialist Programs.**
Microsoft Excel database of educational programs.

# National Association of College Admissions Counseling (NACAC)

www.nacacnet.org/MemberPortal/ForStudents

**NACAC National College Fairs.** Information on college fairs, dates, and exhibitors.

*Steps to College.* Online newsletter that covers a wide range of issues, such as considering an honors program, tips for parents of college-bound students, scholarship advice, and more. You can browse by issue or topic. New stories are added several times a school year—in September, November, January, March, and May.

**Prep for College Calendar** (click on College Preparation). Useful calendars for high school freshmen, sophomores, juniors, and seniors planning for college.

**Publications for Students.** Information on NACAC print and online publications, some of which are available for free download. Free online publications include *What Parents and Students Should Know About Independent Counselors, Educational Consultants,* and *Commercial Counseling Centers and Definitions of Options in Higher Education.*

> **Did You Know?**
> According to the National Association of College Admissions Counseling, nonacademic "tip" factors that play a role in admissions include the admissions interview, extracurricular activities, work history, and demonstrated interest.

**Statement of Students' Rights and Responsibilities.**
Information for students before they apply, as they apply, when they are offered admission, if they are placed on a wait or alternate list, and after they receive their admissions decisions. Also available in Spanish.

**Which College Admission Process Best Suits You?** Provides information on regular decision, rolling admission, early action, early decision, and restrictive early action.

Additionally, at the NACAC's home page (www.nacacnet.org) click on Products and Services/Publications to access the following resources:

**Countdown to College: Tips for Parents With Middle School Teens.** Offers college-planning advice to parents of children in grades six through eight. Includes advice on activities at home, recommended classes, standardized tests, identifying career interests, and financial planning for college.

**Countdown to College: Tips for Parents With High School Teens.** Offers college-planning advice to parents of children in high school. Includes advice on recommended classes, college entrance exams and practice tests, searching for a college, the college application process, and financial planning for college.

# National Association of Dental Laboratories

**www.nadl.org/educational_institutions.cfm**

**Education Institutions.** Lists dental laboratory technology schools in the United States.

# National Association of Independent Colleges and Universities (NAICU)

**www.naicu.edu**

**Member Directory** (click on Member Center). Directory of NAICU-member schools listed alphabetically. Member schools include liberal arts colleges, research universities, faith-based institutions, black colleges and universities, colleges for women, performing and visual arts schools, two-year institutions, and schools of business, engineering, law, medicine, and other disciplines.

**Independent Colleges and Universities: A National Profile** (click on Publications/Publications Order Form/PDF). Offers sections on minority students, college costs, financial aid and scholarship options, and facts and figures about colleges and universities across the country.

**Twelve Facts That May Surprise You About America's Private Colleges and Universities** (click on Publications). Details surprising facts (i.e., most of the financial aid undergraduates receive at private colleges and universities is based on financial need) about U.S. private schools. The brochure's three sections (Affordable, Diverse, and Successful) present useful text, graphs, and pie charts to support the 12 Facts.

# National Association of Independent Schools

**www.nais.org** (click on Admission & Financial Aid)

**School Search.** Database of independent colleges and universities in the United States and abroad. Searchable by school name, city, state/province, school type, student type, religious affiliation, and other criteria.

**Admissions Facts for Families.** Touts the benefits of attending an independent school and a list of questions to ask when choosing a college.

**Financial Aid Facts for Parents.** Information on need-based financial aid and merit awards.

**School and Student Service (SSS) for Financial Aid.** The SSS is "used by more than 2,400 K-12 schools and organizations across the country to help assess a family's ability to pay for independent education."

# National Association of Intercollegiate Athletics

**http://naia.cstv.com/member-services/attend.htm**

**A Guide For the College-Bound Athlete.** Features information on financial aid, eligibility regulations, and the advantages of competing as an Association athlete.

**A Guide For Students Transferring from Two-Year Institutions.** Offers information on eligibility regulations, financial assistance policies, and recruitment policies.

Visit naia.cstv.com/member-services/about/members.htm to access the following resource:

**Member Institutions.** Lists the nearly 300 colleges and universities that are members of the Association. Schools are listed alphabetically, by state, and by athletic conference.

# National Association of Judiciary Interpreters and Translators

www.najit.org

**Frequently Asked Questions About the Field of Judiciary Interpretation and Translation.** Provides answers to FAQs about the field including What is the difference between interpretation and translation?, How does one study to become a judiciary interpreter?, and Which languages are most in demand?

**Links to Related Websites and Resources.** Provides links to college-level interpreting and translation programs.

## FYI

Legal assistants are also known as paralegals. There are approximately 238,000 paralegals and legal assistants employed in the United States, according to the U.S. Department of Labor.

# National Association of Legal Assistants

www.nala.org/whatis.htm

**Evaluating Paralegal Programs.** Details nine points to consider when choosing a paralegal educational program.

**Educational Programs.** Provides an overview of the most common type of educational programs for paralegals.

## National Association of Neonatal Nurses

www.nann.org/edu_jobs/jobs/index.html

**A Career in Neonatal Nursing.** Provides answers to questions such as What is it like to be a neonatal nurse?, How do I prepare to be a neonatal nurse?, and What can I expect as a neonatal nurse.

**Neonatal Nurse Career Path Scholarship.** Provides information on a scholarship for college neonatal nursing students provided by OVATION Pharmaceuticals.

## National Association of Pediatric Nurse Practitioners

www.napnap.org

**Pediatric Nurse Practitioner School List** (click on Education/For Students/PNP Programs Information). Lists U.S. schools that offer pediatric nurse practitioner training.

# National Association of Professional Band Instrument Repair Technicians

**www.napbirt.org** (click on Resources/Repair Schools)

**Repair Schools.** Lists colleges in the U.S. and Canada that offer training in musical instrument repair. Also includes an overview of job duties, educational paths, and advice on choosing a school.

# National Association of School Psychologists

**www.nasponline.org**

Click on Students to access the following resources:

**List of NASP-Approved Programs.** Lists school psychology graduate programs in the United States.

**School Psychology Training Program Information.** Provides detailed information on school psychology graduate programs in the United States.

**Minority Scholarship Program.** Offers information on the Association's financial aid program for minority students at the master's level.

Click on About School Psychology/Become a School Psychologist to access the following resources:

**A Career in School Psychology: Selecting a Master's, Specialist, or Doctoral Degree Program That Meets Your Needs** (click on Student Fact Sheets). Provides tips on assessing your career goals, defines degree types and designations (as well as presents the advantages and disadvantages of each degree), and provides references and suggested readings.

**Frequently Asked Questions.** Provides general information about training and employment in school psychology and answers to questions about the field, including What do school psychologists do?, What education is required?, How do I select a good school psychology training program?, and Will I be admitted to a school psychology program if my undergraduate major was in another field like English?

**Becoming a School Psychologist.** Information on selecting a school, levels of training/degrees awarded, admissions requirements and deadlines, and financial assistance.

**Who Are School Psychologists?** Provides an overview of educational requirements and career options for school psychologists.

**School Psychology: A Career That Makes a Difference.** Provides an overview of the career, including information on educational and training requirements, job duties, necessary personal skills, and work settings.

*An art teacher instructs a student. (Photo courtesy of Comstock)*

# National Association of Schools of Art and Design (NASAD)

http://nasad.arts-accredit.org

**FAQ: Students, Parents, Public.** Provides answers to frequently asked questions about accreditation, applying to art and design schools, and preparing to major in art or design.

**Member Lists.** Database of NASAD-accredited schools of art and design. Searchable by institution name, city, and state.

## National Association of Schools of Dance (NASD)

http://nasd.arts-accredit.org

**FAQ: Students, Parents, Public.** Provides answers to frequently asked questions about accreditation, applying to dance schools, and preparing to major in dance.

**Member Lists.** Database of NASD-accredited schools of dance. Searchable by institution name, city, and state.

## National Association of Schools of Music (NASM)

http://nasm.arts-accredit.org

**FAQ: Students, Parents, Public.** Provides answers to frequently asked questions about accreditation, applying to music schools, and preparing to major in music.

**Member Lists.** Database of NASM-accredited schools of music. Searchable by institution name, city, and state.

# National Association of Schools of Public Affairs and Administration (NASPAA)

**www.naspaa.org**

**FAQ.** Includes answers to questions about pursuing a graduate degree in public administration (MPA) or public policy (MPP). Questions include Is a graduate degree a worthwhile investment?, Why should my graduate degree be an MPA/MPP?, What types of undergraduate students pursue an MPA/MPP degree?, What are the admissions criteria for an MPA or an MPP program?, and Should I choose a NASPAA-accredited MPA or MPP program?

**Find a Graduate School.** Database of graduate programs in the United States offering programs in public administration, public policy, and related disciplines. Searchable by state, type of degree, specialization, and accreditation status. A program summary is provided that includes an overview of the university and graduate program, degrees offered, tracks or specializations, and admission requirements.

**Undergraduate Programs** (click on For Students/Find a Graduate School). Lists NASPAA-member schools that offer bachelor's degrees in public administration.

**Financial Assistance** (click on Careers and Resources). Links to information on loans, scholarships, grants, and other financial aid for students.

**PublicServiceCareers.org.** This sister site features information on careers and undergraduate and graduate programs in public service.

# National Association of Schools of Theatre (NAST)

**http://nast.arts-accredit.org**

**FAQ: Students, Parents, Public.** Provides answers to frequently asked questions about accreditation, applying to theatre schools, and preparing to major in theatre.

**Member Lists.** Database of NAST-accredited schools of theatre. Searchable by institution name, city, and state.

## Did You Know?

Social workers are employed in public agencies, hospitals and mental hospitals, clinics, schools, courts, private businesses, elderly daycare programs, nursing homes, private practices, police departments, and prisons.

# National Association of Social Workers (NASW)

https://www.socialworkers.org/students

**Social Work Profession Overview** (click on Careers). Includes information on career specialties, typical work responsibilities, and educational requirements.

**Scholarship Information.** Details graduate financial aid programs offered by the NASW Foundation.

# National Association of Student Personnel Administrators

www.naspa.org/gradprep

**Graduate Program Search.** Directory of U.S. graduate programs in student affairs administration. Searchable by state, keyword, and institution name. Information for each school includes a program description and degree options.

# National Association of Veterinary Technicians in America

www.navta.net/education/index.php

**Frequently Asked Questions.** Answers questions about educational requirements for veterinary technicians and veterinary assistants, scholarships, and employment prospects.

**AVMA-Accredited Distance Learning Program.** Provides contact information for distance learning programs in veterinary technology.

**Veterinary Technician Programs.** Lists veterinary technician programs in the United States and Canada that are accredited by the American Veterinary Medical Association.

# National Athletic Trainers' Association (NATA)

**www.nata.org/student**

Click on the link for high school students to access the following resources:

**Education.** Includes educational requirements and clinical education guidelines for students enrolled in accredited athletic training education programs.

**Accredited Athletic Training Programs.** Provides links to U.S. athletic training programs accredited by the Commission on Accreditation of Allied Health Education Programs.

**Jack Cramer Scholarship.** A scholarship for high school seniors planning to study athletic training in college.

Click on the link for college students to access the following resources:

**Athletic Training Career Information** (click on Become an Athletic Trainer/Career Information Brochure). Provides an overview of work settings (including secondary schools, colleges and universities, professional sports, sports medicine clinics, the military, and industrial and commercial) and information on educational requirements and financial aid.

**Undergraduate scholarship information** is also available from the NATA Research and Education Foundation (www. natafoundation.org/scholarship.html).

# National Auctioneers Association

**www.auctioneers.org/web/2007/06/education.aspx**

**Auction Schools.** A list of schools in the United States that offer training in auctioneering.

# National Center for Homeopathy

**http://homeopathic.org/resources/educational.jsp**

**Educational Directory.** Lists homeopathic training programs in the United States, Canada, and New Zealand.

## National Christian College Athletic Association

www.thenccaa.org

**Tips on Choosing a College** (click on Member Schools). Offers advice on choosing an academic institution from a Christ-based perspective.

**Member Schools.** Lists member colleges [small Christian colleges (Division I) and Bible colleges (Division II)] that offer sports programs. Unfortunately, the site does not provide links or contact information for these institutions.

## National Clearinghouse for Professions in Special Education

www.special-ed-careers.org/career_choices

**Career Profiles in Special Education.** Features information on 19 career options for people who major in special education, educational requirements, and classes and activities that will prepare students for the field.

**Getting Started.** Discusses educational paths for people interested in special education, whether they are high school students, recent college graduates, mid-career changers, or general education teachers.

**College and University Programs.** Database of more than 800 colleges and universities offering degree programs in special education. Searchable by type of degree, state, area of training, and institution name.

**Financial Aid to Become a Special Educator.** Information on financial aid options for special education students.

> **Did You Know?**
In 2003-04, only 2 percent of high school athletes received scholarships to play at the collegiate level, according to the National Collegiate Athletic Association.

## National Collegiate Athletic Association (NCAA)

www.ncaa.org

**Diversity & Inclusion** (click on about the NCAA). Information about diversity programs, gender equity (Title IX) task forces, research statistics, and scholarship opportunities at Division I, II, and III schools.

**Eligibility and Recruiting.** NCAA rules for student-athletes.

**Statistics.** Statistics for Division I-III NCAA sports.

*The NCAA News.* Online version of the NCAA's biweekly newspaper.

**Guide for the College-Bound Student-Athlete** (click on Academics and Athletes/Eligibility and Recruiting). Features detailed information about amateurism-eligibility requirements, academic-eligibility requirements, questions to ask when considering colleges, details for high school counselors and administrators, and information for parents and guardians.

**Scholarships & Internships** (click on Academics and Athletes/Education and Research). Provides information on athletic scholarships and internships.

**NCAAStudent.org.** Sister site that helps student-athletes find a balance between academics and sport.

## National Commission for Cooperative Education

**www.co-op.edu**

**About Co-Op.** An overview of cooperative education that will help students better understand the goals and possible benefits of co-op programs and decide if these programs might be right for them.

**Frequently Asked Questions.** Provides answers to questions about co-op education, including What are the chief benefits of co-op?, What if I don't have a major or career plan yet?, Will this extend my time in college?, and How do I pick a college with a good co-op program?

**Best of Co-Op Guide.** Lists participating community colleges, four-year institutions, and employers (such as Capital One, Hershey Foods, and Xerox Corporation) that participate in co-op programs.

> **FYI**
>
> Cooperative or "co-op" education combines college study with paid work experience in a related field.

**Annual Scholarships.** A scholarship for high school students who plan to attend one of the Commission's Partner Institutions (see the organization's website for a complete list).

# National Commission on Orthotic and Prosthetic Education

**www.ncope.org**

**Fitter Education.** Lists orthotic fitter educational programs in the United States.

**Accredited Schools.** Provides information on orthotic and prosthetic practitioner and technician training programs in the United States.

# National Conference of Gerontological Nurse Practitioners

**https://www.ncgnp.org/gnp-academic-programs.html**

**GNP Academic Programs.** Lists gerontological nurse practitioner educational programs in the United States.

*An elementary school teacher shows a bird's nest to her students. Employment of teachers at this level is expected to grow faster than the average for all careers through 2016, according to the U.S. Department of Labor. (Photo courtesy of PhotosToGo)*

# National Council for Accreditation of Teacher Education (NCATE)

**www.ncate.org** (click on Public)

**FAQs about Careers in Education.** Provides answers to FAQs such as What is the benefit of attending an NCATE-accredited college of education?; How do I discover which schools are best for me?; I want to be a teacher, but cannot afford college tuition; and How do I get a loan, grant, or scholarship to a college?

**Why Attend an Accredited School?** Touts the benefits of attending an accredited school of education.

**What to Look for in a Teacher Preparation Program.** Provides a list of questions to ask when choosing a program.

**NCATE-Accredited Schools, Colleges, and Departments of Education** (click on Accredited Institutions). A searchable database of undergraduate colleges and universities that offer education training programs. Includes list of majors offered and education level available.

**Financial Aid Resources.** Provides information on outside sources of financial aid.

## National Council for Science and the Environment

http://ncseonline.org/o2education

**University Affiliate Program.** List of 150 member institutions.

**EnvironMentors!** Mentorship program that prepares high school students from underrepresented backgrounds for college programs in environmental and related science fields.

The Society for Conservation Biology, a sister organization of the NCSE, offers an international directory of **Academic Programs in Conservation Biology.** Program listings include information on degrees offered, program specializations, and faculty. The directory can be accessed in English, Spanish, Portuguese, French, and Chinese. To access this directory, visit www.conbio.org/SCB/Services/Programs.

## National Council on Education for the Ceramic Arts

www.nceca.net/resources/programd.html

**U.S. Ceramic Education Programs Database.** List of U.S. colleges and universities that offer degrees in ceramics. Available in Microsoft Excel and Adobe Acrobat formats.

## National Court Reporters Association (NCRA)

www.ncraonline.org

**Certified Schools** (click on Education/Schools and Programs). Lists approved court reporting educational programs in the U.S. and Canada.

> **Did You Know?**
> To graduate from a court reporting school, students must perform machine shorthand at a speed of at least 225 words per minute.

**Trends and Analysis** (click on Education/Schools and Programs). An interesting overview of court reporting educational programs and the students who attend them.

**Scholarship & Grant Information** (click on Foundation). Details financial aid for current court reporting students from the NCRA and the National Court Reporters Foundation. Includes awards for students with disabilities.

Additional information on careers and education can be obtained by reading **Careers in Court Reporting and Broadcast Captioning,** a sister website from the NCRA. It can be accessed by visiting www.bestfuture.com.

*A paralegal manages documents in a law office. (Photo courtesy of Photos.com)*

# National Federation of Paralegal Associations (NFPA)

**www.paralegals.org**

**What is a Paralegal?** (click on CLE/Getting Started). Covers job responsibilities, educational requirements, work settings, and earnings.

**How To Choose a Particular School?** (click on CLE/Getting Started). Offers information on choosing a paralegal education program, including the following online resources: Suggested Curriculum for Paralegal Studies, A Guide to Quality Paralegal Education, and How To Choose a Paralegal Program.

## National Funeral Directors Association

**www.nfda.org** (click on About Funeral Service/Funeral Career Center)

**Exploring a Career in Funeral Service.** Includes an overview of the career, educational requirements, and the funeral service educational curriculum.

**Mortuary Science Programs.** Lists accredited U.S. mortuary science education programs. Includes program type and information on distance education options.

**Baccalaureate Completion Programs.** Information for students and current funeral professionals interested in pursuing a bachelor's degree in mortuary science.

Includes answers to Frequently Asked Questions, a Step-By-Step Guide for Adults Planning to Return to College, Mortuary Science Schools Offering On-Campus Baccalaureate Degrees, and Directories of Online Baccalaureate Degree Programs.

**Funeral Service Scholarships.** Details financial aid available for funeral service students.

# National Junior College Athletic Association (NJCAA)

**www.njcaa.org**

**Find Your College** (click on Membership). Lists member junior colleges by geographical region, state, college name, and sport.

Click on Forms/Eligibility to access the following resources:

**Prospective Student-Athlete Brochure.** Information for athletes planning to attend NJCAA schools.

**Eligibility Rules Pamphlet.** Lists eligibility rules for NJCAA student athletes.

# National Junior Horticultural Association

**www.njha.org**

**Career Videos** (click on Careers). Videos that provide an overview of nine career options in the field.

A horticulturist (l) and plant pathologist study plants in a greenhouse. (Photo courtesy of Rob Flynn, USDA)

**University Departments** (click on Resources). List of U.S. colleges and universities that offer horticulture and related programs.

**Scholarships.** Information on financial aid for student members.

# National League for Nursing Accrediting Commission

**www.nlnac.org/Forms/directory_search.htm**

**Accredited Nursing Programs.** Database of nursing education programs in the U.S. and abroad. Searchable by degree level, state, country, and institution name.

# National Press Photographers Association

www.nppa.org/professional_development/students

**Photojournalism Education.** Advice on choosing a photojournalism education program, including financial considerations and locations.

**Scholarships and Foundation Information.** Details undergraduate and graduate scholarships for print and television photojournalism offered by the National Press Photographers Foundation.

**Getting Started in Photojournalism** (click on Entering the Job Market). Provides information on important personal qualities for success in the field, a discussion on the merits of professional education, and information on landing and succeeding in an internship.

# National Recreation and Park Association

www.nrpa.org

**Considering a Career in Parks and Recreation?** (use the site's Search feature to locate this document). Provides an overview of job duties and educational and training requirements for careers in recreation administration, commercial recreation/tourism management, natural resources/park management, and therapeutic recreation.

**Academic Accreditation** (click on Accreditation/Certification). Lists accredited U.S. undergraduate programs in leisure services management, natural resources recreation management, leisure/recreation program delivery, and therapeutic recreation.

**Master's Programs in Parks, Recreation Resources, and Leisure Studies** (click on Education & Conferences/Higher Education). Lists master's programs in the United States and Canada.

**Doctoral Programs in Parks, Recreation Resources, and Leisure Studies** (click on Education & Conferences/Higher Education). Lists doctoral programs in the United States and Canada.

# National Restaurant Association

www.restaurant.org/careers/
education.cfm

**High School Hospitality Programs.** Information on the National Restaurant Association Educational Foundation's (NRAEF) ProStartr program, a restaurant and foodservice management study program at more than 1,100 schools in 45 states and territories.

**List of Culinary and Restaurant Schools.** Lists nearly 1,000 U.S. colleges and universities that offer restaurant or hospitality management education programs. Searchable by state.

**Scholarship Opportunities.** Lists scholarships for high school seniors and undergraduates offered by the NRAEF.

*There are countless opportunities available in the restaurant industry for people with all types of educational backgrounds. (Photo courtesy of Photos.com)*

# National Science Teachers Association

http://careers.nsta.org/advice.asp

**Planning a Career in Science Education.** Offers advice for students planning to enter the field, information on financial aid, and details on certification.

# National Society for Histotechnology

www.nsh.org (click on Student Center)

**Why Should I be a Histotechnologist?** Covers job duties and educational requirements for histotechnologists.

**Schools/Programs.** List histotechnology training programs in the United States, including those with online options.

**Scholarships.** Information on financial aid for college students who are studying histotechnology or a related field.

# National Society of Genetic Counselors

www.nsgc.org/career

**Become a Genetic Counselor.** Brochure that details career responsibilities and educational requirements.

**Graduate Training Programs in Genetic Counseling.** Directory of U.S. and international master's-level training programs in genetic counseling.

**How to Become A Genetic Counselor.** Offers advice on exploring educational programs, putting together a college application, interviewing for acceptance into a graduate program, and other topics.

Approximately 2.5 million registered nurses are employed in the United States. (Photo courtesy of Photos.com)

# National Student Nurses' Association (NSNA)

www.nsna.org/career/
ultimate_adventure.asp

**Nursing: The Ultimate Adventure.** Provides an overview of nursing today and answers frequently asked questions, including How do I apply to nursing school?, What is nursing school like?, and What are the educational pathways available to becoming a registered nurse?

**Is Nursing For You?** Details educational paths and personal and professional qualities needed to be successful in the field.

**Tips to Surviving Nursing School.** Ten tips from a nursing educator to help nursing students study more effectively.

**A Formula for Academic Success.** Advice from two experienced nurses on achieving academic success. Topics include time management, organization, and proper scheduling.

**Preparing for a Graduate Education in Nursing.** Details the benefits of pursuing graduate nursing education, including the wealth of career options available to nurses with advanced degrees.

Info on **scholarships and other financial aid** for enrolled nursing students is available at the Foundation of the NSNA's website, www.nsna.org/foundation.

# Newspaper Association of America

**www.naa.org/Resources.aspx** (click on Newspaper Careers/Career Resources)

**Newspaper Careers in Finance: Accounting Manager.** Provides info on job duties and educational requirements for the field.

**Newspaper Careers in Finance: Treasurer and Chief Financial Officer.** Provides info on job duties and educational requirements for the field.

> **Did You Know?**
> Reporters employed by newspaper, periodical, book, and directory publishers earned mean annual salaries of $40,420 in 2007, according to the U.S. Department of Labor.

# North American Society of Homeopaths (NASH)

**www.homeopathy.org/directory_entrance.html**

**School Directory.** Directory of NASH member schools in the U.S., Canada, and Spain.

# Nuclear Energy Institute

**www.nei.org** (click on Careers & Education)

**Education.** Alphabetical list (by region) of U.S. colleges and universities offering programs in nuclear technologies.

**Scholarships, Internships, and Fellowships.** Information on financial aid for aspiring nuclear science students.

# Nurses for a Healthier Tomorrow

**www.nursesource.org/career_info.html**

**Career Profiles.** Provides information on job duties, work settings, earnings, and educational requirements for 17 nursing specialties.

**The Nurse Career.** Presents an overview of nursing careers and answers FAQs such as How do I apply to nursing school?, What is nursing school like?, and What are the educational pathways to becoming a registered nurse?

## Nursing World

**www.nursingworld.org**

This site is sponsored by the American Nurses Association.

**About Nursing** (click on Careers & Credentialing). Offers an overview of nursing careers, educational requirements, and tips on funding your nursing education.

## Oncology Nursing Society (ONS)

**www.ons.org/ceCentral/education**

**Graduate Programs in Oncology Nursing.** Lists graduate programs in oncology nursing in the United States. Information provided for each school includes program type, type of specialty, clinical focus, education requirements, and distance education options.

**Educational Scholarships.** Information on bachelor's, master's, and doctoral scholarships offered by the ONS Foundation.

> **> Did You Know?**
> Optical engineers are employed by companies that produce robotic technology, fiber optics, laser technology, and electro-optics technology. Other employers include hospitals, laboratories, colleges and universities, and the construction and telecommunication industries.

## Optical Society of America/ International Society for Optical Engineering

**www.opticseducation.org**

**Optics Education: International Directory of Degree Programs in Optics.** Lists certificate, associate's, bachelor's, master's, and doctoral optics programs. Searchable by institution name, city, country, optics specialties, degrees offered, and tuition range. Information listed for each school includes department name, current enrollment, and type and description of degrees offered.

## Orthotics & Prosthetics: Make a Career of Making a Difference Everyday!

**www.opcareers.org**

This site is sponsored by the American Academy of Orthotists and Prosthetists. It is also available in Spanish.

**Education Pathways.** Provides information on certificate, bachelor's, master's, and doctorate programs and orthotics and prosthetics.

**O&P Education Programs.** Lists academic programs that prepare students for careers as technicians, assistants, fitters, pedorthists, and practitioners.

**FAQs.** Answers questions such as Where can I find information on careers and schooling in O&P? and What are my schooling options if I studied marketing in college? Had a masters in engineering? Have already been a registered nurse for five years?

**Scholarships.** Offers information on financial aid for college orthotic and prosthetic students.

# Perfusion Program Directors' Council

**www.perf-ed.org/cfm/listprograms.cfm**

**Perfusion Training Programs: United States and Canada.** Lists accredited perfusion education programs. Includes length of program and contact information.

# Pharmacist.com

**www.pharmacist.com**

Click on Careers/Student Resources to access the following resources:

**List of Pharmacy Schools.** List of undergraduate and graduate programs by state.

**Shall I Study Pharmacy?** Provides a wealth of information on pharmacy education and careers including work settings, personal requirements, recommended high school courses and activities, choosing a school, paying for school, and typical college curricula.

**Pharmacist Education.** Provides an overview of educational requirements for entry into the field.

**Preparing for the Pharmacy Admissions Process.** Provides an overview of types of educational programs (including distance learning), recommended high school courses, pharmacy school rankings, college course requirements, and admissions tests.

## Physician Assistant Education Association

www.paeaonline.org

**What Is a PA?** (click on For Applicants). Provides information on the career, details on the Central Application Service for Physician Assistants (where students can apply to the majority of accredited PA programs online), and answers to FAQs about the career and educational preparation.

**Physician Assistant Programs** (click on For Applicants). Database of physician assistant training programs in the United States.

## Population Association of America

www.popassoc.org (click on Publications)

**Careers in Population.** Lists colleges and universities in the United States, Canada, and Great Britain that offer population and demographic studies programs. Includes contact information and Web addresses. Also provides information on career options and educational requirements.

## Presbyterian Church (USA)

www.pcusa.org/navigation/ministryvocations.htm

**Preparing for Ministry.** Comprehensive information on preparing for the Presbyterian ministry.

**Presbyterian Seminaries.** Lists Presbyterian Church seminaries in the United States. Each school listing includes information on its history, mission, size, and degrees offered.

**Financial Aid for Students.** Information on undergraduate and graduate scholarships and other financial aid offered by the Presbyterian Church (USA).

## Printing Industries of America/ Graphic Arts Technical Foundation

www.gain.net

Click on Programs and Services/Education to access the following resources:

**Print and Graphics Scholarship Foundation Directory of Schools.** Lists technical schools, colleges, and universities that offer courses in graphic communications. Includes information on degrees awarded, curriculum, academic calendar, enrollment, faculty, and academic departments. Also includes a section on secondary and postsecondary schools accredited by PrintEd, the printing industry's national accreditation program.

**Print and Graphics Scholarship Foundation.** Information on undergraduate and graduate scholarships offered by the Foundation.

# SAE International

http://students.sae.org

**Choosing a College.** Presents a brief discussion of undergraduate educational options and lists colleges and universities in the United States that offer master's degrees in automotive and motorsports engineering.

**Scholarships and Loans.** Provides an overview of financial aid, including scholarship information for high school seniors, undergraduates, and graduate students.

# SNM

www.snm.org

**Careers in Nuclear Medicine** (click on Career Center). Provides detailed information on the careers of nuclear physician, nuclear medicine technologist, nuclear pharmacist, and nuclear medicine physicist and engineer. Also includes information on educational paths and accredited training programs.

**Grants, Awards, and Scholarships** (click on For Technologists). Provides information on financial aid for high school seniors, undergraduate students, and graduate students studying nuclear medicine technology.

# Society for American Archaeology

www.saa.org/careers

**Archaeology & You: Archaeology as a Career or a Vocation.** Information on ways to explore archaeology while in high school, a description of undergraduate and graduate requirements and curricula, and an overview of career options for archaeologists.

**FAQs About a Career in Archaeology in the U.S.** Answers archaeology-related questions, including What kind of education do I need to become an archaeologist?, What classes should I take in high school if I want to be an archaeologist?, What college should I attend if I want to major in archaeology?, What do archaeologists do?, and Where do archaeologists work?

**University Programs.** Lists U.S. and international colleges and universities that have at least one archaeologist on the faculty.

## Society for Historical Archaeology

**www.sha.org** (click on Students & Jobs)

**Types of Careers in Archaeology.** Details the career of historical archaeologist and provides information on educational requirements.

**Guide to Higher Education in Historical and Underwater Archaeology.** Lists U.S. and international graduate degree programs in historical and underwater archaeology. Includes information on types of degrees awarded, faculty, department focus, and laboratory/research facilities.

---

### FYI

You will need at least a bachelor's degree in archaeology or anthropology, including training in archaeological field and laboratory techniques, to work in this field. Many archaeologists have master's degrees and doctorates. Recommended high school courses include math, science, English (especially writing), history, statistics, foreign language, and computer science.

---

## Society for Industrial and Applied Mathematics

**www.siam.org**

**Comprehensive List of Mathematics Departments from The Math Archives** (click on Students). Link to The Math Archives' list of U.S. and international mathematics departments.

**Internships in Computational Science and Engineering** (click on Careers & Jobs). Provides information on internships available from at government agencies and laboratories such as Argonne National Laboratory, Lawrence Berkeley National Laboratory, and the U.S. Department of Energy.

## Society for Industrial Microbiology

www.simhq.org/careers/careers.aspx

**Careers in Industrial Microbiology and Biotechnology.**
Provides information on career paths (antibiotics/antimicrobials,
vaccines, health-care products, oil recovery/mining, etc.) and
educational requirements.

## Society for Integrative and Comparative Biology

www.sicb.org/careers

**Frequently Asked Questions.**
Provides answers to questions such
as Why should I become a biolo-
gist?, What do biologists do?,
What major should I choose?,
What are some of the subdisci-
plines in biology?, and How much
training will I need? Should I go to
graduate school?

**Did You Know?**
Biologists work in a
variety of settings,
including academia,
industry, government,
zoos and aquaria,
environmental consulting
firms, and museums.
They typically have at
least a bachelor's degree
in biology or a related
field.

## Society for Marine Mammalogy

www.marinemammalogy.org

**For Students.** Provides answers to FAQs about career options,
educational requirements, and ways for those interested in
marine mammal science to locate university programs.

## The Society for Mining, Metallurgy, and Exploration

www.smenet.org

**Exploring Opportunities: Careers in the Mineral Industry**
(click on Students & Education/on Teaching Aids and Resource
Materials). Provides a comprehensive overview of the following
career areas in the mineral industry: geology, geological engineering, mining, mineral processing, health and safety, and environment. Also features Academics: Making the Right Choices,
which details important criteria for selecting a school for a minerals career, including type of school, academic programs, faculty,
cost, and financial aid.

**Links to Minerals Schools** (click on Students & Education/Student Center). Links to U.S. and international schools that offer programs and curricula related to materials engineering, mining, and minerals.

**SME Scholarships** (click on Students & Education/Student Center). Information on undergraduate financial aid options offered by the Society.

## Society for News Design

**www.snd.org/resources/cndp.html**

**College News Design Programs.** List of U.S. and international colleges and universities that offer programs in visual journalism and new media.

### Did You Know?
Only nine postsecondary range management programs are accredited by the Society for Range Management. They are the University of Arizona, Colorado State University, the University of Idaho, New Mexico State University, Oregon State University, Texas A&M University, Texas Tech University, Utah State University, and the University of Wyoming.

## Society for Range Management (SRM)

**www.rangelands.org**

**Universities and Colleges** (click on Education). Lists SRM-accredited range management programs at U.S. universities.

**Masonic-Range Science Scholarship** (click on Students). Scholarship available to a high school senior, college freshman, or college sophomore planning to or currently majoring in range science or a related field.

## Society for Technical Communication (STC)

**www.stc.org** (click on Education)

**Academic Programs.** Searchable database of two- and four-year colleges and universities throughout the world that offer training in technical education. Database is searchable by degree level, country, state/province, and availability of online degrees or certificates.

**Scholarships.** Information on financial aid for undergraduate and graduate students from the STC.

# Society of American Archivists (SAA)

www.archivists.org/prof-education/edd-index.asp

**The Archival Profession.** Details the work of archivists and educational requirements for employment.

**Archival Education.** Provides information on graduate study and financial aid.

**Directory of Archival Education.** Lists archival education programs in the United States and Canada. Program listings include information on degrees and certificates offered, faculty, program philosophy, facilities, and research opportunities.

**Guidelines for a Graduate Program in Archival Studies.** Standards for graduate education in archival studies developed by the SAA.

# Society of American Foresters (SAF)

www.safnet.org/aboutforestry/forestrymajor.cfm

**Forestry: Is It For You?** Details the career of forester, educational options, and work settings.

**Getting Started in Forestry.** Discusses important issues for students who are planning to major in forestry, including types of educational programs, geography, emphasis on research, curriculum, and job placement.

**SAF-Accredited Professional Forestry Degree Programs.** Lists (by U.S. state) SAF-accredited forestry degree programs at the baccalaureate level and higher.

> **About Forestry**
> According to the Society of American Foresters, forestry is defined as the "science, art, and practice of creating, managing, using, and conserving forests in a sustainable manner to meet desired goals, needs, and values." Foresters have a four-year college degree, while forestry technicians have a two-year technical degree.

**SAF-Recognized Technology Forestry Education Programs.** Lists (by U.S. state) educational programs that offer two-year associate degrees in forest technology or equivalent areas.

# Society of Diagnostic Medical Sonography (SDMS)

www.sdms.org/career

**So You Want to be a Sonographer?** Includes an overview of the career and educational paths.

**Selecting an Educational Program.** Presents 12 important questions to ask when choosing a diagnostic medical sonography (DMS) program.

**Accredited Programs.** Link to a list of DMS programs in the United States accredited by the Commission on Accreditation of Allied Health Education Programs (CAAHEP).

**Distance Learning Educational Clearinghouse.** Lists educational programs that offer distance education opportunities in sonography.

**Sonography Higher Education Pathways.** Chart that details sonography educational paths for people with varying education and experience levels.

**Make a Sound Decision: Diagnostic Medical Sonography.** Provides information on educational requirements, job responsibilities, types of sonography, and earnings.

**Career Video.** Provides an overview of educational requirements and career paths in the field.

The SDMS Educational Foundation offers **scholarships** to undergraduates enrolled in CAAHEP-accredited programs. For more information, visit www.sdms.org/foundation/scholarships.asp.

# Society of Environmental Journalists

www.sej.org/careers/index1.htm

**Environmental Journalism Programs and Courses.** List of courses and programs in the United States.

Additionally, the School of Journalism and Mass Communication at the University of Wisconsin-Madison offers a searchable **Directory of Science Communication Courses and Programs** at its website, www.journalism.wisc.edu/dsc.

# Society of Fire Protection Engineers (SFPE)

**www.sfpe.org/profession.aspx** (click on Colleges and Universities)

**Undergraduate and Graduate Programs in Fire Protection Engineering.** Provides links to U.S. and international colleges and universities that offer programs in fire protection engineering.

**Scholarship Opportunities.** Links to SFPE chapters, colleges and universities, and other professional associations that offer scholarships.

Additionally, **Careers in Fire Protection Engineering,** a supplement to *Fire Protection Engineering* magazine, is available at www.fpemag.com/careers.

# Society of Illustrators

**www.societyillustrators.org/students/index.cms**

**Students.** Provide advice for high school, college students, and current illustrators.

**Scholarship Database.** Lists art schools that offer courses or majors in illustration, cartooning, graphic design, or visual communications.

# Society of Manufacturing Engineers (SME): Manufacturing is Cool!

**www.manufacturingiscool.com**

**Cool College.** Link to directory of colleges and universities that offer manufacturing education programs. Searchable by country, state, city, accreditation status, size of student body, setting, and tuition. Information for each school includes degree programs offered, tuition, average ACT/SAT scores, and setting.

**Cash for College.** Information on financial aid (for high school through graduate school students) offered by the SME and other organizations.

**Science, Technology & Engineering Preview (STEPS) Academy.** A summer day camp for middle school students interested in learning more about manufacturing. Camps are available in California, Colorado, Connecticut, Illinois, Missouri, New York, South Carolina, Tennessee, and Wisconsin.

This website also includes fun quizzes and facts and information on competitions, activities, and careers.

# Society of Naval Architects and Marine Engineers

**www.sname.org**

Click on Education to access the following resources:

**Careers in the Maritime Industry.** Provides an overview of careers for naval architects, marine engineers, and ocean engineers; suggested courses for high school students interested in these careers; and a list of more than 20 schools in the United States and Canada that offer training in these disciplines.

**Undergraduate and Graduate Scholarships.** Information on scholarships offered by the Society.

Click on K-12 to access the following resource:

**Career Information.** Provides information on career options (naval architect, marine engineer, and ocean engineer) and educational requirements.

# Society of Petroleum Engineers (SPE)

**www.spe.org/spe-app/spe/career/index.htm**

**Petroleum Engineering and Technology Schools** (click on University Programs). Lists U.S. and foreign schools that offer courses of study in petroleum engineering, petroleum technology, and related disciplines. Information includes degrees offered, accreditation status, curriculum, admission requirements, and faculty information.

**Petroleum Scholarships** (click on University Programs). Information on scholarships for high school students and undergraduate and graduate students offered by the SPE Foundation and other petroleum engineering organizations.

# Society of Physics Students

**www.spsnational.org/cup**

**Careers Using Physics . . . It's Not Just Equations Anymore.** Features comprehensive information for students interested in physics, including essays about training and career development and profiles of people who use physics in their careers (searchable by job sector and highest degree attained).

**Scholarships** (click on Programs and Awards). Information on financial aid for undergraduates studying physics.

## Society of the Plastics Industry (SPI)

**www.plasticsindustry.org/outreach/institutions**

**Education and Training in Plastics.** Lists two- and four-year U.S. and Canadian colleges that offer plastics-related training. Information includes department focus and program length.

**Scholarships and Training Support** (click on Outreach and Education). Provides information on scholarships offered by SPI's Molder and Moldmaker divisions for students pursuing careers in the plastics molding industry.

## Society of Toxicology

**www.toxicology.org/AI/APT/ careerguide.asp**

**Resource Guide to Careers in Toxicology.** Detailed information on the career of toxicologist. Includes answers to frequently asked questions, including What is toxicology?, Why consider a career in toxicology?, Where do toxicologists work?, and How do I prepare for a career in toxicology?

> **Did You Know?**
> *Toxicologists* are scientists who study the effects of toxic levels of drugs, pollutants, pesticides, and other chemicals on humans, animals, and the environment.

**Academic and Post-Doctoral Toxicology Programs and Websites.** Lists (alphabetically and by region) U.S. colleges and universities that offer undergraduate and graduate degree programs in toxicology. Information provided includes types of degrees offered and program strengths.

## Society of Vertebrate Paleontology

**www.vertpaleo.org/education/faqs.cfm**

**PaleoFAQs.** Answers to FAQs such as What is a vertebrate paleontologist?, How do you become a vertebrate paleontologist?, and What should I study in school if I want to be a vertebrate paleontologist?

## Society of Women Engineers (SWE)

http://aspire.swe.org

**Your Road to College** (click on Do Engineering). Offers advice on high school preparation (recommended classes and activities) and campus visits.

**Do Engineering.** Provides information on after-school programs, engineering competitions, summer camps and programs, and more.

**Scholarships and Awards.** Details information on scholarships available to female undergraduate and graduate engineering students.

## Society of Wood Science and Technology

www.swst.org (click on Education)

**Directory of Schools.** Lists North American colleges and universities offering baccalaureate and graduate degree programs in wood science and technology. Detailed information on program offerings at each school is provided.

**Accreditation.** Lists colleges and universities that are accredited by the Society.

## Southern Baptist Convention (SBC)

www.sbc.net

**Theological Education** (www.sbc.net/aboutus/sem.asp). Lists SBC seminaries in the United States.

**Colleges and Universities** (www.sbc.net/colleges.asp). Lists SBC-affiliated Baptist colleges and universities.

## SPIE—The International Society for Optical Engineering and the Optical Society of America

http://spie.org/x2576.xml

**Optics Education-International Directory of Programs in Optics.** Link to database of optical and photonics education programs searchable by institution name, U.S. state, country, optics disciplines, degrees offered, and tuition range. School descriptions include department name, current optics program enrollment, and types and descriptions of degrees offered.

**Scholarships.** Offers information on financial aid information for high school, undergraduate, and graduate students who are planning to pursue or who are already pursuing an optics education.

**Pre-College Students Membership** (click on Student Members). Information on complimentary membership for high school students interested in optics.

# Sports Turf Managers Association

**www.stma.org/GetInvolved/STU**

**Extension & University Links.** Links to college sports turf management training programs in the United States.

**Scholarships.** Information on scholarships for students in college sports turf programs from the SAFE Foundation.

# Start Here, Go Places in Business and Accounting

**www.startheregoplaces.com**

This website is sponsored by the American Institute of Certified Public Accountants. (Note: Free registration is required to access certain content on the site.)

### Did You Know?
More than 64,000 students earned a bachelor's or master's degree in accounting in 2006-07, according to the AICPA—the highest number of graduates in 36 years.

**Colleges & Scholarship.** Features information on recommended high school courses, top accounting and business schools, and details on scholarships and other financial aid.

# Student Academy of the American Academy of Physician Assistants

**www.saaapa.aapa.org**

**General Physician Assistant Profession Information** (click on Pre-PA). Offers answers to questions such as What is a physician assistant? and How are physician assistants trained?

**PA Program Information** (click on Pre-PA). Offers a list of more than 130 accredited physician assistant programs (including email and Web addresses) and information on applying to PA schools using the Central Application Service for PAs, job shadowing, and financial aid.

**Pearls From PA Students** (click on Current Students). Current PA students offer advice on applying and getting into PA school, interviewing, being accepted into PA school, and surviving school.

---

**FYI**
You might be surprised to learn that the following products are made from paper: surgical gowns, accordions, coffins, fiber board, surgical dressings, photographs, seedling planting pots, flashlight batteries, and sutures.

---

# TAPPI—The Leading Technical Association for the Worldwide Pulp, Paper and Converting Industry

**www.tappi.org/paperu**

**Paper University: Where Students and Teachers Explore the World of Paper.** Well-designed website that features information, games, and activities for those who are interested in learning more about paper and careers in the industry. When I Grow Up is the most useful section for students. It details career options (process and design engineering, timber operations, manufacturing, research and product development, technical sales and marketing, and administration) and what to study (including an attractive chart that presents suggested college classes by career option) as well as presents lists of U.S. and international colleges and universities that offer training in paper-related careers.

TAPPI offers a variety of **scholarships** to high school seniors, undergraduate students, and graduate students interested in a career in the paper industry. Visit www.tappi.org for more information.

# United Methodist Church: General Board of Higher Education and Ministry

**www.gbhem.org/highed.html**

**Guide to Choosing a School.** Offers detailed advice on picking a college.

**Benefits of United Methodist Schools.** Touts the benefits of attending one of the 122 schools, colleges, universities, and theological schools related to the United Methodist Church.

**Colleges and Universities.** Lists (alphabetically) two- and four-year Methodist colleges and seminaries in the United States.

**The UM Historically Black Colleges.** Lists 11 colleges in the United States.

**Loans and Scholarships.** Provide information about financial aid that is offered by the United Methodist Church.

Click on Ministry to access the following resources:

**Beginning Candidacy.** Provides information for people who are considering entering the Methodist ministry.

**Licensing & Course of Study.** Provides an overview of the curriculum for seminary students.

**United Methodist Theological Schools.** Lists United Methodist theological schools in the United States.

# U.S. Department of Agriculture

www.csrees.usda.gov/qlinks/partners/state_partners.html

**Land Grant Colleges and Universities.** List of more than 100 land-grant colleges and universities in the United States.

# University Aviation Association

www.uaa.aero

**Colleges and Universities.** Lists contact information for its 115 member colleges and universities in the U.S. and Canada.

**Collegiate Aviation Scholarship Listing.** Features information on 777 college aviation scholarships totalling more than $1.2 million.

# Water Environment Federation

www.wef.org

**Career Paths** (click on Membership & Careers/Jobs)Resources). Overview of 50 careers in the water environment field. Includes personal skills and educational requirements.

Additionally, information on the **Canham Graduate Studies Scholarship,** which is offered by the Federation to graduate students pursuing study in the water environment field, is available at www.wef.org/AboutWater/ForStudents/UniversityCenter/ StudentProgramsServices.htm.

## The Wildlife Society

**www.wildlife.org** (click on TWS for Students)

**Universities and Colleges Offering Curricula in Wildlife Conservation.** Lists North American colleges and universities that offer study in wildlife conservation and management. Organized alphabetically by state/province.

## Women in Engineering Organizations

**www.engineering.tufts.edu/wieo/girls.htm**

**Find Programs in Your Area.** Searchable database of summer programs, enrichment programs, and other engineering education resources.

**Scholarships.** Provides information on financial aid for female engineering students.

## Worldstudio Foundation

**www.worldstudio.org/home.html**

**Scholarships.** Information on scholarships for economically disadvantaged high school seniors and college students who plan to or who are currently pursuing the study of art direction, animation, architecture, cartooning, crafts, environmental graphics, film/theater design (including set and costume design), film/video direction or cinematography, fine arts, furniture design, graphic design, illustration, industrial/product design, interior architecture, interior design, landscape architecture, new media, photography, surface/textile design, and urban planning.

# Counselor Associations on the Web

## NATIONAL/ INTERNATIONAL

**American Counseling Association**
www.counseling.org

**American School Counselor Association**
www.schoolcounselor.org

**Canadian Counselling Association**
www.ccacc.ca

**Higher Education Consultants Association**
www.hecaonline.org

**Independent Educational Consultants Association**
www.educationalconsulting.org

**National Association for College Admission Counseling**
www.nacacnet.org

## U.S. STATE

**Alabama Counseling Association**
www.alabamacounseling.org

**Alaska School Counselor Association**
www.alaskaschoolcounselor.org

**Arizona School Counselors Association**
www.azsca.org

**Arkansas School Counselor Association**
http://arsca.k12.ar.us

**California School Counselor Association**
www.calif-schoolcounselor.org

**Colorado School Counselor Association**
www.coloradoschoolcounselor.org

**Connecticut School Counselor Association**
www.ctschoolcounselor.org

**Delaware School Counselor Association**
www.desca.org

**Florida School Counselor Association**
www.fla-schoolcounselor.org

**Georgia School Counselors Association**
www.gaschoolcounselors.com

**Idaho School Counselor Association**
www.idahoschoolcounselor.org

**Illinois School Counselor Association**
www.ilschoolcounselor.org

**Indiana School
Counselor Association**
http://isca-in.org/index.html

**Iowa School Counselor Association**
www.iowaschoolcounselors.org

**Kansas School
Counseling Association**
www.kssca.com

**Kentucky School
Counselor Association**
www.kyschoolcounselor.org

**Louisiana Counseling Association**
www.lacounseling.org

**Maine School
Counselor Association**
www.meschoolcounselor.org

**Maryland School
Counselor Association**
www.mdschoolcounselors.com

**Massachusetts School
Counselors Association**
www.masca.org

**Michigan School
Counselor Association**
www.mich-sca.org

**Minnesota School
Counselors Association**
www.mnstate.edu/msca

**Mississippi Counseling Association**
www.mscounselor.org

**Missouri School
Counselor Association**
http://schoolweb.missouri.edu/msca

**Montana School
Counselor Association**
www.mtschoolcounselor.org

**Nevada School
Counselor Association**
www.nvsca.org

**New Hampshire School
Counselor Association**
www.nhschoolcounselor.org

**New Jersey School
Counselor Association**
www.njsca.org

**New Mexico School
Counselor Association**
www.nmsca.org

**New York State School
Counselor Association**
www.nyssca.org

**North Carolina School
Counselor Association**
www.ncschoolcounselor.org

**North Dakota School
Counselor Association**
www.sendit.nodak.edu/ndsca

**Ohio School Counselor Association**
www.ohioschoolcounselor.org

**Oklahoma School
Counselor Association**
www.okschoolcounselor.org

**Oregon School
Counselor Association**
www.oscainc.org

**Pennsylvania School Counselors
Association**
www.psca-web.org

**South Carolina School
Counselor Association**
www.scschoolcounselor.org

**South Dakota School
Counselor Association**
www.counselors.k12.sd.us

**Tennessee School
Counselor Association**
www.tnschoolcounselor.org

**Texas School
Counselor Association**
www.geocities.com/txsca

**Utah School Counselor Association**
www.utschoolcounselor.org

**Vermont School
Counselor Association**
www.enosburg.k12.vt.us/vsca

**Virginia School
Counselor Association**
www.vsca.org

**Washington School
Counselor Association**
www.wa-schoolcounselor.org

**West Virginia
Counseling Association**
www.wvcounseling.org

**Wisconsin School
Counselor Association**
www.wscaweb.com

**Wyoming School
Counseling Association**
www.wyoca.org/WySCA

# State Financial Aid and College Planning Associations and Websites

## ALABAMA

**Alabama Commission on Higher Education**
www.ache.state.al.us

## ALASKA

**Alaska Commission on Postsecondary Education**
http://alaskaadvantage.state.ak.us

**Alaska Department of Education & Early Development**
www.eed.state.ak.us

## ARIZONA

**Arizona Commission for Postsecondary Education**
www.azhighered.org

## ARKANSAS

**Arkansas Department of Higher Education**
www.arkansasgovernorsscholarship.com

www.adhe.edu/challenge

## CALIFORNIA

**California Student Aid Commission**
www.csac.ca.gov

www.calgrants.org

## COLORADO

**Colorado Department of Higher Education**
www.collegeinvest.org

www.state.co.us/cche

## CONNECTICUT

**Connecticut Department of Higher Education**
www.ctdhe.org

## DELAWARE

**Delaware Higher Education Commission**
www.doe.k12.de.us/high-ed

## FLORIDA

**Florida Office of Student Financial Assistance**
www.floridastudentfinancialaid.org

## GEORGIA

**Georgia Student Finance Commission**
http://gacollege411.org

## HAWAII

**Univ. of Hawaii Board of Regents**
www.hawaii.edu/offices/bor

## IDAHO

**Idaho State Board of Education**
www.boardofed.idaho.gov

## ILLINOIS

**Illinois Student
Assistance Commission**
www.collegezone.com

## INDIANA

**State Student Assistance
Commission of Indiana**
www.in.gov/ssaci

## IOWA

**Iowa College
Student Aid Commission**
www.iowacollegeaid.org

## KANSAS

**Kansas Board of Regents**
www.kansasregents.org

## KENTUCKY

**Kentucky Higher Education
Assistance Authority**
www.kheaa.com

## LOUISIANA

**Louisiana Office of
Student Financial Assistance**
www.osfa.state.la.us

## MAINE

**Finance Authority of Maine**
www.famemaine.com/education/
education.asp

## MARYLAND

**Maryland Higher
Education Commission**
www.mhec.state.md.us

## MASSACHUSETTS

**Massachusetts Office
of Student Financial Assistance**
www.osfa.mass.edu

## MICHIGAN

**Michigan Bureau of
Student Financial Assistance**
www.michigan.gov/mistudentaid

## MINNESOTA

**Minnesota Office
of Higher Education**
www.getreadyforcollege.org

## MISSISSIPPI

**Mississippi Office
of Student Financial Aid**
www.ihl.state.ms.us/financialaid

## MISSOURI

**Missouri Department
of Higher Education**
www.dhe.mo.gov

## MONTANA

Montana Office of the
Commissioner of Higher Education
http://mus.edu/che/che.asp

## NEBRASKA

Nebraska Coordinating Commission
for Postsecondary Education
www.ccpe.state.ne.us/publicdoc/ccpe

EducationQuest Foundation
www.educationquest.org

NebraskaCareerConnections.org
www.nebraskacareerconnections.org

## NEVADA

Nevada Office of the State Treasurer
http://nevadatreasurer.gov

## NEW HAMPSHIRE

New Hampshire Postsecondary
Education Commission
www.nh.gov/postsecondary

## NEW JERSEY

New Jersey Higher Education
Student Assistance Authority
www.state.nj.us/highereducation

## NEW MEXICO

New Mexico Higher
Education Department
http://hed.state.nm.us

## NEW YORK

New York State Higher
Education Services Corporation
www.hesc.com

## NORTH CAROLINA

North Carolina State
Education Assistance Authority
www.ncseaa.edu

College Foundation of North Carolina
www.cfnc.org

## NORTH DAKOTA

North Dakota University System
www.ndus.edu

## OHIO

Ohio Board of Regents
http://regents.ohio.gov

## OKLAHOMA

Oklahoma State
Regents for Higher Education
www.okhighered.org

## OREGON

Oregon Student
Assistance Commission
www.getcollegefunds.org

## PENNSYLVANIA

Pennsylvania Higher
Education Assistance Agency
www.pheaa.org

## RHODE ISLAND

Rhode Island Higher
Education Assistance Authority
www.riheaa.org

## SOUTH CAROLINA

South Carolina
Commission on Higher Education
www.che.sc.gov

## SOUTH DAKOTA

South Dakota Board of Regents
www.sdbor.edu

## TENNESSEE

Tennessee Student
Assistance Corporation
www.collegepaystn.com

## TEXAS

Texas Higher Education
Coordinating Board
www.collegefortexans.com

## UTAH

Utah Higher Education
Assistance Authority
www.uheaa.org

## VERMONT

Vermont Student
Assistance Corporation
http://services.vsac.org/ilwwcm/
connect/VSAC

State Council of
Higher Education for Virginia
www.schev.edu

## VIRGINIA

State Council of
Higher Education for Virginia
www.schev.edu

## WASHINGTON

Washington Higher
Education Coordinating Board
www.hecb.wa.gov

## WEST VIRGINIA

West Virginia Higher
Education Policy Commission
www.hepc.wvnet.edu/students

www.promisescholarships.org

## WISCONSIN

State of Wisconsin Higher
Educational Aids Board
www.heab.state.wi.us

## WYOMING

Wyoming Department of Education
http://www.k12.wy.us

Wyoming Community
College Commission
http://communitycolleges.wy.edu

# Glossary

**A**

**Academic advisor**
A counselor that assists students in picking out classes to meet program requirements.

**Academic standing**
Label that describes a student's academic performance. For example, a student in good academic standing might be on the Honor Roll. Conversely, a student in poor standing could be on academic probation.

**Academic year**
The time period of educational instruction, usually September through June.

**Accreditation**
The process of determining whether an educational institution or academic program meets standards set by regional or national organizations of professionals. Ensures that curriculum and faculty members are of high quality.

**ACT**
See American College Testing Program.

**Adjusted Gross Income (AGI)**
All taxable income that is reported on a U.S. income tax return.

**Admit/Deny**
Student is admitted to the college but not awarded financial aid.

**Advanced Placement (AP)**
Credit for passing certain high-level courses and exams that high school students can use to obtain college credit or skip prerequisite courses.

**American College Testing (ACT) Program**
More commonly used in the Midwest, South, and West Coast, this test measures aptitude and skill in English, math, reading, and science reasoning. Test scores are used to estimate aptitude for college work.

**Apprenticeship**
A hands-on training process where students learn a skilled trade. Student participants, called apprentices, work

under a trained craftsman for a certain period of time and are generally paid at a low wage.

**Aptitude test**
A test designed to measure an individual's likelihood of succeeding in future schoolwork or in a specific career.

**Army College Fund**
A program that covers the cost of a college education for enlistees with certain job skills.

**Assets**
Cash, stock shares, investments in real estate (excluding the home), and income-producing property, equipment, and inventory. Assets are considered in determining Expected Family Contribution (EFC) when applying for financial aid.

**Assistantship**
A form of financial aid offered to graduate students in exchange for part-time work in teaching or research.

**Associate degree**
Degree earned after a student completes a two-

year postsecondary program. Sometimes used to transfer into a four-year bachelor's program.

**Audit**
Taking a class solely for educational purposes; not eligible for a grade or academic credit toward a degree.

**Award letter**
The formal document spelling out all the terms of a financial aid package.

**B**
**Baccalaureate degree**
Latin term for a bachelor's degree.

**Bachelor's degree**
Degree earned after a student successfully completes a four-year undergraduate program at a college or university. Also called a **baccalaureate degree.**

**BIA Grant**
See Bureau of Indian Affairs Grant.

**Blog**
Online journal that presents a record of thoughts and/or information, usually available for others to read and respond to.

**Bursary**
A financial award given to students (based mainly on need) that does not need to be repaid.

**Bureau of Indian Affairs (BIA) Grant**
This federal grant program is aimed at Indian, Eskimo, or Aleut students who are pursuing an undergraduate or graduate degree.

**Byrd Scholarship**
A federally sponsored, merit-based scholarship aimed at high school students.

**C**
**Campus-based financial aid programs**
Federal aid programs administered directly by a college, such as the Perkins Loan (formerly the National Direct Student Loan) and the Work Study Program.

**Career**
A job for which an individual has trained and has possibilities for advancement.

**Certificate**
The document acknowledging the successful completion of a particular program or course of study, particularly in a vocational school, trade school, or junior college.

**Chair**
The head of an academic department or unit at a university.

**Class rank**
A methodology used to compare one student's academic performance with the performance of all other students in the same grade.

**Clinical education**
Academic programs that combine classroom time with supervised, hands-on experience. Most commonly found in science and medical programs.

**COA**
See Cost of Attendance.

**College**
A degree-granting institution of higher learning. Also refers to schools within a larger university, such as a College of Nursing.

**College catalog**
A publication that illustrates an institution's programs, admissions requirements, financial aid options, school and career guidance services, and student activities. May be available in print or online format.

**College-Level Examination Program (CLEP)**
A series of exams in various subjects that evaluate a student's proficiency in each area.

**Common application**
A form that may be used to apply to more than one college.

**Community college**
An academic institution that offers instruction lasting two years or less that results in an associate's degree or a certificate.

**Commuter student**
A student who does not live on a school's campus. This includes students living at home with their parents or living in off-campus housing.

**Concurrent programs**
Two academic programs studied at the same time.

**Conditional acceptance/admission**
Acceptance letter offering a student a place in a university or college program as long as he or she meets specified conditions.

**Consolidation loan**
Allows borrowers to combine different types of loans into a single loan with one interest rate and one repayment schedule.

**Continuing education**
Formal courses of study often taken by adults during the evening hours.

**Cooperative education (Co-op) program**
A program that combines classroom study with work experience.

**Core course**
An academic course that focuses on the subject that a student is studying; it is usually required for graduation.

**Cost of education**
This generally includes college tuition and fees as well as cost of room and board, books and supplies, and transportation expenses. Student loan fees, dependent care, costs for a study abroad or cooperative education program, and/or costs related to a disability may also be included.

**Course load**
The number of courses taken within a period of study.

**Credit**
A measure of academic progress granted for each completed course. Most institutions require students to complete a certain number of credits in order to graduate.

**Curriculum**
Subject matter covered in a course of study.

**Custodial parent**
In cases of divorce or separation, this is the parent with whom the dependent student lives and whose financial information is used in aid applications.

**D**
**Dean**
The head of a faculty, college, or school of a university.

**Deferment (of admissions)**
Temporary postponement of acceptance to a university or college program.

**Deferment (of loan)**
Temporary postponement of loan repayments, generally without further interest.

**Degree**
A designation awarded upon completion of a postsecondary program. Includes four levels: associate's, bachelor's, master's, and doctorate.

**Department**
Faculty members concerned with a specific discipline of study.

**Departmental scholarship**
A financial award that is designated for a student studying within a specific academic department.

**Dependent student**
A student whose parental income and asset information is used in calculating Expected Family Contribution.

**Diploma**
A document bearing record of graduation from an educational institution.

**Direct PLUS Loan**
Long-term loans made available to parents of dependent students.

**Distance education**
An education program that allows students to complete part or all of their program away from the college or university. (For example, taking a class online.)

**Doctorate degree**
The highest university degree conferred.

**Double major**
Completing two courses of study at the same time, such as a foreign language and education.

**Drop/add**
After registering for classes, a student can choose to drop or add courses as he or she sees fit, generally during the first few week of a semester or term. This period is often called drop/add week.

**E**
**Early action**
Like early decision, this option allows students to apply and be notified of acceptance earlier than at most other schools. However, students, if admitted, are not obligated to attend the college.

**Early admission**
A program available at some colleges that accepts students before they receive their high school diploma.

**Early decision**
Allows students to apply to colleges and be notified of acceptance earlier than at most other schools. Accepted students are usually expected to enroll at the college that accepts them.

**Elective**
A course that it not required for a program but is chosen freely by the student.

**Exchange program**
An agreement that permits students to move from one institution to another for short- or long-term periods of study.

**Expected Family Contribution (EFC)**
The amount of money a student and his or her family are expected to

contribute toward college costs. EFC is used to determine a student's eligibility for the student financial assistance programs.

**F**
**Faculty**
The professors and researchers employed by a university.

**FAFSA on the Web**
Electronic method of applying for federal financial aid. See Free Application for Federal Student Aid.

**Federal Family Education Loan (FFEL) Programs**
The collective name for the Federal Stafford, Federal PLUS Loan, and Federal Consolidated Loan programs.

**Federal Pell Grant**
A federal grant program for students who have not yet received their bachelor's degree.

**Federal Perkins Loan**
A campus-based loan program that is long term and low interest.

**Federal PLUS Loan (FPLUS)**
Long-term loans made available to parents of dependent students.

**Federal Stafford Loan**
Long term, low interest loans administered by the Department of Education.

**Federal Work-Study Program**
A campus-based loan program that allows students to meet part of their educational expenses by working in part-time campus jobs.

**Financial aid**
Loans, bursaries, scholarships, work-study arrangements, and fellowships that are offered by government and educational institutions to college-bound students of need.

**Financial aid package**
A combination of different forms of financial aid (loans, grants and/or scholarships) that is awarded to a student on the basis of financial need and academic performance.

**Financial need**
The difference between an educational institution's cost of attendance and the family's ability to pay for it.

**Fraternities**
All-male student organizations formed for social and/or philanthropic purposes.

**Free Application for Federal Student Aid (FAFSA)**
The form required by all colleges that is used to apply for financial aid from the U.S. government.

**Full-time student**
Generally defined as a student who takes at least 60 percent of what is considered a full course load.

**G**
**Gift aid**
Educational funds such as grants or scholarships that do not need to be paid back to the lender.

**Graduate Management Admission Test (GMAT)**
Exam taken as an admission requirement for postgraduate business and management programs.

**Grade Point Average (GPA)**
The average value of all grades achieved by a student during an academic period. GPA is calculated on various scales depending on the school, but the most frequently used system of numerical values is A = 4, B = 3, C = 2, D = 1 and F = 0.

**Graduate**
An individual who earns an academic degree.

**Graduate program**
An academic program leading towards a master's or doctorate degree.

**Graduate student**
A student working towards a master's or doctorate degree.

**Grant**
A form of financial aid awarded on the basis of need that does not require repayment.

**Graduate Record Examination**
Exam taken as an admission requirement for postgraduate programs in fields other than business, law, and medicine.

**H**
**Honors program**
A bachelor's degree program that includes more prerequisite classes, more challenging coursework, a major project or thesis, and sometimes one extra year of study.

**Humanities**
Fields of study that deal with individuals and groups of people and how they relate to one another. Includes history, languages, literature, and sociology.

**I**

**Income**
Money received from wages, interest, sales or rental of property or services, profits, welfare, social security benefits, and child support.

**Independent student**
A student who:
(a) will be 24 years of age by December 31st of the current school year OR
(b) is an orphan or ward of the court;
(c) is a veteran;
(d) is married or is a graduate or professional student;
(e) has legal dependents other than a spouse; or
(f) presents documentation of other circumstances demonstrating independence.

**Independent study**
A course of study designed by a student with approval from a faculty member.

**Intelligence Quotient (IQ) Test**
A test that estimates an individual's supposed mental capacity.

**Interdisciplinary curriculum**
The study of all aspects of a particular field (such as chemistry or engineering) rather than the study of a single area within a field (such as biochemistry or electrical engineering).

**Internship**
A work arrangement, either paid or unpaid, that is related to a student's area of study and may count as academic credit.

**L**

**Learning disability**
A discrepancy between a student's intelligence and his or her academic performance.

**Lecture**
Method of instruction primarily categorized by one-way communication of prepared material from an instructor to his or her students. In colleges or universities, lectures are typically large introductory classes where students take notes and have limited time for asking questions.

**Liberal arts**
The study of the humanities and the social and natural sciences.

**Law School Admissions Test**
Exam taken as an admission requirement for a law degree program.

**Loan**
An advance of funds from a lender to a borrower that requires repayment (usually with interest) by a certain date.

**M**

**Macromedia Flash Player**
A software program that allows users to view moving or static images on the Web. A free download of this program is available at www.adobe.com/ shockwave/download/ download.cgi.

**Major**
The academic focus pursued by a student in a degree program.

**Master's degree**
A degree granted upon completion of an advanced program to students who have already earned a bachelor's degree.

**Matriculate**
To enroll in a college or university.

**Medical College Admissions Test**
Exam taken as an admission requirement for a medical degree program.

**Merit-based aid**
Financial assistance awarded to students with high academic

achievement or talent in a particular area, such as sports, music, or dance.

**Mid-year admission**
Students are accepted to enter college in the middle of the school year rather than in the fall.

**Military scholarships**
See Reserve Officer Training Corps (ROTC) Scholarship Program.

**Minor**
A secondary academic focus pursued in addition to the student's major.

**N**
**National Collegiate Athletic Association (NCAA)**
An athletic governing body of about 1,200 colleges and universities consisting of three divisions.

**Need-based aid**
Financial assistance awarded to a student who otherwise couldn't afford a college education.

**Needs analysis**
The process used to evaluate a student's financial situation to determine how much money is needed to help meet education expenses.

**Non-need-based aid**
Financial assistance awarded to students

based on criteria other than financial need, such as academic, musical, or athletic achievement. Also called **merit-based aid.**

**O**
**Online education**
Education that is conducted using a computer and the Internet.

**Open admissions**
The practice of accepting all school applicants who meet basic requirements.

**P**
**Parent contribution**
An estimate of a parent's ability to contribute to his or her child's educational expenses.

**Parent loan**
See Federal PLUS.

**Part-time student**
Generally defined as a student who takes 20 percent or less of what is considered a full course load.

**PDF**
A popular way to distribute information electronically. PDF, or portable document format, files are compatible with Windows, Macintosh, and Unix-based systems. They retain all the formats of the original version and

can be read on screen and printed by nearly any computer. Visit the Adobe Systems website www.adobe.com/products/acrobat/readstep2.html) to download a free copy of the software.

**Pell Grant**
See Federal Pell Grant.

**Placement test**
An exam used to determine a student's ability in a particular subject area and place them in appropriate-level courses.

**Podcast**
An audio or audio-visual presentation that can be downloaded from a website and played back on a computer or portable digital device.

**Polytechnic**
An academic institution that offers its primary instruction in the applied sciences or technical arts.

**Pop-up**
A separate window that opens at a website that displays advertising or other features.

**Portal site**
A website that act as a promotional tool for one or more websites. Also known as a **gateway site.**

**Postsecondary education**
Schooling that occurs after a student has completed secondary school requirements.

**Practicum**
Work experience that is related to a student's program of study.

**Preliminary Scholastic Assessment Test (PSAT)**
An exam, generally taken in 10th or 11th grade, that gives students an idea of how they will perform on the SAT.

**Prerequisite**
Course required to prepare for a more advanced class.

**Principal**
When referring to loans, this is the amount of money that is borrowed; does not include additional interest or other charges.

**Private institution**
An institution that runs primarily on non-governmental funds.

**Promissory note**
The legal document that details the repayment obligations and other terms and conditions of a loan.

**Public institution**
An institution that runs primarily on governmental funds.

**Q**
**Quarter**
One-quarter of an academic year.

**QuickTime Media Player**
Software that allow users to access video and audio resources on the Web. A free copy of the software can be downloaded at the following website, www.apple.com/quicktime/download.

**R**
**RealOnePlayer**
Software that allow users to access video and audio resources on the Web. A free copy of the software can be downloaded by visiting www.real.com.

**Registrar**
The individual responsible for students' enrollment and academic records.

**Registration**
The process in which students sign up for classes.

**Regular admission**
The admissions schedule used by most colleges and universities. Applications are due January 1st, January 15th, or February 1st; schools notify candidates between March 1st and April 15th; and students have until May 1st to respond.

**Rolling admission**
Admissions policy whereby students are notified of the college's decision as soon as all application materials have been received.

**Reserve Officer Training Corps (ROTC) Scholarship Program**
Scholarship that pays for a student's education as well as provide a monthly living stipend and other benefits in exchange for time spent in the military. ROTC students must participate in drills and classes during their academic year, military camp during the summer, and, upon graduation, must enlist in full-time active duty for at least four years.

**S**
**SAT**
See Scholastic Assessment Test.

**Scholarship**
A financial award (that does not require repayment) given to a student

to help finance his or her education. May be awarded based on academic merit, nationality, group membership, or talent.

**Scholarship search services**
Organizations that claim to help students find little known and unused financial aid funds. Because of possible scams, families who are interested is using such services should thoroughly research the company before submitting any financial information.

**Scholastic Assessment Test (SAT) I**
Two separate reasoning tests, graded on a scale from 200 to 800, which measure students' mathematical skills and verbal ability.

**Scholastic Assessment Test (SAT) II**
One-hour subjects tests covering English, foreign languages, science, history, and math.

**Seminar**
Also called a **tutorial,** this class format is categorized by its small size and emphasis on group discussion.

**Seminary**
An academic institution that prepares students

for the ministry, priesthood, or rabbinate.

**Semester**
The duration of an academic session, generally 15 weeks.

**Sororities**
All-women student organizations formed for social and/or philanthropic purposes.

**Special education**
Instruction tailored to meet the needs of students with educational or physical disabilities.

**Stafford Loan**
See Federal Stafford Loan.

**Student aid**
Financial assistance for students generally based on need or academic performance.

**Student contribution**
An estimate of a student's ability to contribute to his or her educational expenses.

**Student loan**
Money that students borrow for educational purposes. Must be repaid when they are no longer full-time students or the loan acquires interest.

**Student residence**
Student accommodations that are on campus.

**Study abroad**
An educational arrangement in which a student pursues education at an academic institution that is located outside his or her country of residence.

**Syllabus**
An outline of a course of study prepared by the instructor. Includes course requirements, testing methods, papers, due dates, and a weekly schedule of the topics, readings, and assignments that will be covered.

**T**
**Technical school (or college)**
A public or private institution that offers two- or four-year programs in technical subjects.

**Test of English as a Foreign Language (TOEFL)**
An exam used to evaluate the English proficiency of students whose first language is not English.

**Thesis**
Typically a requirement of an academic program, this thorough and generally lengthy paper reflects extensive research and analysis done during the student's degree program.

**Transcript**
Official student academic record detailing courses studied and grades earned.

**Tuition fees**
Money paid toward the cost of academic classes.

**Tuition payment plan**
A method by which tuition payment for present classes is extended by colleges, banks, insurance companies, or financial management organizations.

**Tutorial**
A classroom organization that involves a small number of students. See lecture.

**U**
**Undergraduate**
A student at a four-year college or university who has not yet completed a bachelor's degree.

**Undergraduate program**
Program leading towards a bachelor's degree.

**Unmet need**
The difference between a student's cost of attendance at a specific educational institution and the student's total available resources.

**U.S. Department of Education**
The section of the federal government that administers the following programs: Federal Pell Grant, Federal Perkins Loan, Federal Supplemental Educational Opportunity Grant (FSEOG), Teacher Education Assistance for College and Higher Education (TEACH) Grants, Academic Competitiveness Grant, National Science & Mathematics Access to Retain Talent Grant (National SMART Grant), Federal Work-Study (FWS), Federal Family Education Loan (FFEL) Programs, and William D. Ford Federal Direct Loan (Direct Loan) Program.

**W**
**Waiting list**
Student's application is neither accepted or rejected but rather held in limbo in case an opening develops.

**Withdrawal**
Canceling attendance in a class within the timeframe set by an educational institution.

**Work-study program**
See Federal Work Study Program.

# Financial Aid Abbreviations

The following abbreviations are commonly used in financial aid administration.

**ACT:** American College Testing Program

**BA:** Bachelor's Degree

**BIA:** Bureau of Indian Affairs

**CLEP:** College-Level Examination Program

**COA:** Cost of Attendance

**CPS:** Central Processing System

**EFC:** Expected Family Contribution (also FC, Family Contribution)

**FAFSA:** Free Application for Federal Student Aid

**FFELP:** Federal Family Education Loan Program

**FM:** Federal Methodology

**FPLUS:** Federal PLUS (Parent) Loan

**FSEOG:** Federal Supplemental Educational Opportunity Grant

**FWS:** Federal Work-Study

**GPA:** Grade Point Average

**HHS:** Department of Health and Human Services

**IPA:** Income Protection Allowance

**IRS:** Internal Revenue Service

**MA:** Master's Degree

**PC:** Parental Contribution

**ROTC:** Reserve Officer Training Corps

**SAR:** Student Aid Report

**SC:** Student Contribution

# Career Title Index

Use this index to help you locate information on specific careers covered in the Association Web Resources section.

# Website Index

# Also From College & Career Press

## Books

### *They Teach That in College* series

Looking for information about out-of-the ordinary, cutting-edge college majors? Our *They Teach That in College!?* series will help you learn more about interesting and unique college majors and programs that will provide young people with great job prospects in the next decade. Each book in the *They Teach That in College!?* series provides information about lucrative and cutting-edge college majors unknown to many counselors, educators, and parents. Majors include Bioinformatics, Broadcast Meteorology, Comic Book Art, Entrepreneurship, Horticultural Therapy, Mechatronics Systems Engineering, Motorsports Engineering, Music Therapy, Nanotechnology, Renewable Energy, Satellite Communications, Sustainable Agriculture, and Toy Design. Each title provides descriptions of these majors, contact information for colleges and universities that offer these majors, lists of typical classes and employers, interesting sidebars, and interviews with college professors.

*They Teach That in College: A Resource Guide*
*to More Than 95 Interesting College Majors, 2nd Edition*
ISBN-10: 0-9745251-7-0, ISBN-13: 978-0-9745251-7-4, 352 pages, $19.95, PB, 6 x 9, Indexes, Photographs

*They Teach That in Community College:*
*A Resource Guide to 70 Interesting College Majors and Programs*
ISBN-10: 0-9745251-2-X, ISBN-13: 978-0-9745251-2-9, 320 pages, $17.95, PB, 6 x 9, Indexes, Photographs

*They Teach That in College-Midwest Edition:*
*A Resource Guide to More Than 65 Interesting College Majors*
ISBN-10: 0-9745251-3-8, ISBN-13: 978-0-9745251-3-6, 320 pages, $13.99, PB, 6 x 9, Indexes, Photographs, [Coverage of college programs (at 580 colleges) in IL, IN, IA, KS, MI, MN, MO, NE, ND, OH, SD, and WI]

# Newsletters

### *CAM Report* newsletter

The *CAM Report* is a career resource newsletter geared toward guidance and education professionals and the students they serve. Its mission: to provide time-saving, comprehensive resources to those who assist students with career discovery.

**For Each Issue:** ISSN: 0745-4341; published bimonthly September through May, and monthly in June, July, and August; 4 pages, 8.5 x 11, Two-Color

**Subscription Rates:** 1 year/$75 (20 issues); 2 years/$140 (40 issues); 3 years/$210 (60 issues)

### *College Spotlight* newsletter

*College Spotlight* is a resource newsletter geared toward guidance and education professionals and the students they serve. Its mission: to help those concerned with selecting, applying to, evaluating, and entering college, as well as to provide other alternatives for today's high school graduates.

**For Each Issue:** ISSN 1525-4313, published six times during the school year, 12 pages, 8.5 x 11, Two-Color, Photographs

**Subscription Rates:** 1 year/$34.95 (6 issues); 2 years/$54.95 (12 issues); 3 years/$69.95 (18 issues)

Visit www.collegeandcareerpress.com to read introductions, tables of contents, and sample chapters or copies (newsletters) for all of our products.

# 5 Ways to Order:

**Mail:** College & Career Press, PO Box 300484, Chicago, IL 60630
**Phone/Fax:** 773/282-4671
**Email:** amorkes@chicagopa.com
**Web:** www.collegeandcareerpress.com